Healing Dramas

HEALING DRAMAS

Divination and Magic in Modern Puerto Rico

RAQUEL ROMBERG

University of Texas Press Austin

Printed in the United States of America
First edition, 2009

Requests for permission to reproduce material from this work should be sent to:
Permissions
University of Texas Press
P.O. Box 7819
Austin, TX 78713-7819
www.utexas.edu/utpress/about/bpermission.html

♾ The paper used in this book meets the minimum requirements of ANSI/NISO Z39.48-1992 (R1997) (Permanence of Paper).

Library of Congress Cataloging-in-Publication Data

Romberg, Raquel.
Healing dramas : divination and magic in modern Puerto Rico / Raquel Romberg. — 1st ed.
p. cm.
Includes bibliographical references (p.) and index.
ISBN 978-0-292-70658-3 (cloth : alk. paper)
1. Magic—Puerto Rico. 2. Divination—Puerto Rico. 3. Medicine, magic, mystic, and spagiric—Puerto Rico. I. Title.
BF1584.P9R65 2009
133.4'3097295—dc22

2008042067

To my mother, Lily Hitter-Freiman, the embodiment of courage and unconditional love

Contents

Preface
AFTER EIGHT YEARS

After eight years, I return to the tapes I recorded while conducting fieldwork in Puerto Rico, and a mixed feeling of curiosity and awe overcomes me. Haydée and Tonio, whose voices are imprinted in these tapes, are no longer among the living. But they are, every time their familiar voices resonate through my transcriber's earphones close to my body.

I wonder which of the hidden messages, of the numerous details exchanged during spontaneous conversations, I may have missed then will reappear now—like a genie coming out of an innocuous, unattended bottle—after so many years. Perhaps in some of these tapes there are frozen secret words or half-words not intended for my ears, spoken by Haydée and others during those instances I was noticeably out of hearing range if not out of the room itself, while the tape placed on a side table was rolling from early morning until the end of the day, recording automatically and indiscriminately everything said in her *altar* (altar room).

I am curious about what I will find. Having already transcribed and published selected parts of that corpus in a book and articles, will I still be able to detect important ethnographic clues in these yet-unheard yards of celluloid?

Enigmatically concrete, these seemingly feeble magnetic tapes have fastidiously saved conversations, whispers, and all sorts of noises, available to me now as technological bits of past embodiments. None has been erased, in contrast to what often occurs with biological memory under the effects of our vacillating human emotions. Here lie the power and challenge of undeviating technological memories.

Will they change under the effects of time compression and immobility, of accumulation and condensation? How will the experiential distance from that originating experience affect my own perception?

As I begin to transcribe these old tapes, I am gradually transported back to Haydée's tiny altar room in Puerto Rico. Initially I am taken by the background sounds: birds chirping, dogs barking, chairs sliding, matches lighting, scissors cutting. The monotonous sound of water flowing in the electrical fountain in Haydée's waiting room; the intermittent raindrops hitting the metallic shades—ti, ta, ta, ti, ta, ta—of Haydée's altar-room window; the almost imperceptibly droning whirlpool of heavy tropical air produced by four plastic ventilator arms spinning at full speed: all these sounds reawaken past sensorial memories. Merengue songs, *música santera* (sacred music), and street and engine noises evoke visceral memories of specific situations in which painful, hopeful, premonitory messages, lighthearted comments and laughter, and somber, sobbing reflections were voiced during our trips to *botánicas* (stores that sell religious paraphernalia), distant Marian chapels, the Yunque (rain forest), the seashore, and the cemetery.

The content of the tapes I am transcribing is overwhelming for another reason too. The cumulative effect of listening over the course of a few days to the juxtaposition of hours and hours of taped interactions uncovers recurrent obsessions troubling Haydée. The transcription of several days' worth of recordings reveals her growing physical and emotional pain following her foot operation and the anger and desperation arising from her unwilling dependency on others and her unbearable separation from her lover.

As soon as she had improved a bit during convalescence, Haydée relocated the functions of her altar to the living room, where, from the sofa on which she lay, she could attend to the needs of her clients. My tape recorder was on all the time, capturing Haydée's voice overlapped by the sounds of four or five other women in the room conversing among themselves as they waited to have a word with Haydée, who in the meantime was busy reading the cards and even performing a *trabajo* (magic work) on the sofa. These tapes also revive the resounding thuds, thumps, and bangs of walls being knocked down, reminding me of Haydée's enormous effort and built-up expectation of having a new chapel-like altar for her patron saint, La Caridad, in her newly enlarged living room.

As I play one tape after another, I notice anew something only vaguely realized in Puerto Rico: discursive reiterations. For example, Haydée tells and retells a dream and her plans to travel and give lectures on Spiritism (*espiritismo*, a belief in spirits, encoded by Allan Kardec). She repeats this narrative many times to three or four people over the course of several consecutive days, which makes me wonder about the significance of such repetitive discourse.

This morning I woke up with a mixed feeling of sadness and well-being: I just had a dream about Haydée and, after many years, felt her strong presence. She appears to be radiantly cheerful, in full charge of her altar, and she looks thinner, younger, and darker than in actuality. I visit her and tell her that recently I met another *bruja* (female witch-healer), who—I assure her—pales in comparison to her. She smiles at me, satisfied at my favorable comparison, asserting with her typical self-assuredness, "I know that." We are now in a hotel that has a swimming pool. She is completely happy and content with her life and success, including her rich, older lover. "My lover has lots of fun with me. How can anyone be bored with me?" she says while hanging her bathing suit on a very elaborate open suitcase-trunk. Perhaps listening to her sobbing voice from eight years ago on tape last night affected me more than I could ever have imagined. There is something irreparable, lost, hanging over me.

If I add up all the instances in which she mentions the lectures she will be invited to deliver (that I had interpreted then as promotional devices), will I discover an encoded message left intentionally for me? She knew I was going to transcribe the tapes upon my return to Philadelphia. But I only transcribed some of them. What a mute pain the realization about the repetitiveness and persistence of her statements is causing me now! Was I oblivious to her wishes when I was in Puerto Rico? Or is this the guilt engineered by the mere cumulative effect of her unfulfilled "mission to lecture about Spiritism" as she had "witched" (*brujeó*, a verb she coined) or "manifested" in front of everyone who came to consult with her? Her intentional stating of this invitation loudly and clearly—in the practice of *brujería* (witch-healing, witchcraft), as I now know—is the way *brujos espiritistas* (Spiritist witch-healers) magically claim (*reclaman*) reality, make it happen.

This book is thus as much about *brujos* (witch-healers) and the drama of divination and magic rituals as about fieldwork, ethnography, and my reflections about them.

After years of immobility, tapes and photos of divination and magic, tapes about dreams, and dreams about tapes, bits of reality of another time and space (distant and yet close) are coming into contact with bits of my present reality: new, untried challenges at writing ethnography await.

Acknowledgments

I am indebted to the work of Michael Taussig, whose unique anthropological style has been an inspiration to me no less than have his insights about shamanism, magic, mimesis, viscerality, and public secrets. Writing about my personal involvement with magic and healing and about the dialogic experience of fieldwork has been easier for me than for generations of anthropologists writing before Michael Taussig, Vincent Crapanzano, Paul Stoller, and Michael Jackson. The boldness and skill with which they explored some of the most ethereal research topics in anthropology have been stimulating and challenging for me. My gratitude goes especially to Paul Stoller, whose intellectual generosity, suggestions, and encouragement as well as friendship accompanied this project. Roger Abrahams and Haim Hazan, as always, have been my dear long-term interlocutors, teachers, and friends. My appreciation goes also to the anonymous readers for their comments and suggestions. I am especially grateful to Theresa May for believing in this project from the very beginning and her encouragement all the way through.

It is true—fieldwork is transformative. The brujos, *santeros* (Santería initiates), and *babalawos* (Santería highest priests) with whom I worked in Puerto Rico have taught me not only what spiritual work is but also what it feels. To them I owe this book's content and spirit.

A summer Ford Pre-dissertation Research Grant and a Penfield Fellowship funded my fieldwork in Puerto Rico. A Temple Research Incentive Grant helped finance transcriptions, editing, and the production of photos for this book. My special thanks go to David Romberg for designing the photo sequences published here, Bernard F. Stehle for working with me again in this book as a keen and skilled editor, Lynne Chapman and Tana Silva for making this a better book, and Pablo Delano for giving permission to reproduce Jack Delano's drawings.

My family has been, as always, my intellectual and emotional rock: Osvaldo, my life companion, and our children, Joanna, Noa Maliar, David, and Victoria, each with his or her own insights, have been my closest and most engaging dinner-table interlocutors and critics. My mother, to whom

I dedicate this book, has been a model to our family and friends spread over three continents. A Holocaust survivor who suffered the most inhumane pain, she has shown us all what the essence of humanity really is.

Healing Dramas

Introduction
HEALING DRAMAS

Es como una cadena: los astros, el mar no tiene límites y el cielo tampoco.
[It is like a chain: the planets, the sea, the sky don't have limits.]

—HAYDÉE TRINIDAD, *July 1996*

We cannot describe the aura, the hinterland, without somehow losing it. Our constructions of the beyond are always slippery. They are, in a sense, like a dream. We experience it, we recall it, but our telling it leaves us with a sense of betrayal, even if our telling gives us relief from the anxiety that surrounds it.

—VINCENT CRAPANZANO, *2004*

Close-up, intimate experiences of divination, healing, and magic rituals, along with my own experiences during fieldwork encounters with brujos and their clients in urban Puerto Rico (1995–1996), organize this project. It encompasses both the formal and phenomenological side of ritual experiences, personal stories, dreams, and my own reflections as an ethnographer and participant.[1] Paradoxically, now that the temporal distance from my own personal reflections during fieldwork has grown to be ten years, I find myself finally more comfortable sharing the more personal and intimate aspects of my ethnographic materials, those that fieldworkers usually note separately in their fieldwork diaries (Malinowski 1989 [1967]). A decade after the publication of my dissertation, I am less concerned about typical demands for scholarly detachment and more at ease in situating myself in this ethnography, readily disclosing the more intimate reflections noted in my fieldwork diary about my personal involvement, dreams, vulnerability, and intuitions during fieldwork.

If in *Witchcraft and Welfare* (2003b) I situate the ethnography of brujería practices in the present according to two combined historical lenses (archeological and genealogical, following Michel Foucault), the present project zooms further in, intimating the drama, poetics, imagery, and magic techniques of brujería. In short, the corporeal spirituality of brujería, its phenomenology—as I sensed and documented it being performed—

inspires these pages. Naturally, by zooming in on the phenomenology of its rituals as well as on its poetics and drama from an experiential perspective, the "forest" of power and history, albeit constitutive of the practices of brujería, will fade away momentarily and then reappear for flashes as nested frames of reference. Although this book explores the phenomenology of magic and healing rituals as practiced *in* Puerto Rico, it is not *about* Puerto Rican healing per se; its colonial, national, creole, Caribbean, and transnational trajectories have been elaborated elsewhere (Romberg 1998, 2003a,b, 2005a,b, 2007). Nonetheless, I will include occasional reflections about the historical confrontation of brujos with various sources of state and religious power, this because my only aim here is to evoke as closely as possible the interpersonal, intensely present-oriented, pragmatic space that emerges between healers and their clients.

A few words about the spiritual economy of brujería and its dynamic transformation in relation to economic, political, cultural, and social forces through time and space are in order here by way of some broad contextual strokes. Of course they do not pretend to be exhaustive: "Total context is unmasterable, both in principle and in practice. Meaning is context-bound, but context is boundless" (Culler 1981:24, inspired by Derrida's deconstruction theory).

After three and half centuries of colonial Catholic rule, the Americanization of Puerto Rico began with the American invasion in 1898 and the establishment of the commonwealth status in 1952. Along with a combined consumer and welfare form of capitalism and the separation of state and religion (at least institutionally) arriving to the island, American Catholic and Protestant churches mushroomed, and exiled Cubans established Santería temples with their arrival following Castro's revolution (Agosto Cintrón 1996, Duany 1998, Vidal 1994). As a result, a general "spiritual laissez-faire" atmosphere emerged, opening up the gates to religious eclecticism and competition.

Trusting that the American presence would help modernize and bring prosperity to the Puerto Rican nation after centuries of declining Spanish colonial rule, many (rich and poor alike) began to convert to the newly established American Catholic and Protestant churches on the island (Hernández Hiraldo 2006; Silva Gotay 1985, 1997). As a result many families have ended up being constituted by individuals affiliated with distinct religious traditions in unprecedented combinations.

It was in this eclectic religious atmosphere, with its various logics of practice, that many of the brujos I worked with were raised, shaping in great measure their individual ritual styles. For instance, popular Catholicism,

Spiritism, and creole reworkings of African-based magic practices mark Tonio's style (see Chapter One). Haydée's style follows Tonio's with an added mode emerging from her upbringing as the daughter of a Catholic mother who converted to an American Protestant church and a Spiritist father. The youngest of all the healers I met, Armando, was raised by an espiritista mother in New York, where he had the opportunity to expand his ritual knowledge among Cuban and "Nuyorican" babalawos as well as other healers from South and Central America, continuing his initiation in Santería under Ronny, an exiled Cuban babalawo in Puerto Rico. Basi, a botánica owner in her mid-sixties with whom I lived for several months, was raised by a Spiritist grandmother and blended New Age versions of Spiritism with an ecumenical form of Christian religiosity. Forty-year-old Ken, a Nuyorican healer married to Mora, a Puerto Rican espiritista santera, developed a personal style that combined various Asian, Native American, and New Age modes of healing with traditional Puerto Rican Spiritism. And Mauro, a Cuban babalawo of Spanish-Arab ancestry in his seventies, was raised by Catholic nuns in a predominantly white society and initiated in Santería as a young man, in 1949, in one of the oldest Afro-Cuban *cabildos* (church-sponsored fraternities) in Cuba. After his exile in Puerto Rico in 1971, he and his wife, Lorena, a Puerto Rican espiritista-santera, established their own temple; by the end of the 1990s they had moved to Miami under the sponsorship of several of their rich initiates.[2]

In addition to such eclectic religious trajectories, the working experiences of brujos have also shaped their healing and magic styles. As a result of new commercial and state opportunities afforded by the system of welfare capitalism and American commercial investments, brujos, many of whom have experienced working in American-owned factories or state agencies, begin to expand their previous ritual areas of involvement (Romberg 2003b:210–235).[3] Having acquired additional cultural capital pertaining to new systems of production and redistribution, they are now able to attend not only to the spiritual but also the material welfare of their clients (as will become evident in the pages that follow). Interceding more directly in the business fields on behalf of their clients, they may recommend their unemployed clients to companies headed by their other clients and inform their needy clients of new funding opportunities available in various state agencies. As a result, brujos—no longer persecuted as heretics or vilified as charlatans—begin to function implicitly as "spiritual entrepreneurs" (Romberg 2003a,b), that is, as brokers between state, business, and professional networks. As such, they are sought out when mainstream medicine, psychology, or social work fail to provide solutions to a variety of health, relationship, and economic problems, but more comprehensively, for promoting *bendiciones* (blessings) or ultimate success in clients' lives.

The Moral Economy of Brujería

Defined in terms of both material and spiritual progress, the quest for bendiciones has been molded recently by consumer and welfare capitalist values and sensibilities, which add to the hitherto exclusively Catholic and Spiritist spiritual understandings of bendiciones as a concern for the material conditions of human existence. The connection between spiritual and material blessings is hence established: material success—measured by one's acquisitive power, social status, and overall progress—attests to having been gifted with spiritual blessings (and vice-versa). This redefinition of the meaning of bendiciones, following the values of consumer and welfare capitalism, suggests that brujería has become a form of "spiritualized materialism" (Romberg 2003B) that answers to a new moral economy for achieving and explaining economic success. What all this means in matters of ritual practice will become apparent in the ensuing ethnography.

Informing current brujería practices, this moral economy is, however, the upshot of a series of contentions not just with present but also past global and local religious, economic, and cultural hegemonic forces, broadly sketched above (Romberg 2005a,b). As vernacular responses to these hegemonic forces through time, brujería practices have encompassed dominant symbols and attitudes often decades after they had ceased to be significant in the mainstream (Williams 1980:40), illuminating both their generative quality and specificity in ritual practices over time. They have done so by means of a performative mimesis, or the imitation of hegemonic symbols and gestures that resists their exclusionary power. Therefore, rather than interpreting these forms of incorporation through imitation as a form of submission to economic, civil, or religious hegemonies, I see them as forms of "ritual piracy" (Romberg 2005b). In other words, by means of these forms of vernacular piracy, symbols of power that intend to exclude (and often vilify) the practices of brujería are appropriated and rechanneled to serve ritual and spiritual purposes foreign to the purposes of their imposition by the dominant culture in the first place. Following a "predatory" form of mimesis (Harney 2003), vernacular religions such as brujería plunder the very powers that these symbols embody, rechanneling them in the preparation of their magic works and rituals.

This explains, as will be shown in the ensuing chapters, (1) the infinite sources for legitimation and healing power that Catholic gestures and stories about Jesus' life afford brujos working today; (2) the present power of nineteenth-century Scientific Spiritism, its spiritual laws, and ethos in shaping the purposes and outcomes of consultations, *veladas* (nightly séances), and dream interpretations; and (3) the transmutation of the powers embodied in state agencies and the bureaucratic gestures of their officials during divination, magic, and healing rituals. This points to the dynamism of vernacular rituals and their ongoing interface with hegemonic symbols throughout history (Kelly and Kaplan 1990). Indeed, contemporary values of welfare and consumer capitalism (albeit contradictory) are appropriated, translated, and adapted (or "tamed") to fit the spiritual agendas and ethos of brujería. One can say that symbols of hegemonic power of various historical periods have been localized or folklorized, albeit in ironic ways, "with an attitude": the alluring powers of colonial and modern states pirated by brujos (Romberg 2005b).

An important caveat is needed at this point. Witchcraft and magic in parts of Africa, Asia, the Caribbean, and Latin America have been conceptualized in recent anthropological studies as local idioms of "occult economies or prosperity cults" (Comaroff and Comaroff 2001:24; Geschiere 1997; Palmié 2002; Taussig 1987, 1997). Promising "to yield wealth without production, value without effort," occult economies become necessary, according to Comaroff and Comaroff (2001:23), when an increasingly neoliberal social order fails to provide those who lack fiscal or cultural capital with the legitimate means to fulfill their desires for capitalistic accumulation.

The case of Puerto Rico stands in stark contrast to this portrayal. Given the ambiguous political status of the island as an associated free state (*estado libre asociado*), characterized as a "postcolonial colony" (Duany 2002) or a "modern colony" (Grosfoguel 1997), Puerto Ricans are granted annual transfers of billions of dollars in the form of food stamps and health, education, and unemployment benefits from the metropolitan state; participation in metropolitan standards of mass consumption; metropolitan citizenship; democratic and civil rights; and the possibility of migration to the metropolitan state without the risks of illegality (Grosfoguel 1997:66–67). What "occult economies" seem to help muster elsewhere the "modern colony" status does for Puerto Rico. Witchcraft and magic practices in this context, in fact, work to reproduce, not subvert, the modern colony, even though unwillingly and in oblique ways. Similarly to Korean shamanism under capitalism (Kendall 1996b), the spiritual world of brujería and the cosmological morality it entails are summoned for *promoting* the necessary practical means to achieve mainstream goals, not for *substituting* them. Adding the ethical tenets of Spiritism to the spectral ethos and predicaments of consumer and welfare capitalism, the moral economy of brujería can therefore hardly be seen as being counter-hegemonic in the same measure as witchcraft and magic practices elsewhere in the world.

Spiritual Lingua Franca

Even though a uniquely personal style characterizes each healer's practices, the similarities—especially in regard to basic ritual gestures, communication styles during divination, possession, and even the components of their altars—are too compelling to overlook. These ritual similarities, which will be discussed in detail later on, suggest a kind of spiritual lingua franca that enables individuals of various backgrounds and religious orientations (myself included) to move in and out of these various types of vernacular healing systems with quite a remarkable (and, in my case, even unexpected) ease. Part of this ease, I believe, is the result of historically layered, embodied intertextual traditions enacted by healers and eventually recognized by their clients.[4] Bearing in mind the intrinsically impossible and futile task of tracing the origins of all these heterodox traditions, I take, instead, a pragmatic approach to discuss the basic competencies developed by clients (and further refined by habitués) that explain the relative ease with which they are able to circulate among the various home altars.[5]

This question needs further clarification in light of the essentially urban clients, employed and unemployed alike, who seek healers of various kinds. Rather than being the result of belief in any particular healing tradition, the choices made by these business owners, professionals, homemakers, and blue-collar workers are mostly guided by the perceived fame and success of particular healers and the imagined or real power ascribed to their individual healing styles (cf. Lévi-Strauss 1963b). In addition to the moral economy mentioned above, the spiritual field of brujería (especially in healer-client relationships) is largely shaped by free-market consumer considerations: intense competition, self-promotion, and specialization. Asserting their fame and powers as spiritual entrepreneurs, healers often define their expertise in relation to mainstream "cloak professions": Armando, for example, defines himself as a "spiritual consultant," Haydée as a "doctor of the soul," and Mauro as a "mystical adviser."

Sensuous Dramas

This book seeks to illuminate the performative significance of healing rituals and magic works, their embodied nature, and their effectiveness in transforming the emotional, proprioceptive, and (to some extent) physiological states of participants by focusing on the visible, albeit mostly obscure, ways in which healing and magic rituals proceed. Heavily dependent on carefully crafted gestures, meticulously manipulated objects, and poetically strung words, healing and magic rituals among heterodox urbanites challenge some assumed notions about the centrality of belief (de Certeau 1984:177–189) as well as deterministic historical, political, and self-oriented approaches to imagination, the body, the senses, experience, and affect (Aretxaga 2005, Crossley 2001, Desjarlais 1997, Lock 1993, Navaro-Yashin 2007, Scheper-Hughes and Lock 1987, Turner 1984).

The sensuousness of magic and divination has been discussed in the last three decades from various anthropological perspectives on experience, the body, and performance, as well as from such theoretical orientations as phenomenology, poststructuralism, and postcolonialism.[6] While inspired by these studies, the questions I pose here, only tangentially theoretical, emerge directly from the particular pragmatics of brujería, shaped by the eclecticism of its rituals, the heterogeneous character of its participants, and the heterodoxy of its moral economy. How is it that people of diverse social class, ethnicity, and gender—most of whom actually "do not believe in these things"—come to consult with brujos and other types of healers when they feel their lives are coming apart? How could I, also among those who "do not believe in these things," sense even for a flash the presence of entities that had been foreign to my life until then and be moved and transformed, albeit unwillingly, by them?

The issue of belief, murky though it might be, seems inescapable. What, if any, is the role of belief in magic and healing rituals? Posed extensively by anthropologists studying traditional societies, this question becomes even murkier due to the heterogeneity and heterodoxy mentioned above. For one, the classic assumption that belief in the system itself or in the individual healer is the a priori condition for the effectiveness of magic rituals is almost impossible to make within the spiritual field of brujería. Belief in the existence of a spiritual world that becomes manifest during ritual may account for only some part of the ritual experience: it might comprise one fleeting aspect of it; it might be embedded in the somatic-practical and thus not be acknowledged at all; or occasionally it might not even be relevant. "To what extent is belief ever an unflawed, totally confident, and uncontradictory thing anyway?" Taussig asks with respect to shamanism. "How much does one have to 'believe' for shamanism to work?" (1998:229).

Far from settling these dilemmas, two fictional characters in Umberto Eco's *Foucault's Pendulum* (1989) illustrate some of the tensions between belief and the reality of ritual as embodiment, which like two magnetic poles attract and repel each other. At an Umbanda *gira* (spiritual gathering) in Rio de Janeiro, mediums are possessed effortlessly by different *orixás* (deities of African origin) and *egúns* (ancestors of indigenous and Afro-Catholic origin) to the increasingly fast and loud beat of drums.[7] A blond German psychologist—a habitué of these gatherings—stands out in the group, having failed to become possessed despite her exceedingly energetic attempts (211–212). In contrast, another woman, a Marxist student of political science who is of mixed indigenous, African, and European ancestry, becomes possessed by the very spirits she refuses to believe in "for being another opium of the plebeians" (214–215).

This fictional situation has analytical import in illuminating the constitutive nature of what Michel de Certeau aptly terms "the discourse of possession" (1990 [1970]). Tracing the historical production of possession in Loudun in seventeenth-century France, he reveals the particular forms it took, the places in which it occurred, and the modes of its public recognition and interpretation, which in turn shaped not only collective perceptions about possession but also individual experiences of it, in particular the apparent ease or difficulty if not impossibility of some to become possessed.[8]

Indeed, the problematic place of "belief in magic" is not only fictional or theoretical; it is an experiential dilemma for those urbanites who come to consult with healers and brujos, best expressed by a woman who, while waiting for a consultation with a bruja, said, "I don't believe in magic but it works" (Romberg 2003b:3–6).[9] Contradicting the expectations of healers about their clients' predispositions regarding magic (no less than some anthropological interpretations of it), the distinction between belief and efficacy, inexplicable as it might be to some skeptics, highlights the critical role of the performative in the spiritual economy of brujería.

Although "ritual piracy" answers some questions about the past in the present, the still intriguing (albeit not fully answerable) question remains: How do past discourses on possession enter into the performative experience of ritual in the here and now? Victor Turner provides one type of answer: "Meaning arises when we try to put what culture and language have crystallized from the past together with what we feel, wish, and think about our present point of life" (1986:33). But then other questions arise: Are our feelings and wishes in the present not also shaped by what culture and language have crystallized from the past? How is affect effected other than by the self, acting in the present? Perhaps another paradox can illuminate these questions.

Turning "the problem of the past in the present" into a new irony about the perceived uniqueness of the self and human experience, Clifford Geertz ends his epilogue for *The Anthropology of Experience* (1986) by addressing the following question posed by an eighteenth-century aesthetician: "How Comes It that we all start out Originals and end up Copies?" The answer, Geertz concludes, "is surprisingly reassuring: it is the copying that originates" (380). If, indeed, copying originates, what happens to the assumption that possession is innately ingrained in some and is impossible for others? Is trance a personal experience, a subjective bodily reaction to some force that is as uncontrollable as blushing, or rather (contra its own discourse) a group-defined and learned aptitude? If the latter, one might ask whether it is our cognition or the body or flesh—as suggested by Eco's Brazilian mediums—that remembers (Young 2002). Even when acquired, "motor habits" might flow seamlessly and effortlessly so that no learning is even suspected and as such are experienced as "second nature."[10] Like *hexis* (body memory), the performative memory of possession might be as ingrained as the athlete's "muscle memory" and "feel for the game," concealing its having ever been acquired in the first place. Indeed, as a form of practical mimesis, the body learns from other bodies, moving from practice to practice without passing through discourse and consciousness (Bourdieu 1990 [1980], Mauss 1979 [1950]).

Where does belief stop, and where do memories of the flesh begin? While these are questions that philosophers and anthropologists of religion ponder, they acquire a different meaning when asked from an ethnographic perspective. In the case of brujos, for instance, the reality of their own possession—unlike that of Eco's fictional characters—is never questioned or predicated on their belief in spirits. Furthermore, since no theological learning is involved in brujería practices, training their bodies to surrender to the will of the spirits during veladas is the only type of learning brujos will ever acknowledge. And yet, to assure the effectiveness of their rituals, they do expect their clients to (cognitively) believe; they achieve this via performative means (not unlike the theatricality of possession analyzed by de Certeau) that often conceal this very purpose, a point I develop throughout the book.

In the middle of a consultation one day, Haydée suddenly stormed out of the altar (leaving behind the client she was consulting) into the waiting room and harshly addressed one of the women: "You! Why are you here? You don't believe! What are you searching for? Are you just being nosy?" Everybody was astonished by these words (see Chapter Three), for they indicated that brujos can "sense" everything (including one's skepticism). Reassuring those silent and perhaps skeptical women waiting to be consulted of the power of brujos to "sense" or "see" beyond, this dramatic interchange resolved, at least for the moment, the inherent tension between skepticism and belief that underlies consultations with brujos.

Artifice and Ritual Efficacy

In light of this inherently irresolvable tension between belief and skepticism, what I find particularly challenging in vernacular religious practices such as brujería is the performative reality of its consultations. Marked by "continuous and relentless deferral," the truth of healing and magic "is a truth continuously questioning its own veracity of being" (Taussig 1998:247). Given that brujería practices are structured neither by initiation hierarchies nor by a prescriptive theological or ritual corpus (as with Santería and Korean shamanism), their legitimation depends heavily on the charisma of practitioners, making the potential fragility of each consultation a constitutive feature of its very experience. Indeed, the performative reality of consultations is highly indeterminate. While they manifestly depend on the performative excellence of brujos, consultations are ultimately experienced as the result of the whims and dictates of spirits. "It's not me," brujos often clarify. "It's the spirits telling me to tell you." When brujos reveal that they do not direct the proceedings of consultations—that they are not the ones performing—they are artfully revealing suspicions of their skilled concealments. As will become apparent later in the book, it is in such ambiguous intersubjective spaces (Jackson 1998, Csordas 1997), created during consultations, that the charismatic performances of brujos with their "studied exercises in unmasking" (Taussig 1998:246) interweave the practical beliefs and skepticism of clients with the uncanny presence of the spirits.

In spite of demands made by healers that their clients believe in magic to assure its ritual effectiveness, the drama of ritual may have just as overpowering an effect on skeptics as on believers when the adroitness of its performance is such that it connects through invisible chains of resemblance and artifice the here and now with unseen social and spiritual imaginaries.[11] Such is the power of theatricality and impersonation—once devalued (as were all the senses) by Platonic philosophies for being deceptive, for diverting us from the apprehension of ultimate realities through our cognition (Diamond 1974). Yet, perhaps, on those rare occasions when artifice is such that we are made to forget impersonation (and cognition), the sensorial excesses of ritual drama can transform mere corporeal manifestations into spiritual realities, aesthetics into emotion.

Indeed, the efficacy of ritual can be paralleled to that of rhetoric (Tambiah 1990:81–83) in that they depend on artifice and roundabout appeals for inducing desired actions and emotions among both visible and invisible audiences. The tricks of magic (like the tricks of the rhetorician) "are not mere 'bad science'; they are an 'art'" (Burke 1969:42). As suggested above, at the core of this artifice is the skillful, fluid display not just of correspondences (or performative mimesis) but also of sharp-witted rites of unmasking (Taussig 1998). To address this artful deftness of magic, I draw on a wide range of studies within the performative paradigm in folklore, anthropology, sociolinguistics, and theater, a list too extensive to mention here.[12]

While the familiar intangibles of everyday life are intimated in art through the playful display of reality (Abrahams 1977, 2005), the intangibles of magic are manifested by the added dramatic denial of any playful artifice of correspondences, illustrating a form of embodied knowledge and feeling by proxy that connects the body of healers to the spiritual world by means of chains of resemblances and their skillful erasure. In the chapters that follow, the artful flow of ritual display or "deictic" verisimilitude (mimesis) and concealment take various forms.[13] Chains of resemblances in discourse, body movement, the manipulation of objects, and the senses will become apparent when I discuss embodied memories (Chapter One), the interpretation of dreams (Chapter Two), and the drama and poetics of possession, cleansing, healing, divination, and magic rituals (Chapters Three, Four, Five, and Six). Indeed, brujos are not only like poets in their dexterous management of resemblances, correspondences, and parallelisms but also quick-witted charismatic performers and manipulators of discourse, corporeality, and revelation.

Drawing on Roman Jakobson (1964) and others of the Prague School, I suggest that ritual correspondences, like metaphors and poetic devices, cause us to be aware of and be moved by intangibles while also mobilizing us to take some form of action. This became evident during my participation in rituals when I saw the emotional impact on clients of repetition and parallelism—of words and gestures—as well as of the shifting voices uttered but not always authored by healers in trance. In short, what I show here is that the aesthetics of mimetic correspondences as well as their masking create a multisensorial ritual drama that is in itself healing by means of igniting the imagination and the senses, stirring emotions, persuading, and mobilizing participants and presumably also the spirits in answering their pleas.

What I argue throughout this book is that this obsessively mimetic corporeal aesthetics, exposed as manifestations of the otherwise concealed world of spirits, is at the basis of the technologies of magic and healing and essential to their ethics, affectivity, and effectiveness. And yet, if one is to be true as much to the immediacy of ritual experiences (Turner 1992) as to their indeterminacy and corporeality, a deconstruction of these technologies might have just the reverse effect: creating the illusion of a neatly coherent system that would, in fact, hinder the very experiential sensing of their ethics and affectivity no less than their effectiveness. Something about the multisensorial, intersubjective experience of ritual, as in other fieldwork experiences, is thus disappointingly irrecoverable in spite of one's best-intended attempts in contextual maneuvering and textual evocation (de Certeau 1984).

The Seduction of Ethnographic Representation and Revelation

As an anthropologist I have attempted to document—in writing, in sound recordings, and in photographs—the corporeal and sensorial aspects of brujería as well as, indeed, to experience them myself (as viscerally as possible). Far from being representative, of course, my own experiences are primarily suggestive instances of a particularly situated and empathic, if at times also complicit, vulnerable participant (Behar 1996, Marcus 2001). Hence my taking of sequential photographs during rituals was not merely a data-collecting device and *aide de memoire* (Ruby 2000:54) but the enactment of a dialogical (and often witty) understanding of my identity and role as a fieldworker, reframed as that of a *reportera* (reporter) in Haydée's eyes.[14] Vestiges of my professional persona (reinterpreted as it might have been during the course of fieldwork interactions), these photos are traces of my own and, obviously, the participants' attention to the sensuous, dramatic, and poetic nature of magic and healing.[15]

Even though magic and healing rituals might appear as some of the easiest ethnographic materials to document empirically because of their performativity, visible gestures, palpable substances, and audible sounds, these very qualities are also at the root of the various challenges for ethnographic textual authority and representation as well as theorizing (Clifford and Marcus 1986, Hazan 1995, Marcus and Cushman 1983, Stoller 1994).[16] How do these essentially sensorial and grounded acts accomplish anything beyond the manifestly visceral?

When brujos reveal that it is not they who speak when they deliver the messages of the spirits, or when they unmask unsuspecting clients waiting to be consulted for being skeptical about the efficacy of magic, they are skillfully performing the theatricality of magic, dispelling the craving for certainty that the secrecy of magic elicits.[17] Having been puzzled, seduced, and then moved by the opacity of the discourse of magic (its trickery, corporeality, and acts of skillful unmasking), perhaps my own textual rituals of revelation of magic and healing experiences (of their poetics and gestures) remain a surface intimation of occasions in which the suspension of disbelief has successfully coexisted with skepticism.

The organization and content of this book loosely mimic the energetic-moral ethos of Spiritism, embodied in Haydée's epigraph, particularly the idea that energies—bad and good, past and present—are never lost, just transformed. Intimating this kind of Spinozean worldview, the sequence of chapters about embodied memories, dreams, possession, divination, the body, and space dwell on a number of specific and intimate, yet hardly exhaustive, instances and approximations of that ethos. The photos that are included here, some of which are arranged in strips that follow the sequence of ritual actions, adhere to this same logic. Even though technologically produced, these photos acquire a spiritual significance following the moral economy of brujería as *manifestaciones* (manifestations) of the power of healing and magic practices: like magic they intimate some form of presence in spite of an irrevocable absence.[18]

Unraveling the technologies of magic and healing, indulging in their magnificent performativity and expected effects, I have touched only "the surface, the fold, the skin, the appearance" (Taussig 1998:243) of magic and healing experiences. Even though in this exercise I may have become an unwilling accomplice in the ritual unmasking of magic, its truth will be exposed in its corporeality, sensed through its performance; beyond that, magic, in spite and because of several wrenching attempts to know and dissect it, will continue to escape cognition and stubbornly resist analysis.

Chapter One

A FLIGHT PERFECTED AT DEATH

Mimetic Memories of a Brujo

The first time I saw Tonio, in July 1995, he was sitting in his wheelchair watching television, dressed in a worn-out robe, his short-cut hair in a net fashioned from a piece of what looked like a woman's dark-skin-colored panty hose. He was about ninety years old at the time. Someone at the library of Loíza had told me that he was one of the most renowned brujos of Puerto Rico.

His house was only a few minutes away from the local library. When I arrived, a man in his sixties—his son—opened quite hesitantly the outside iron gate and invited me to wait for Tonio on the porch. I was gazing out across the road when Tonio wheeled himself onto the porch a moment later. He pointed with pride to the Cave of Loíza across the road from his house and told me about its significance for Puerto Ricans. A mystical place inscribed in the nationalist history of Puerto Rico, it is the place where a very powerful Taíno female *cacique* (native chief) by the name of Loíza (probably Yuisa or Luysa originally and baptized as Luisa) lived. The township of Loíza takes its name after her. Legends say she ruled the area of the Jaimano on the margins of the river Cayrabón (today's Río Grande de Loíza). As in many other conquest miscegenation stories, she was abducted and forced into "marrying" Pedro Mejías, a mulatto Spanish conquistador. She fought valiantly against the Spaniards (and possibly also the Caribs, an indigenous population believed to be in constant warfare with the Taíno), and both she and her husband were killed in the fighting. Adding to the mysticism of the cave, a natural stream runs under Tonio's house, providing the "blessed" water of the earth for drinking and irrigating. Everything around him—people and plants—"grow" fast and strong, I later heard from other brujos.

I ask him about brujería and espiritismo. Without a word, he uncovers a small silver medal of the Virgin of Mercy carefully pinned to the underside of his pajama-shirt collar. She was the one who appeared to him when he was seven years old, promising him spiritual guidance and protection; her metal image has protected him ever since. He begins to pray in Latin, showing off his knowledge of Catholic prayers, which he uses to heal, he tells me. I gather that he is Catholic; Jesus and the saints protect him and direct his healing practices.

Tonio also speaks as a popular Spiritist medium in the tradition of Scientific Spiritism. A fashionable secular-transcendental practice created in France by scientist and man of letters Allan Kardec during the second half of the nineteenth century, Spiritism was based on the belief in human communication with enlightened spirits and reincarnation. European Romantics believed that enlightened spirits could direct people in creating a progressive, morally sound world, and this is why Spiritism was embraced by nineteenth-century liberal, anticolonial, and progressive elites as a counterforce to the hegemony of Spanish Catholic rule in Puerto Rico and became through the decades a legitimate sphere for alternative transcendental practices (Romberg 2003a, 2003b:54–80). Today, a follower of espiritismo, whether in its orthodox or popular form, is generally called an *espiritista*. Tonio, like many other brujos, adopted the form and content of Spiritist practices such as holding monthly veladas. Following a minimalist symbolism, Scientific Spiritists believe that at these types of gatherings the white tablecloth, the white candles, and the Bible they use attract spirits of light or enlightened spirits who will eventually appear and give their messages.

Hundreds of novice mediums who are now practicing brujos developed their mediumship under the auspices of young Tonio, who used to be the head or *presidente* of these veladas for more than a half-century. He also consulted some who needed special spiritual treatments in his private consultation room, or altar. This is how Haydée, the bruja I got to know through Tonio, met him. As a child she used to accompany her father at dawn—as early as four or five o'clock in the morning—to Tonio's altar in order to assure they would be able to consult with him since, Haydée once told me, hundreds used to come from all over the island to see him. At his home I often heard Tonio speak of the goodwill, charity, and positive energies that inspired his work as a healer. As I would hear among other healers during my fieldwork, Tonio asserted his mission as a healer by uttering the Spiritist motto, *Fé, esperanza y caridad* (Faith, hope, and charity), commonly used as a greeting among healers and in consultations.[1]

But I also remember people telling me that Tonio Lacén was a famous brujo, implying that he was an espiritista who was also knowledgeable in performing all sorts of magic works, or trabajos, and especially in managing and controlling any evil forces that were or might again be involved in harming his clients.

An espiritista who not only communicates with enlightened spirits but also tames and exorcises evil ones is considered to be a brujo. Bolina, the bruja I had met in Loíza a few months earlier, had mentioned that Tonio was a famous brujo who unfortunately was not working any more due to his old age and deteriorating health. Indeed, besides possessing strong spiritual powers, having a strong *materia* (matter) is necessary to withstand the dangerous effects of evil spirits possessing the body of a healer. Why was Tonio covering up this aspect of his work and highlighting only his Catholic devotion and Scientific Spiritist ethics?

I hesitantly ask, in keeping with the academic questions I had proposed back at home for my investigation:

> What are the African aspects of what you do?
> *None.*

He immediately points to a young boy getting a haircut in the yard and calls the child to come to him. As the boy approaches, Tonio says to me,

> You see this dark black kid, a relative I take care of? *He's* of African origin.

I am astounded by Tonio's reaction to my question and its implication that he is not black, for he looks phenotypically black to me, his complexion only a bit lighter than the boy's. Sensing that he does not want to be associated with anything related to Africanness, especially to slavery in Puerto Rico, I question the appropriateness of my asking him about the African aspects of his healing practices. I do not wish to offend him. Evidently he sees himself not at all as a black person, but simply as "just" a Puerto Rican. As a resident of Argentina who moved to the United States, I had already learned that American racial categories are not invariably applicable elsewhere. A connection to Africa is not what Tonio wants me to see in him in our first meeting. I gather that for Tonio, as for many other Puerto Ricans who do not engage publicly in the politics of race and color—things African are still cast in a problematic light.

Tonio tells the boy, "Here, take some *chavos* [money] for candy," sending him off. That was the end of my probing into the African connections of Tonio's healing practices.

As I continue to listen attentively to bits and pieces of his life history—the names of living and dead neighbors and family members who had consulted him throughout the years—he begins gradually to add the minute details of his true path as a brujo. He tells me about a miraculous healing he experienced after he had surgery for appendicitis. The incision got badly infected; he instructed a hospital cook to fetch him a piece of fresh bacon, which Tonio placed on the infected scar. "I was immediately cured of the infection," he tells me. The doctors, who had been waiting for the results of all sorts of tests to medicate him, could not explain how he had been suddenly cured.

He knows of all sorts of prayers and healing plants, he tells me. And whenever I might need them, he advises me to get them at Siquito's botánica in Río Piedras, which also carries some good-quality printed Spiritist prayers and Kardec's *The Gospel According to Spiritism*.

> You know, for stains and varicose veins, *persipipí* [folk term for a healing plant] and baths with *saúco* [folk term for *sirrio*] or also boiled milk with raisins and Oilatum [sensitive-skin soap bar] are very good.[2]

He then lists a series of ailments and their possible cures with plants, which I manage to jot down quickly if only partially:

> *Sándalo* [sandalwood], *mejorana* [marjoram], *geranio* [geranium], *yerba buena* [spearmint]; and for the stomach, a mixture of leaves of *guanábano* [cherimoya tree, *annona muricata*] and *Juana la blanca* [angel trumpet, *datura arborea*] should be rubbed with olive [San Rafael] oil or oil of camphor, on the navel.

I wonder if he thinks I came for a consultation, but then he begins to reminisce:

> I used to go to the *monte* [rain forest, mountain] to get the bark of *mabí* [seaside buckthorn, *Colubrina elliptica*]. I harvested it at night and used it during the day. I also made *ditas de higuera*, bowls made of the fruit of the calabash tree [*Crescentia cujete*], which I learned from an African healer who used to wear golden earrings and had a red dragon to overpower *malos pensamientos* (bewitchments).

This reminds him of his own protections:

> I used to have a *Gaspar, Melchor y Baltasar* [The Three Kings] made of stone, but it broke during the last hurricane—I cried so much.

We speak about that hurricane, which hit the island a few months earlier. I tell him how worried I became before the hurricane hit the island, seeing all the preparations people were making and not knowing what exactly I should do. I also tell him how difficult it was for me to drive on the flooded road along the shore of Loíza in the aftermath of the hurricane. As if giving the recipe for a cake, he says,

> Indeed, if you take the *resaca* [debris] that the undercurrent from the bottom of the sea washes to the shore after a tempest, you can make very good incense of it; you can burn it and cleanse yourself.

Shifting the topic slightly to other aspects of his past as a healer, Tonio continues:

> I used to harvest the fruits of the jagua [genipap tree, *genipa americana*]. I could recognize this tree from afar because cattle always gather around it to eat its leaves and fruits. Its fruits are good for the bladder, heart, kidneys, and for alleviating retention of water in the body; for headaches, you take the inside parts of the fruits and use them in a bandage over the head.

Suddenly he shifts from plants to people, apparently remembering that I am from Philadelphia, and begins to tell me about a neighbor of his, a woman who used to live in Philadelphia and then regularly traveled between Loíza and Philadelphia to collect Social Security and visit her son, Luis Ortiz Cruz, who ended up being "burned to death in Philadelphia." Have I understood him correctly—"burned to death"?

> When she came to see me, she didn't yet know about this tragedy but felt very ill. When she learned the truth about her son—that he had been murdered—in complete disbelief she insisted on seeing at least his trousers, but they had been burned as well. She never recovered.

Tonio, I gather, is reviewing the cases he encountered during his many years as a healer. Reminiscing about another of his neighbors, he says,

> Doña Estefania Febre, *negra prieta* [dark, black woman] used to bring me potatoes and eggs as gifts for my spiritual consultations.

Somewhat shifting his tone and expression, Tonio begins to enact an apparent duel between himself and an old bruja, Isidora Osorio, now deceased. While he swings his long hands in front of me, he says,

> She, with her big red-and-white dress, told my apprentice Rafael, *Te voy a sacudir el vestido dos veces* [I will waggle my dress two times in front of you]. It was a bewitchment—and he got sick. With the leaves of *albahaca* [basil] and *ruda* [rue, *ruta chalepensis*] I made a cleansing bath [to free him from Isidora's bewitchment]. Isidora had [an effigy of] Rafael tied to a plant of *guineo* [plantain]. She asked me, "You set him free from my bewitchment?" Apparently she had [spiritually] smelled the scent of the cleansing bath that I had made for Rafael and asked me, "Are you now going to do something against me?"[3]

Aware that he could be the object of Isidora's revenge, Tonio then instructed Purita, a woman who was apprenticing with him,

> When you go to Isidora, check whether she prepared something against me.

Turning to me, he says,

> You know, Raquel, the rosary protects you, especially *el Salve* [Hail Mary].

Thinking about the oddity of Catholic prayers used as shields against the threats of bewitchments, I nonetheless nod and register this as personal advice. Tonio is obviously very well versed in Catholic worship, I think to myself, but he might not know that as a Jewish-born woman I have only a superficial sense of what saying "the Salve" entails.

Lunchtime is approaching, and Tonio's daughter-in-law, a woman in her fifties who is taking care of him, announces that it will be ready shortly.

> You know, Raquel, I used to cook a lot. I was very good at it. I even helped a poor woman who did not know how to cook—not even potatoes. In my house there were always desserts made of grated coconut flakes. We used to put them to dry on a type of wooden block you can't get anymore.

I also share with him a similar recipe for a candy made with grated coconut, the Brazilian *cocada*, which I learned to make during my yearly trips to Brazil, and which, I stress to him, is dried in exactly the same way, showing the connection between the ecology and slave history of Puerto Rico and Brazil. As he continues describing old ways of cooking all sorts of meats and vegetables that entail covering them with banana leaves in outdoor cooking hearths, I can see him delighting in those past flavors as much as he delighted himself in recalling the recipes of the cleansing baths and healing bandages he used to concoct as a healer.

At that moment a tall, chubby black man comes by to visit Tonio. He has just arrived from the United States. He has known Tonio and his household since his childhood, when he used to spend most of the day hanging around and eating at Tonio's house. He announces to Tonio,

> I've come for the fiestas of Santiago Apóstol [the patron saint of Loíza].

To me the man explains,

> I always come back to Loíza. I'm a *loiceño* [native of Loíza] and a *puertorriqueño* [Puerto Rican].

Seeing that Tonio is busy, the man takes his leave:

> I'll come back later to consult with you.

Tonio tells me nothing about this man, not even his name. But a few days later I meet this same person again during the procession of Santiago Apóstol and take a picture of him standing next to one of the masqueraded *caballeros* (knights) at the procession. Dressed in Bermuda shorts, a T-shirt, and a baseball cap—a combination that loudly asserts "I'm an American"—he tells me that before he left for the United States he was destroyed by drinking; his wife left him, and he then drank even more—until he was totally lost. He was always drunk until one day he sat down in front of the church—the one at the center of the Santiago Apóstol procession—and had a vision, implying that Tonio and the cleansing works he had performed for him had something to do with it. Now he is very successful; he lives in the Bronx and has a wonderful job as an ambulance nurse. When he retires he plans to come back to his hometown of Loíza.

After this man leaves, Tonio resumes telling me about certain families he had helped all over the island, naming places, people, and their treatment. I ask him when he began working as a healer.

> At the age of six. One day I had gone as usual to fetch some fresh water from a stream far from the house. I saw a mysterious woman wearing a long dress, down to her feet. I filled one of the buckets with water and then lay down to rest at the center of some palm

A Nuyorican *loiceño* at the fiesta of Santiago Apóstol.

> trees. When a woman approached me, I asked [seeing that she was distraught], "Señora, what's the matter with you?" The woman said, "Give me a little water." She took my bucket and said, "O, My Father, San Antonio [Tonio's full name is Antonio], child of God, help me. They are persecuting me. Where should I go?" After filling another bucket of water for her, I told her to follow me to my house. But she arrived at my house before me. When I got there, my Aunt Jacinta scolded me for arriving so late. "You should have come earlier," she said. "You left about three o'clock to get water." But what Aunt Jacinta did not know was that I had had a miraculous encounter. Seeing that I had gotten into trouble for helping her, the Virgin said to me, "I won't say anything more to you, but I'll leave you with something." That something was the power to "see" and to heal.

Reinforcing the fact of his gift to heal, Tonio tells me he was born in a *zurrón* (caul, birth membrane), believed to be an omen of good luck and special *facultades* (spiritual powers). The historian of religion Keith Thomas (1971:188, 625) mentions similar sixteenth- and seventeenth-century English beliefs in the good fortune of being born with an intact caul wrapped around one's head. The historian Carlo Ginzburg, in his study (1983 [1966]) of the first trial of a *benandante* (fighter of evil witches, often mistaken for the latter) in 1580, tells us that such a birth is a precondition for becoming a benandante. Tonio recalls,

> As a child of five years, I used to say to people, "You have a *causa* [bewitchment]." My mother had to lock me in the house to protect me from the constant flow of people seeking my help.

He then refers to his spiritual powers.

> I see the spirits and they talk to me, but above all is God; faith in God is the most important thing.

I understand what he is trying to tell me: he wants me to know that whatever I have heard about him being a brujo (implying his connection to what people commonly see as black magic), he is a Catholic healer who believes in and draws on the power of the Christian God in his healing practices.

As if sensing that my presence obligates him to give me spiritual advice (although I was not asking for it), Tonio volunteers the recipe for a good-luck bath solution. Though puzzled at such uninvited instructions, I jot them down without objection or question as he dictates them:

> Mix Baño de Flores de Colores y Raíz de Pacholí [bath of various colors and root of patchouli], Agua Divina [divine water], and Flor de Blasón [blazon flower].

As he recites the names of these mass-produced bottled concoctions, he tells me that a wave of *fluídos* (spiritual fluids, ethereal fluids by means of which mediums receive the messages of the spirits) runs through his spine—a sign, I later learn, that the spirits have inspired this recipe for me.

In this, our first conversation of many, Tonio tells me he used to work in the sugarcane fields of the area. I read about them before coming to Puerto Rico. Loíza is known, among other characteristics, for its past as a plantation area where slaves of African ancestry lived and worked. He simply adds, "There used to be lots of cane in this area."

Driving west along Route 187, which borders the sea all the way from Isla Verde to Piñones, one passes pristine pine groves extending along the banks of the biggest mangrove lagoon of the island. Crossing the bridge over the famous Río Grande, one then enters what Puerto Ricans characterize as the blackest and poorest—and remarkably also the most picturesque—town of Puerto Rico: Loíza. Its poverty is a living memorial of the slave society that sustained the numerous sugar plantations of the area during the sugar boom in the second half of the nineteenth century under Spanish rule—and its continued operation with the aid of U.S. capital after the invasion of 1898. Its "local color" is a living postcard crafted by the intense state, tourist, and scholarly attention given to Loíza's "African folkloric expressions," touted in its township brochure as "The Capital of Tradition," following Operation Serenity, the 1950s state-sponsored cultural program that constructed a creole Hispano-Taíno-African tripartite symbol of the newly established commonwealth nation.

Tonio remembers the plantation owner—a man from New York—who used to give him a few coins when he was a child to watch over some areas of the plantation, a role that increased as he became an adult to, eventually, overseer of the entire plantation. But I am surprised that he tells me no horror stories about that time. He remembers, instead, the communal sharing of food—the *arroz y habichuelas* (rice and beans) he ate with the sugarcane workers—during breaks. He does tell me some stories, which I only partially grasp, about the few occasions on which he caught some cane workers getting drunk or having illicit sexual relations during work time on the plantation and how, by means of his spiritual power as a healer, he managed not only to discipline them without jeopardizing their jobs but more generally to address the love, health, and family issues that had caused some of these contraventions in the first place.

He would like to help me, but now, he says, *Soy pájaro con el ala cortá* (I'm a bird with a cut wing). Only a few weeks later did I understand the full meaning of this aphorism when, during another visit, he said, "Spirits are birds."[4]

And because they are birds, he was able "to catch the saints" (*coger santos*, enter into trance) even when he was visiting his sister in New York many years ago. *Los santos se cogen igual en los Estados Unidos* (You can catch the saints the same way in the United States), he says and begins to illustrate this by listing a number of birds one can find in the United States: "doves, swallows, pelicans, parrots . . ." To make his point even stronger, he reminisces:

> At 310 103rd Street in New York City, there was a *centro* [center for mediums and healers]. I went there with a friend and her husband, who was white—like you. I saw Santos Bausa, a medium, enter in trance [with spirits that spoke] in English.

But as a way to distance himself from Santería practitioners, he steadily refused to participate in their rituals because, Tonio tells me, they "do bad things." He explains:

> Once on 115th Street a guy who was performing animal sacrifice [probably offering a chicken] and handling plantains [a direct reference to the offerings made to some of the orishas of Santería] addressed me, saying *trigueño* [colored man], when in fact he was darker than I am [showing me his bare arm]. "Come here to perform some trabajos," he said. I told him, *Cambia el catre que te cae gotera* [Get another cot because water is dripping over this one—You're misreading who I am and what I might do for you]. If you show you're submissive, you're in trouble. Of course I told him, "No!" Also, to another woman, Isidora, nicknamed Tindora, I responded [as a form of dare], "If your lemon has spines, my orange tree will spike them" [I will overpower you].

Tonio was voicing a warning with bravado that I would hear recurrently among various healers who, in spite of working on similar grounds with others, feel the need to assert their unique spiritual powers as stronger than those of all others, in no small measure as a professional survival strategy.[5]

After almost three-quarters of a century treating hundreds—perhaps even thousands—of clients from dawn to dusk, he had to stop a few years ago, Tonio says. Trance and spirit possession had become too strenuous for his frail body. Even his *protecciones* (guardian spirits), which had helped him "overpower any brujo in the past," could not shield him in his condition now. So he refers me to Haydée, "a very positive medium and powerful espiritista bruja," one of his spiritual godchildren, with whom I would go on to work intensely as an apprentice.

I kept visiting Tonio every week, with and without Haydée, until I left Puerto Rico at the end of 1996. I often brought him foods that he liked or gave him some money for shopping. During these visits I would witness a host of his clients and friends from all parts of the island parade through his house, asking for advice, even though formally he was no longer working. I also heard him conducting numerous overseas consultations on the phone and saw packages containing trabajos being mailed to cities on the mainland such as Kansas City, New York, and Chicago. He was not a bird with a cut wing, after all.

Every time I came to visit him, alone or with Haydée, he would suggest recipes for food as well as for healing and cleansing preparations and share his knowledge about medicinal and magical plants. But with her he also compared notes, and that was exciting to observe. I particularly liked to see them spontaneously engage in "ritual gossip" about clients they had in common and about trabajos they had made, as well as current ruminations on their personal lives. The intensity and speed of their exchanges was hard to follow. Whenever I was unclear about a word or part of a story, I was able to clarify it with Haydée afterward. This is what I did once when they mentioned a plant named *bora bora* in the midst of talking about women and love affairs. By their giggles, gestures, and half-words, I managed to understand they were talking about the *chocha* (slang for vagina)—which of course increased my curiosity. Haydée told me furtively,

> You can't find this plant at a pharmacy or botánica. It is used to shrink the chocha—ha! ha! ha! In Santo Domingo they use the nuts of *guapana* [folk term].

I was struck by how intimate the clients get with their brujos and by how complicitous I felt in learning such secrets.

After Tonio's wife died suddenly of a stroke when I was on one of my short visits home in Philadelphia, the traditional *novenas* (communal prayers of the rosary for nine days) were offered for her at their home. Upon my arrival on July 17, the closing day of the novena, I went to his home with Haydée and Reina, her assistant, to take part in it. All of their children, each an experienced medium, had assumed the organization and performance of the prayers. Many people gathered in the living room, sitting in a circle and chanting the rosary, presided over by Tonio's oldest son. I moved to an inconspicuous space outside the circle when the praying began, feeling awkward at not being able to follow the litany. At the end of the novena and after cupcakes and refreshments had been served, everyone but Tonio moved to the small altar house built for him in the yard behind his house, where a closing velada was going to be conducted, again with Tonio's oldest son presiding, in the presence of family members, well-known espiritistas, and other acquaintances. This presented a unique opportunity for me to enter the altar house, which had remained shut once his practice was formally closed. A thirty-by-thirty-foot one-room building, it is one of the oldest altar houses in Puerto Rico.

Before anyone entered, strong incense was burned to cleanse the place. Haydée and I had to stay outside longer than the others because of our asthma; when we finally entered, I saw several rows of santos aligned with candles and flowers in an elaborate display, conveying a clear sense of the myriad spiritual forces Tonio had acquired over the years as a brujo. The number of chairs set around the Spiritist table in concentric rows is evidence of the popularity of the monthly veladas Tonio used to hold for professionals, politicians, and working-class people over the course of a half-century.

The walls were covered with chromolithographs, many of Jesus and of the Buddha in addition to those of various saints. Flowers and all sorts of figurines were placed in rows on shelves all around the walls. At the center, a white table was set in the traditional Spiritist manner: two glass bowls filled with water for cleansings and occasionally for divination; three white candles; a bottle of consecrated water containing herbs and perfumes, used for cleansings and blessings; a Bible; a Spiritist prayer book; and a small bell used to open the velada and, during it, to alert people of the presence of spirits.

The lights went off, the bell was rung, blessings were said, and the velada began. During the whole velada a number of messages were given to specific participants by mediums in trance. When I heard one of the mediums call, "*Esa de* brown" [That one in brown], my heart started racing. The only person dressed in brown, I had to stand up and receive the message meant for me. "I see a book that is being closed," was the cryptic message given to me by the spirit, after which I was induced to approach the table and cleanse myself, especially the area of my head, with the water in one of the bowls. Confused, and threatened a bit, I let go of the tension when we all had to tap our feet and hold our arms up in spiritual communion to frighten off some evil spirit who was disclosed as pestering one of the participants. When I later asked Haydée what the message to me meant, she replied that somebody had bad thoughts for me, and that was the reason I had to cleanse myself.

Perhaps as a result of the increasing intimacy and ease of subsequent conversations over the year, I learned not only about Tonio's deeds as a divinely inspired espiritista but also as a *brujo malo* (wicked brujo, an espiritista who also performs black magic). I also learned about his desire "to fly over the Yunque," the rain forest of Puerto Rico only a few miles southeast of Loíza. Haydée and Tonio would often tease each other: "So when are we going to fly over the Yunque?"

When Tonio, the "Brujo of Loíza," spoke of flying over the Yunque, he was connecting the world of 1996 with the Spanish colonial imaginary of flying witches during the Inquisition, as well as with four centuries of colonial nightmares and fantasies, often misrepresented as typical of Latin American "magic realism." But as the spiritual godfather of many present-day Puerto Rican brujos espiritistas, he was also more than likely referring, via a Spiritist metaphor, to the experience of mediumship following the Spiritist tradition of Allan Kardec. Who knows, perhaps he was also referring to the postmortem flight of spirits to the abode of ancestors, typical of ancestor-worship beliefs found among Bantu-speaking people in the Angola-Congo region of West–Central Africa and their descendants in the Americas as well as among the indigenous pre-Columbian Taínos.

Healers of many disparate traditions in Puerto Rico consider the Yunque to be the abode of spiritual entities of African, Creole, and Amerindian origin, as well as a mystical realm over which brujos hover during their nocturnal flights.[6] Are these the same spiritual flights outsiders have referred to as flying witches over the centuries? Greco-Roman lore traces these flights to the power of witches to transform themselves into birds, especially owls and ravens. A strange connection arises. Tonio said spirits are birds. Books on European medieval witchcraft have plenty of stories about the flight of witches—on brooms, forks, or shovels, or with cats—circling over villages as embodiments of the devil. In sixteenth-century Italy, for example, the benandanti, mentioned earlier, claimed to use their nightly flights to fight witches (the devil) in the name of Christ. They were nonetheless persecuted and tried—the alluded benevolence of their flights disregarded by the Inquisition (Ginzburg 1983 [1966]). The Puerto Rican folklorist Teodoro Vidal recorded stories (1989:13–23) about the flight of witches circulating among Puerto Ricans, mainly peasants, he met between 1968 and 1974 and again in 1987 in various places on the island, such as Loíza, Sabana Grande, San Germán, and Carolina. These stories, assumed to have been passed down from parents to children over generations, depict how Puerto Rican female witches were seen, again, flying like birds, often naked, beating their arms (or a pair of palm branches held underneath their armpits), or thrusting multilayered starched skirts against the wind.

Flying witches (drawings by Jack Delano published in Vidal 1989).

These stories reflect the "inherited" fear (and scorn) that flying witches have produced in the imagination and folklore of Puerto Ricans. Most importantly, these nocturnal voyages, patterned upon similar stories in medieval Catholic Europe, were commonly thought of as intended to cause harm—and often death—to fellow villagers. These flights, occurring mostly on Tuesdays and Thursdays but always begun at midnight, were initiated—stories tell—by special rubbings of oils and by spells that were essentially meant to voice the rejection of the existence of God, Mary, and the saints—refutations that not surprisingly mimic the evil motivation of accused witches assumed by the Inquisition. Before engaging in nocturnal flights, witches would declare, *Sin Dios ni Santa María, con el diablo me voy* (Without God and Saint Mary, with the devil I go). Folk stories also tell of flying mishaps that befell malicious witches, exposing their carelessness and stupidity along with their malevolence. There are other stories about some witches who, hiding at the last minute before nocturnal departure from their loved ones and neighbors, mispronounced their spell. Instead of declaring, *Sin Dios ni Santa María*, they accidentally said, *Con Dios y Santa María* (With God and Saint Mary). They found themselves, as a consequence, lying flat on their faces, not hovering in the air over their village houses, and—as a moral conclusion to the story—the object of the scorn and punishment by villagers (Vidal 1989:13–23).

Tonio knows the whereabouts of healing plants and animals in every niche and mound of Puerto Rico; in our conversations he recalls hundred of the names of families and individuals he has helped out in Loíza and other neighborhoods all over the island. The recitation of places evokes the names of specific healing and magical plants that grow only in one of those places—on a certain mountaintop, for instance, or on the bank of a certain river. The names of healing plants trigger, in turn, their effects: the *llantén* (a broad-leaf plantain, *Plantaginaceae*), for example, produces *llanto* (tears). The natural effects of plants anticipate, finally, their spiritual effects: the effervescence of the *mabí* (soldierwood, *Colubrina reclinata*) produces renewed energy.[7] A first lesson in the chain of mimesis is being rendered to me. People, plants, and plants' desired effects on people—as Sir James Frazer (1960 [1922]) may have phrased it—are magically connected by various types of contact: by being parts of a whole and being connected by physical, metaphoric, semantic, and emotional proximity. Plants and their healing and magical effects also are connected to humans by the principle of similarity: the degree of resemblance and correspondence between the sounds and meanings of words and their referents, that is, a linguistic similarity semantically connects plants and human emotions. A personal name that is part of a location, a location that contains a plant, and a plant whose signifier and some of its attributes denote its magical effects on human emotions are all looped in chains of similarity and contact.

I am not permitted to tape our conversations or take photographs of Tonio, for mechanical copies of his voice and face would then be available for abuse (in trabajos, for instance) if they fell into the wrong hands. As an unfortunate consequence, rapidly spoken invaluable information vanishes before I can render it in writing. And because of the esoteric nature of much of his communication, many words remain unintelligible even to me, a native Spanish speaker. (It also does not help that he is missing a lower denture!) I find myself drawn even more to his eyes and hands instead, searching for the gestural equivalents of those meanings I lose when attending only to his words. The antics of his huge hands recreate past worlds and events in front of me. Mesmerized, I follow his arms and head as they move suggestively yet precisely, mimicking his career as a brujo. Detailed recipes for the preparation of magical potions and healing mixtures are dramatized in front of my eyes, his long fingers modeling sizes, quantities, and modes of extracting potent juices that had been injected into a dead lizard or wax figurine. He says,

> I use the round leaf, not the long one. I take a *cantito* (bit) like this, and then—*¡pángana!* [boom!].

While his hands are measuring the size of the toxic plant he is reminiscing about having used for the preparation of a strong trabajo, he grimaces from the acidity of the magic potion as if he were tasting it right there; and as his arms are knocking down some imaginary enemy, he shouts a passionate *pángana* that converts his grimace into a wicked, victor's smile. He is not only a Catholic healer, then, but a savvy, powerful brujo who never hesitates to perform a "strong" trabajo when needed to revoke a misfortune sent against a client.

Tonio confirms what others said of him; he is a *brujo malo*. But, he explains to me, he only makes a *trabajo malo*—what the literature on Africa and Latin America refers to as "black magic" and *magia negra*, respectively—when he wants to punish somebody else's evil actions. His trabajos are never inspired by evil motives—quite the opposite: they are meant to *revocar* (invalidate, revoke, and retaliate against) black magic. *Brujos malos hablan malo* (brujos who perform trabajos malos use profanity), he also points out, because they have to *hablar claro y directo* (speak in a clear and direct manner). The voices of the spirits are above social conventions; they *llaman las cosas por su nombre* (call things by their names, tell it like it is).

On my visits to his home, I saw several reenactments of that powerful, mysterious instant when the magic inflicted upon a dead lizard reaches—through what Frazer (1960 [1922]) termed "sympathetic magic" in reference to the principle of similarity (in an iconic way)—its real victim miles away. At times I saw Tonio draw in the air with his thumb pressed against his index finger, as if holding a thin string, the circumference representing the waist of a person. He was mimicking a familiar movement he used to perform to magically tie lovers or estranged couples together. Pieces of clothing worn by individuals who were the object of magic works would be stretched ethereally in front of my eyes between Tonio's hands and placed in imaginary boxes or containers, modeling another principle of magic: contact or contagion, by means of which a part of the whole can affect the whole in a synecdochic way.

In fact, what I was experiencing whenever Tonio mimicked the trabajos he used to perform was a reenactment, a copy of those trabajos he had performed years ago. These were copies of copies; also, each reenactment was a piece of *that* whole. It was a mimesis of mimesis as much as it was a part that belonged to a whole (his whole life as a brujo): the mimetic memory of instances of magical mimesis and contagion. I could not grasp the whole of it then. And even now I can sense those moments only for a flash before losing them. This is a different way of knowing. Was that the lesson Tonio wished for me to learn?

If it is through copies and contact that magic works, these must bridge the space between the *here* and the *there* in order to connect the object of the magic with its simile (in iconic or synecdochic ways) so as to affect the victim through its representation. Similarly, Tonio's mimetic gestures have bridged over time, connecting the performance of *that* magic act with *this* embodied mimetic memory. Tonio had bewitched me with the magic of mimesis—with the power of similes twice removed. I had entered the sensuous realm of witchcraft through its chamber of reflecting mirrors. Its various histories flickered in our meetings through chains of similarity and contact, through images, gestures, grimaces, people, and events displaced in space and time. These histories embodied in Tonio's gestural lexicon were replicas, parts that stood for the whole, for the entirety of his life as a renowned powerful brujo.

These somatic accounts are cunning histories, indeed. As I write these lines I wonder: Would this rendering be a third-level replica, a mimetic enactment, a metonymic rendering of those parts that stood for previous wholes? Michael Taussig has reflected on these issues in *Mimesis and Alterity* (1993), characterizing ethnography as "Embodied Retelling": if ethnographies *instantiate*, or make *concrete*, they illustrate the magic of mimesis wherein the replication, the copy, acquires the power of the represented. Are readers of these examples thereby "lifted out of [themselves] into these images?" (16). Just as witches and shamans capture and create power by making models (copies) of agents and objects of social power, so do ethnographies when they set to "model" realities in writing. Making an analogy between ethnographic writing and the magician's art of reproduction with the intention of estranging writing itself, Taussig further puzzles over the ethnographer's model: "If it works, [the model] gains through its sensuous fidelity something of the power and personality of that of which it is a model," showing "the capacity of the imagination to be lifted through representational media, such as marks on a page, into other worlds" (16). Comparatively, for shamans and witches the mimetic faculty is used "to capture that very same spirit power" of the original, while for ethnographers it is employed to graph the essence of the ethnos (the group). Yet in the latter form of copying reality, Taussig suggests, "the stakes are no less important" than for the former (17).

I realize now that I engage here in a kind of "gossip style" anthropology, not only by the way I learned about Tonio's past deeds but also in the way I convey his stories to you, the reader. Not coincidentally, Taussig has followed this form of reporting—narrativizing or, following Bauman and Briggs (1990), entextualizing—his field notes in *Shamanism, Colonialism, and the Wild Man* (1987). Apparently, the subaltern—in this case the shaman—speaks better through gossip, a form of speech classically relegated to the margins of the Enlightenment, in general, and the knowledge society, in particular. Magic and witchcraft, it seems, can only reappear in an experience-based discourse that escapes the disciplinary techniques of rational and empirical proposition making.

At noon on a day when I am visiting Tonio, the phone rings. In a flicker, he crosses himself over his chest and, before picking up the receiver, over the ear against which he will press the receiver. It is a client from Manhattan. He gives her precise and detailed instructions, suggesting that she pray before going to work; buy some herbs, oils, and prayers at a nearby botánica on 117th Street; and wait until he mails her a package with a special magic work. Puzzled, I ask him why he crossed himself before picking up the phone and murmured the rosary after hanging up.

> My enemies might still be trying to bewitch me using every possible means, such as a phone, especially at noon, when magic works most effectively. [Remember,] I'm a brujo malo.

Oblivious of any scholarly, rationalist separation between religion and magic, Tonio, being a faithful follower of the Gospels and their reinterpretation by Spiritism, constantly invokes the powers of Catholic symbolism without revering its institutions. His knowledge of Catholic worship, for example, proves critical (as a matter of life and death) after the performance of a magic work that involves "catching" evil spirits and then praying the rosary to exorcise them.

One thing I regret, as I am writing now, not asking then is this: Why did Tonio cross his ear? I had only seen people touch their foreheads and cross their chests. Probably it was an additional protection, the cross acting as a material, literal shield, following the mimetic faculty of magic, against malicious, poisoned words. Jesus, represented on the cross, had protected priests and Spaniards in Spain and its colonies from brujos and all other sorts of evil since the Inquisition. That same cross, once the symbol of European hegemony—used by colonizers as a spiritual shield against brujos and many others who were perceived as fearsome polluters in Spain and the colonies—was now being invoked to protect a brujo against other brujos in Puerto Rico. By what kind of mimetic cunning has the spiritual power that was once monopolized by priests been seized by witches? Why have those considered the repositories of evil appropriated the very power that was meant to destroy them?

After Catholicism had been imposed by force and the threat of annihilation, indigenous and marginal creole populations crossed themselves and prayed (in innumerable instances, probably) for protection against a host of newly imported evils anathema to Catholicism as well as for protection against the evils of colonial oppression itself. Since the cross was intimately associated with colonial rule, it was most likely seen not only as a religious symbol but also as a symbol of power—a power that was as much coveted and ritually appropriated as it was feared: the power invested in the cross pirated by those who were meant to fear it (Romberg 2005b).

Accessing chains of similarities at cosmic crossroads between this and other worlds, between North, South, East, and West through ritual symbolic gestures of crossing oneself, might have been unexpectedly familiar for some. After all, the European cross might have elicited, via infinite chains of resemblances, safe memories of other crosses, those that used to summon the Congo gods unwillingly left across the ocean.[8] The ability to tap into and intervene in chains of similarity or sympathy—using all sorts of

A magic work hanging from a cross.

magical rites that concretize displaced images (of desired referents)—might have informed this unforeseen fascination with the colonial cross and its symbolic power.

Taussig ponders where this wondrous chain of sympathy begins and ends (1993:72). Suggesting that these wonders are not limited to sorcerers, he writes, they surely "have also been displaced by the expansion of European colonialism from the sixteenth century on" (ibid.). All those gestures encompassing "first contact" between colonizers and colonized at the point of conquest were marked by an essential mishap and misrecognition of chains of similarity, forever permeating future interactions between indigenous and marginalized populations and hegemonic colonial forces as well as the colonial boundaries between good and evil, Catholic and pagan, civilized and wild (Taussig 1987, 1993).

But the civilizing power, which for centuries and under many guises had aimed at taming the unruly, wild sphere of African and Amerindian healing and magic through Catholicism (and later through modernity), was transformed by brujos and reflected back on the civilized world in uncanny ways: the fascination of brujos with the symbols of civilizing powers that had meant to subdue them was rechanneled into actual magic power. How can one not be amazed by such magic?

Proximity—imaginary or cognitive, but always imperceptible—of physically distant or unrelated elements both defines and defies mimesis. Is that what Taussig (1993) and Cantwell (1993) were thinking when they suggested, each in his own terms, that mimesis is intrinsic to the making of culture? What Taussig calls "the mimetic faculty" is universal: "the nature that culture uses to create second nature, the faculty to copy, imitate, make models, explore difference, yield into and become Other" (1993:xiii). Impersonation or embodiment is part of this culture-making process; it involves both taking on the lives and roles of others and subliminally and physically participating in this enactment as audiences (Cantwell 1993:5). Cantwell regards this impersonation, "at once mostly unconscious and spontaneous and thoroughly ubiquitous in human social relations . . . as the vital medium of social communication and hence ultimately culture" (5).

But, most frighteningly, impersonation at the cultural level—even as it is motivated by the desire and fascination with the exploration of difference—can also produce irrational violence, as vital established differences (of class, gender, or race) are jeopardized by imitation. For the "wonder of mimesis lies in the copy drawing on the character and power of the original to the point whereby the representation may even assume that character and that power" (Taussig 1993:xiii). Symbolic and other forms of violence are inescapable, since "once the mimetic has sprung into being, a terrifically ambiguous power is established; there is born the power to represent the world, yet that same power is a power to falsify, mask, and pose" (Taussig 1993:42–43).

The controversial literary critic René Girard (1965 [1961]) invites us to look at the relations of power, control, and hidden violence that such impersonation, driven by a "mimetic desire," entails from a psychological, Lacanian perspective, suggesting that it encompasses a triangular motivational relationship between the desiring Subject, the Model of desire, and the Object of desire (see also Cottet 2000, Livingston 1992). Inspired by the trajectories of key characters in literary masterpieces by Cervantes, Stendhal, Proust, and Dostoyevsky, Girard suggests that the mimetic desire is based on a fascination with the Model, who has something the Subject lacks and therefore wishes to possess, and which is materialized in the desire to possess the Object of desire of the Model. In the case of Don Quixote (the Subject), for example, his expressed wishes to imitate in every detail the life and adventures of the Amadis de Gaule or his chivalrousness (the

Object of desire of the Model) mediates his envy of and wish to become the Amadis de Gaule (the Model), a wish that responds to a basic lack Don Quixote perceives in himself. This apparently cumbersome but quite obvious proposition makes sense also in the ethereal space that informs social interaction in that it implicates an apparent absence that mediates between the fascination with the Other and the envy of not being the Other. The Model's fear and even repulsion of being imitated (the threat of the erasure of significant differences, mentioned earlier)—the other side of the mimetic desire—adds to the implied social-symbolic violence of mimetic desire.

If one applies this insight to figuring out the practices of brujos, not literary characters, then the imitation and incorporation of the sacred gestures of Catholicism during centuries of Catholic colonial rule seem less indicative of mere submission and more a desire to posses its power, which brujos lacked and envied. Their impersonation, a direct result of their marginality, responds to their mimetic desire to appropriate the transcendental (and in Latin America, also civilizing) power of the Church (Romberg 2005b).[9] Hence the violence that every act of irreverent impersonation generates for hegemonic institutions, whose monopoly depends on keeping social and moral categories separate and clear—not tarnished by imitation and therein by the dangers of counterfeit and pretense (Bhabha 1994).

In post-emancipation and post-independence eras, such irreverent impersonations turned into pollution nightmares that endangered the very fabric of nation-building projects in the Caribbean (Romberg 2005b). In Puerto Rico and elsewhere in the Americas, state agencies persecuted vernacular healing practices for being "atavistic remnants" of a "premodern, irrational" past that threatened the order of rational nation-states. And yet, when agents of development and progress needed to resolve, if only temporarily, their own modern ailments, they often sought the wild, enchanting world of brujos (forged as such by colonial fears and misconceptions). This imagined world inhabited by fierce Amerindians and mischievous Congo spirits must have stirred "Mr. Allen"—an American accountant for a U.S.-owned plantation where Tonio worked as an overseer of cane cutters—to seek Tonio's help in the 1950s. Several geographic and moral boundaries that separated the order of the corporation and the disorderly realm of coastal plantations and the color line of imagined danger and impurity as well as sensuousness were crossed each time Mr. Allen came to consult Tonio. Attracted by the desire to seize upon the power, in his eyes, of this tall, "black" brujo, he knew that when Tonio in trance embodied an indigenous hunter-spirit of the rain forest, no person or spirit who was the target of his spiritual performance could resist his power. Mr. Allen must have been told time and again, for example, that estranged lovers could not resist Tonio's love incantations, and he must have witnessed the famous *ligas* (ties) Tonio used to perform (and which I have witnessed him miming), pleading with Changó (the Afro-American spirit of seduction) to reunite lovers and seal their love forever in the cosmos.[10]

Tonio no doubt executed this work in the same slow and profound voice I hear him now recount Mr. Allen's long-ago appeal to him. As Tonio utters the magical words of the past, his eyes open wide; I feel that Changó himself is there in front of me, directly casting his spell on me. I watch Tonio trace in the air with his long fingers the contours of an invisible calabash, delightfully taking his time to mime with exquisite care the motions of stuffing it with honey, pieces of bark, fresh aromatic plants, and all sorts of inebriating perfumes, before offering it to Changó in exchange for his interventions in bringing back estranged spouses or lovers.

I can only imagine Mr. Allen's fascination with the copy of him produced by the dexterous hands of Tonio manipulating the tiny wax figurine (simile) of his body with penetrating aromas and exquisite oils before performing a trabajo for him. I feel a fleeting vertigo in savoring the copy of that copy being reenacted in front of my eyes as I recognize in Tonio's face the lavishness I have learned to recognize in Changó, the irresistible African seducer. Perhaps this is the same vertigo that Mr. Allen felt as he saw himself reflected in the copy of him crafted and manipulated by Tonio.

Through the magical power of mimesis and contact with Tonio (and, through Tonio, with Changó's attributes), Mr. Allen had experienced, if only for an instant, the moral elsewhere of magic; he had possessed the uncanny, unruly, uncultivated space of the Other. Mr. Allen, the agent of development and progress, saw himself reflected in the image Tonio had created of him, an image that reflected his own desires to possess the sensual, polluted world of the Other. When Mr. Allen came to Loíza from Washington, D.C., he not only had crossed the Atlantic, separating the U.S. mainland from Puerto Rico, but had also surreptitiously traversed into a space and time foreign, in his mind, to the organizational sphere of progress and development. Through the power of mimetic desire he had entered the mysterious yet equally powerful ancient world of Amerindian and African spirits.

Was I also mesmerized by the magical power of mimesis, enacted in front of my eyes in Tonio's gestures, in the innumerable, scattered mimetic memories of his life as a brujo? I could only see a rendering, an imperfect, incomplete copy of that copy of the object of that magic work. Yet, even imperfect copies, as Taussig reminds us (1993:17), are effective in acquiring the power of the original, in appropriating the essence of the object represented. Paul Stoller tells us (1997:12–13) that the sorcerer knows that while the arrow he shoots—carrying sickness to a rival—may fall idle on the floor, the "inside arrow" flies, if the sorcerer's aim is good, above the sky to meet its target. The shooting light that the rationalist Edward Evans-Pritchard reported (1976 [1937]:11) seeing in the middle of the night and interpreted as a bonfire might have been, Stoller suggests, the "fire" of witchcraft (as the natives later assured Evans-Pritchard), an "emanation" of the witch's body, dispatched to cause death to an unsuspecting victim in a nearby compound (Stoller 1997:12–13). That is how magic works. Outwardly imperfect copies may carry the internally perfect copy.

How many imperfect copies had the earth seen Tonio bury, had the rivers seen him deposit for the current to take away, had the forests seen him hide beneath its foliage! Now, I see his fingers touch, prick, stuff, cover, and powder invisible doves, lizards, snakes. In a parallel realm their targeted doubles may have sensed the pain, the restraint, or the liberation that these animals had suffered or enjoyed on another plane. I follow Tonio's stand-in performance, as he moves his mimicking hands through the antics of sewing a calf's tongue stuffed with hot peppers, severing the throat of a chicken, and mixing an enemy's semen with bitter herbs. Some of these mimetic memories trigger the names of lawyers who won "lost" cases thanks to their suddenly "overpowering tongues" in the courtroom. Such memories elicit a vindictive smile, a reenactment of the joy he must have felt when seeing how accusing witnesses literally lost their voices or abusive husbands lost their sexual powers while their wives neutralized their female competitors. Meticulously pointing to the locations where these magical works had been placed or buried, his long arms move, drawing in the air the directions that correspond to a distant rain forest or nearby cemetery and river. Putting his hands in front of me, Tonio says,

> All the trabajos I have made the earth ate them. How many magic works have I done with these hands!

The embodied memories I see Tonio enacting before my eyes are current reflections of past reflections of power that had once bewitched brujos and now serve their magic works.[11] These are habits acquired through centuries of Catholic indoctrination and repression (and, more recently, through the enticements of modernity and the state), all of which I can now sense and transmit as sensuous renditions.

I think I understand: the gestures of magic bewitch not only once but twice. In his *Sensuous Scholarship* (1997), Stoller argues that although inscribed in the body, the gestures of magic and spirit-possession are not, as postmodern and feminist theories had once suggested, "readable as discourse." They are to be sensed, smelled, and felt in order to be "understood." Even academics, as Stoller himself exemplified when he became inexplicably ill in the field after falling in disgrace with one of his informants, cannot escape their own bodies as knowing vessels. They too could be bewitched.

"Remember, Raquel," Tonio said, "we brujos have a power that makes things we say, in whatever form, happen that same way." I remember him wishing to fly over the Yunque. I wonder, was it a flight that meant to mirror those other ones of pre-conquest Taínos, of enslaved Africans on American soils longing for Africa, or of flying witches on brooms imagined in the Spanish Inquisition? Or maybe it was a flight that encompassed all those flights altogether. After all, contact, an essential precondition for magic to work, pervades the history of witchcraft in Puerto Rico to this day.

After their usual long gossip session on one of the many occasions I visited Tonio with Haydée, she asked him, half-jokingly in order to lift his spirit in light of his declining health,

> So, Tonio, when are we going to fly over the Yunque?

As if to alleviate her concern, he responded as a true brujo malo,

> Weed never dies.

He smiled in complicity and continued gossiping. He must have known that flying over the Yunque as a brujo was no longer a possibility for him as much as that flying as a spirit would take just a bit longer.

The last time I saw Tonio was on the day I left Puerto Rico. He was in bed, and for the first time in the eighteen months I had known him

The last day Haydée and I visited Tonio.

he let me take his picture—and videotape a conversation between him and Haydée. With his usual overtly sensuous self, he seemed to enjoy our attention to his playful self-display. He smiled and posed for my camera, even though he was bedridden and clothed in baggy pajamas. It was a joyful occasion for all three of us, one worthy—we all seemed to realize at that very moment—of being documented as a commemorative trophy. I kept a copy of these photos for myself and mailed two other sets to Haydée to share with Tonio.

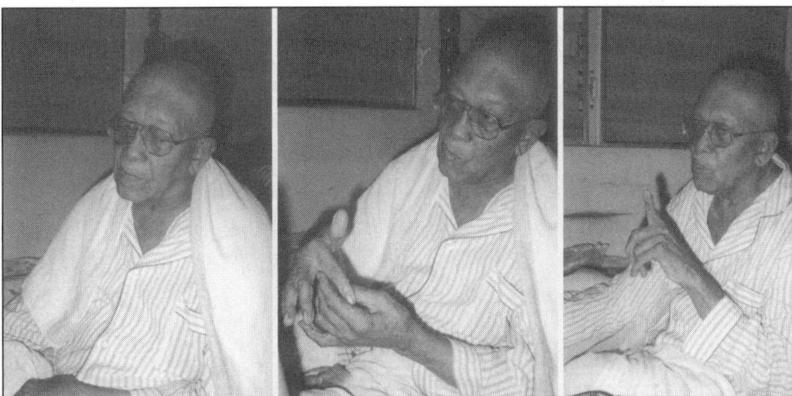

Tonio describing the trabajos he used to make.

Tonio's hands.

Now I have a copy of Tonio for myself. Possessing a part of him, his reflection on paper, makes me feel empowered. Somewhat like a bruja seizing one of the infinite links of chains of resemblance, I can invoke my memories of Tonio. But, curiously, I still feel apprehensive about showing these pictures for the first time in public. When I left that day, Tonio said that the next time I came to Puerto Rico he would not be *there* any more. I would like to regard his last gesture of allowing me to photograph him as a gift to me.[12]

On one sad day in December 1998, Haydée phoned me, crying, telling me that Tonio, her spiritual father, had just died. His wake and burial were like those of the most esteemed public figures. Hundreds of flower crowns, including the one I had sent from Philadelphia in recognition of his generosity to me, accompanied his way to the Loíza cemetery, where the mayor, in line with his public and personal duty to the Brujo de Loíza, delivered the eulogy, lending to the event the official status usually accorded only to public figures. His eulogy was again a copy, empowering anew.

As the successor of a long line of brujos in his father's lineage, the Lacéns, who had originated in Antigua, Barbados, during the slave past, Tonio had mimed their memories in countless magical works, visions, and spirit possession. Flying over the Yunque might have been a quest to fly the

Tonio, the Brujo of Loíza.

Their desired flight over the Yunque perfected at death.

imagined journeys of European witches or those of African sorcerers or maybe still to flutter in the ethereal space of creole saints, Congo deities, and nature and ancestor spirits—of the fierce Taíno, national heroes, and enlightened free-thinkers. His quest might have been aimed at mirroring the stages of spiritual development envisioned by espiritismo that guide the upward path connecting the recent dead, the near-spirits, the ancient spirits and deities, and the enlightened ones. His material death, what espiritistas refer to as "disincarnation," might have initiated his path through several spiritual realms, bringing him into contact with the spirits of other powerful brujos and closer to his intended and much anticipated flight over the Yunque, the paradise of brujos and timeless spirits: a flight perfected at death.[13]

Coda

On March 21, 2000, at the age of fifty-five and only two years after Tonio's death, Haydée died of a massive heart attack while in the Dominican Republic. She had gone there in hopes of recovering from the overwhelming sorrow and depression brought on by the death, three months earlier, of Eliseo, the youngest and last surviving of her three children.

Chapter Two
DREAMS

While dreaming is common to all human beings, not everyone makes the recording, telling, interpreting, and circulating of them an important part of the everyday experience of dreaming. As soon as I arrived in Puerto Rico in the summer of 1995 to conduct an exploratory research on the circulation of spiritual practices between the island and the U.S. mainland, I realized that describing one's dreams and asking others to interpret them is a common practice, even among quasi-strangers, as I was for many. In various situations since my first days in Puerto Rico—at the university, in stores, and obviously in botánicas and at any gathering of healers—people spontaneously shared their dreams with me as soon as they learned I was interested in espiritismo and brujería, although at the time my research did not encompass dreams. Oftentimes people shared with me not only their own dreams but also others' dreams that they considered worth telling. These were not just any dreams; they were assumed to have had a decisive role in the waking lives of the dreamers, especially in the life-changing choices they made as a consequence.

Indeed, in the context of espiritismo, sharing dream narratives acquires a singular religious meaning, for they are thought to be messages from the otherworld. Composing a speech genre almost in itself, dream narratives are recognized as an appropriate form of communication among close and not so close interlocutors. Memorable and decisive, these dreams are viewed as messages from their dead loved ones, messages that are considered—as in many other well-documented ancient and present-day societies—omens and prophecies for the living. These accounts were told to me, a foreigner, as proof of the intimate relationship between humans and spirits, as evidence that communication with the world of the dead and the spirits is a fact. That humans need to pay close attention to dreams is the implied message communicated to me time and again in these early stages of my research.

I was introduced to Mani, a man in his thirties, on a street in Old San Juan by a mutual friend and colleague of mine from Philadelphia, and he began telling me about his dreams as soon as he heard about my research. His unforgettable, life-changing dreams were related to his protecciones, especially to his long-dead grandmother, "who always tells me things in dreams, for me and my family." Once he dreamt that his grandmother, "who had long dark hair, performed a singing rosary [*rosario cantado*, healing prayer] for my aunt who was sick with cancer. Some time later, when my aunt underwent all sorts of tests, everything came out negative!" When he has such "healing dreams," he added, he wakes up "with an incredible sense of peace."

During the first months of my fieldwork I rented a tiny bedroom in Old San Juan. It was there that I befriended Sara and Julia, two elderly neighbors (the first an espiritista-santera, the second a fervent churchgoing Catholic). Narrated in a casual tone similar to that of a kitchen talk about a recent visitor, their dreams conveyed, however, important messages they received at night from their loved ones. Sometimes they warned them of impending dangers and trips they should not make or reminded them of basic everyday precautions they should take in order to be safe, such as locking doors more carefully or distancing themselves from certain people and places. At other times their dreams forecast impending conflicts with their loved ones or provided the two of them with guidance on making important health-related and emotional decisions. Had they missed following the suggestions given to them in dreams, they would have suffered a lot, they told me. It was thanks to their special sensitivity and belief in God as well as the quality of their mediumship abilities, both women held, that they were able to regularly decipher these encrypted messages.

One morning I accompanied Sara to the administrative office at the national Parliament, where she did some volunteer work for her party representatives. There I met Clara, one of Sara's friends, whose mother was an espiritista. Her mother, Clara told me, would divine the problems of her loved ones either in trance or through visions she had, most of which were given to her in dreams. Her "seeing a lot in dreams" meant that she was also good at deciphering the messages given to her in dreams by the spirits.[1] If, however, relatives and friends fail to interpret them, dreamers need to seek the expertise of healers and mediums. This is what motivated Eric, a young man in his twenties and a friend of Haydée's son, to seek her help. Although he did not tell me what it was about, he just said he recently had a very unsettling dream and thus needed to come consult with Haydée urgently, for he felt that the dream encoded some important message for him, one that might have tragic consequences if he failed to decode it in time. Though not sure of its precise meaning, Eric evidently had enough experience participating in collective dream interpretation sessions to characterize this one dream as potentially threatening for his future.

In the course of a few months of work with healers and mediums, I listened to dreams and their interpretations and was able to learn, even if unsystematically and unreflectively, about the ways in which interpretations are delivered following espiritista practices. Intrigued by this particular system for deciphering dreams, I purchased in a botánica a cheap booklet on dream symbols, which I kept as a sort of handy if popular consulting resource. Interestingly, although not a medium myself—only one who worked with a few—I was sometimes asked to offer my interpretation when I was present at the telling of a dream. Feeling quite awkward, I usually piggybacked on the interpretations of others, as I guess any novice would have done when trying to figure out appropriate, face-saving ways to respond.

But on one memorable occasion I was alone. I had begun to work with Haydée and systematically take pictures, regularly dropping off my film the next morning to be developed and printed at a Kodak store in Isla Verde, where I first met Chelo, one of the store's employees. When she realized, having seen some of my photos, that I was doing research on espiritismo, she challenged me one morning, saying, "Let see what do you have to say about this," and she began telling me the lengthy dream she had the previous night. I knew that the telling of a dream very soon if not right after having it is an invitation for interpretation. I, of course, was not taking notes at the store, but I remember that the dream was about some rather unpleasant, dangerous situations and that at the end of her dream she was immersed in water: "Somebody—I could not see who—came from behind and covered me from head to toe with a yellow cape." Not knowing what the entire dream meant, I nonetheless ventured an interpretation, if not of its entirety, at least its conclusion. Having already worked with healers for some months, I had a sense of what "to be covered" (*ser arropado*) signified, as well as the color yellow. Several times I had heard mediums say they had felt while in trance or in dreams that they had been "covered" by their guardian sprits, a sign they interpreted as being protected and healed by them. I therefore answered in the best way I knew in that moment, which ended up meeting her expectations and concerns: "Whatever happens [to you], La Caridad is protecting you."[2]

All of these vignettes appear in my field notes as short daily observations on my exploratory research. They are the result of impromptu reactions to people with whom I interacted casually and sporadically, definitely not the kind of in-depth relationships I needed to cultivate for my later ethnographic work. But still, when considered cumulatively, these impromptu responses gathered over a relatively short period show a general trend that, coming at the beginning of my fieldwork, made me reflect on the centrality of dreams for espiritismo and brujería. These initial impressions proved critical for the continuation of my fieldwork. "I wish I took my camera and tape recorder every time I was in the street!" I wrote in my field notes just a few weeks after my arrival in Puerto Rico. Next to it I had jotted: "Dream narratives, an oral popular tradition?"

Embodied Messages

The prophetic aspect of dreams is but one of many frameworks human beings apply in making sense of their dreams. Several resources on dreams mention philosophical, literary, and scientific reflections made through the ages—from Plato, Aristotle, Democritus, Lucretius, Cicero, and Maimonides to Descartes, Leibniz, Montaigne, Locke, Goethe, and, in the twentieth century, to Bergson, Jung, and Freud—about the puzzle dreaming poses for human attitudes toward reason, imagination, imagery, reality, transcendence, and the mind, to mention just a few enigmas. In anthropology, dreams occupy a central role during the first half of the twentieth century, especially but not only in culture and personality studies (see Eggan 1949, Firth 1934, Kluckholn and Morgan 1951, Lincoln 1970 [1935], Radin 1936, Rivers 1923, Seligman 1923, and Wallace 1958). After a few decades in which anthropological research interests shifted away from dreams altogether, the seminar convened by Barbara Tedlock in 1982 at the School of American Research rekindled scholarly attention to dreams from a "postmodern" perspective as a way to move beyond structuralist approaches to the latent and manifest meanings of dreams. The main argument Tedlock makes in the volume she edited based on this seminar, *Dreaming: Anthropological and Psychological Interpretations* (1987), and which she further elaborates (1987a, 1991, 1994), concerns the insurmountable gap that separates the dream experience from the dream account. Edward Bruner cogently highlights this predicament in his 1989 review of Tedlock's edited volume: "To go from experience to telling is to go from images to verbalization. The telling of a dream is situated discourse and is doubly retrospective" (603), once when the dream images are recalled and once when the dream is narrated in a form that might not be coherent but is at least interpretable according to culture-specific criteria. In this sense, "any telling involves self-construction and is not only a social and cultural act but also a political one" (ibid.).[3] Addressing the problematic relation between dream and narrative, Vincent Crapanzano notes that Moulay Abedsalem, an old, illiterate Moroccan pallbearer and shroud maker, once explained that what one dreams is what the soul has witnessed. "Dream distortion results, he said, from the mind's (*'aqel*) inability to translate accurately what the soul has experienced. Insofar as mind has to make use of words to convey dreams, it is words that distort them. How else, Moulay Abedsalem asked with terrible irony, would we know our dreams?" (1992:145–146).[4]

Further addressing this dilemma, Crapanzano suggests that

> we cannot describe the aura, the hinterland, without somehow losing it. Our constructions of the beyond are always slippery. They are, in a sense, like a dream. We experience it, we recall it, but our telling it leaves us with a sense of betrayal, even if our telling gives us relief from the anxiety that surrounds it. It is not simply that our words do not do justice to what we dreamed; it is that they change experiential register. They create a distance between the experience of the dream and its articulation. The dream loses its immediacy, that sense of immanence, of imposition, of entrapment (so evident in nightmares) that we may perhaps liken, as an analogue, to our sense of destiny, nemesis. (2004:21)

Imagine the sense of immanence, imposition, entrapment, and destiny that lingers among dreamers who believe, unlike those engrossed in psychological or biological explications, that dreams are one of the ways in which spirits communicate with the living. For generations of Puerto Rican espiritistas since the nineteenth century, as for many in other parts of the world since ancient times, this entrapment is further complicated by the held belief in the premonitory nature of dreams and the special attention they require of dreamers.

Historian of ideas Merle Curti was able to trace (1996) the different attitudes toward dreaming in colonial America thanks to the custom of seventeenth-century colonists of documenting their dreams (and ruminations about them) in diaries. An examination of these diaries reveals that European attitudes about dreaming continued in the Americas, requiring that dreamers always give serious attention to their dreams. Attitudes that were imported to the colonies included, for instance, "the Biblical view of the dream as a divine or devilish monitor of things unseen and otherwise unknown" (393). Also imported were "folklore notions about the premonitory character of the dream . . . [based on] age-old assumptions about the supernatural and allegorical character of dreams" (ibid.).

Indeed, the need to document dreams in the middle of the night, immediately after they were dreamt, was a recognizable activity in preindustrial western Europe. As historian A. Roger Ekirch demonstrates (2001), sleeping through the entire night is a modern phenomenon; in preindustrial times, due to the lack of artificial light in most households, people went to bed soon after sunset. "Western Europeans on most evenings experienced *two major intervals of sleep* bridged by up to an hour or more of quiet wakefulness. . . . Both phases lasted roughly the same length of time, with individuals waking sometime after midnight before ultimately falling back to sleep" (29). During the "intervening period of consciousness—what [Robert Louis] Stevenson poetically labeled a 'nightly resurrection'" (ibid.), people engaged in all sorts of creative, social, and reflexive activities such as smoking tobacco, making love, visiting friends, or pondering the dreams they had during the "first sleep" and before the "second sleep," from which they awoke in the morning (2–3).[5]

Most relevant to my purposes, during these nightly intervals or segmented sleeping patterns, people even discussed and documented their impressions, inner thoughts, meditations, and feelings. Believed to occur when people were at their best, free of the burdens of daily life, these waking periods would be optimal times for engaging in transcendental reflections and, occasionally, for deciphering dreams and visions. For example, Ekirch notes,

> seventeenth-century merchant James Bovey reputedly from age fourteen kept a "Candle burning by him all night, with pen, inke, and paper, to write downe thoughts as they came into his head." Indeed, by the mid-eighteenth century, in order to better preserve midnight ruminations, methods were devised to "write in the dark, as straight as by day or candle-light," according to a report in 1748. (37)

Attentive to the profits potentially gained from this unique form of nightly expression, a London tradesman advertised in the 1760s a "Nocturnal Remembrancer,"

> an enclosed tablet of parchment with a horizontal aperture for a guideline whereby 'philosophers, statesmen, poets, divines, and every person of genius, business or reflection, may secure all those happy, often much regretted, and never to be recovered flights or thoughts, which so frequently occur in the course of a meditating, wakeful night. (Ibid.)

Especially when the allegorical and premonitory character of dreams is assumed, every element is meaningful, and thus recording them in exact detail is fundamental, the premise being that the dream experience and the dream account are analogical to or part of each other, neither one subordinate to the other. Corresponding to each other, the vision and its narration (or images and words) are supposed to be tied by a transcendental, cosmic connection: both present (rather than represent) in different modes of experience the spirits' message, and thus to decode one is to decode the other.

The folk system of dream interpretation among the Ilahita Arapesh of northern New Guinea is a good cross-cultural example of this analogical connection. Rather than assuming the disguised meanings of dream symbols, Donald Tuzin shows (1975) that the Arapesh interpret dreams according to their beliefs and practices surrounding the dead. Depending on the relative temporal distance between the living and the dead, they distinguish between "recent" and "ancestor" ghosts. The former are those of the recently deceased, and the latter are benign spirits whose "bones have dried" and whose now-mature spirits move to their "eternal resting place" with their own clan (557). The Arapesh, among other many other groups in the world, "do not admit that dreams are fantasies at all; rather they take them to be *literal experiences* of the dreamer's soul as it wanders on another plane of reality" (563, my emphasis). The gripping reality of the dream while it is being experienced carries over into the waking afterthought, and thus when an Arapesh individual ponders his dreams, the very literality in which dreams are accepted "diverts waking reflection into essentially noninterpretative channels" (563). Indeed, the Arapesh experience their dreams of the more recently deceased as proof that such ghosts exist and are night prowlers whose desocialized nature (shown by their absurd and inappropriate behaviors) does not preclude them from being often dangerously interested in the affairs of mortals, hence the terrifying character of these dream encounters (566).

This distinction between the spirit of the recently deceased and those of remote ancestors is also relevant to the practices of brujería. The difference is that brujos and espiritistas can use their powers to control and recruit the spirits of *muertos* (the dead), however obnoxious. For example, when muertos possess mediums in trance, mediums forcefully instruct them to "enlighten" and "raise themselves high to the celestial mansions" (farther from human affairs) to become *espíritus de luz* (enlightened spirits) or, following Arapesh cosmology, to "mature" and become benign ancestors.

Embodied Dreams and the Circulation of the Imaginary

Oftentimes, dream visions need to be immediately recorded and decoded as well as continuously recounted and circulated to publicly recognize (and in some cases, celebrate) their providential occurrence. Subject to all the typical hazards of circulating stories, their content and form are undoubtedly further refined to fit conventional patterns of prophetic, allegorical dreaming. The circulation of dream visions thereby reinforces and socializes listeners into the belief system that provided the interpretative frame for these dreams. In Puerto Rico, the circulation of dream accounts in general and of dream visions in particular is part of everyday life experience and is recognized as an appropriate form of communication and socializing.[6] Many people told me that when they were young, all the family members would gather in the morning, share their dreams, and interpret them. This is why telling dreams, for a majority, appears as a natural form of verbal exchange.

When the magical and revelatory power of dreams is assumed, the sharing and interpreting of dreams among close relatives, friends, colleagues, and even random acquaintances become, in most cases, a matter of major life-changing import. The telling of the dream and its details is of critical importance because "the dreamer's retrospective narrative, based on the memory of what happened during sleep, represents the *only* evidence for the dream" (Stewart 1997:877). For espiritistas, this evidence confirms the existence of spirits, as among the Arapesh, and their ability to communicate with the living. In fact, the magical nature of dreams and, by extension, the telling of them defines a moral etiquette guiding their circulation. This is best illustrated by Crapanzano, who remembers that Moroccans with whom he worked "saw great and potentially dangerous power in the dream. In telling a dream for the first time, they said, the dreamer transferred its power—good or evil—to his or her audience. Bad dreams were first told to a rock to neutralize them, but how could one be sure . . . ?" (2004:21).[7]

The Evocation of Images and the Intertextuality of the Imaginary

In Stewart's ethnography of dream telling on the island of Naxos, Greece, this moral etiquette is evident each time a miraculous dream about the wonder-working power of saints is narrated and circulated (1997:880). As soon as dreamers (usually women) learned about Stewart's research interest, they shared their dream visions about miraculous healings the power of saints prompted. A sizeable collection of these dream tellings allowed him to notice that the dreams' content corresponded to various nondream texts, such as the Old and New Testaments, the stories behind icons in churches, and women's funeral laments.[8] Stewart suggests that the latter genre provides dream narration and interpretation with means for dispelling uncertainty and thus anxiety. Becoming "a hybrid genre that conjoins distressed complaint with attempts at achieving divinatory revelation," such dream accounts are indeed "laments for the living" (885)—reminding me of Bruner's comment about the politics of retelling dreams, mentioned above.

Stressing interlocution and its role in shaping the experience of dream telling more specifically, Crapanzano suggests (2004:21) that even though the dream is a singularly personal experience at a basic experiential level, the telling experience "is the product of complex interlocutory forces." In this respect, and by the standards of waking life, its "faulted communication" is what gives the dream experience its particular quality. "It is neither addressed to a definable interlocutor nor subject to ordinary communicative and linguistic conventions" (ibid.). And yet, Stewart finds (1997:879), if widely circulated, dream accounts might become in themselves "cultural objects in the world," resembling or even merging with such fantastic narratives as folktales and myths.[9] "These widely circulating cultural stories may then reenter individual dreams precisely because of their presence in the waking environment; they become residues of the day" (879). Furthermore, in the process of exchanging dream accounts, Stewart adds, "codes of dream interpretation also exercise a tailoring effect of dream experiences. Although these codes were initially developed only to interpret dreams, they have become so familiar to individuals that they shape the narrations, if not the very experiences, of dreams" (ibid.).[10]

But the initial experience of dreaming, as all who have tried to tell about it know, is not easily narrativized. Images in dreams exceed words: "They are the point at which language is unequal to the task of representing the felt intensity of emotion" (Favret-Saada 1990:198). Think about the immediate agitation one has upon awakening from an intense dream and the ensuing sensation one carries the rest of the day following such a dream. It is a wordless sensation, if you wish, filled with a profusion of images that do not easily make sense when one wishes to narrativize them. Even if we often experience dreams as vivid sensations not unlike those often experienced when viewing movies on the big screen, dream images, unlike foreign films, do not come with ready-made subtitles. Dreaming is par excellence an experience that "exceeds the capacity to represent it" (Good 1994:139), so much so that recalling a dream is almost impossible unless one immediately writes it down upon awakening.

Disconnected images of dreams escape one's attempt at affixing or recalling them, for they seem to be experienced as sensations rather than decodable signs. Crapanzano suggests (2004:21–22) Freud would add that it is because dreams consist of "perceptual—mainly visual—and verbal debris, the residues of the day or days that immediately preceded it" and because the "grammar of desire and taboo," which conjoins them, is unknown to the dreamer. Dream sensations consequently resist narration or even visualization; they linger as unnamable, amorphous emotions, feelings, and predispositions. And yet, dreams demand narration to fully exist and be recognized as such.

Dreaming, Narration, and Time

Temporality and repetition, it seems to me, mediate our experiences of dreaming and dream telling. Counterintuitively, the closer the narration is to the dream experience, the more difficult it will be to narrate it smoothly, to verbally convey the sensorial experience in its fullness due to the elusiveness and disconnectedness typical of dreams and the lingering vividness of their sensations. The more distant in time is the narration from the actual dream sensations, the more coherent the account may become. For as time passes, the original elusiveness of the dream experience may be resolved through ready-made constructions and collectively recognized styles of narration (typical of folk narratives), which provide the various narrative tropes that help transform arrays of previously disconnected vivid images into culturally recognizable, coherent tellings.

Thus, what we interpret and circulate are not dreams but rather, as Lacan notes, "dream texts"—whose dynamics psychoanalysis attributes to condensation and displacement and linguists to metaphor and metonymy (Crapanzano 2004:22). Yet, the "dream account," however distorting, is evocative, Crapanzano insists, of the "dream-experience, perhaps even formative of it. It is appellative. It evokes our experience of the dream, and presumably those of our interlocutors. It is what is called forth—the dream—that gives the dream recitation value" (ibid.).

"They Speak to Us in Dreams"

As a consequence of the equal impact of Spiritism on Catholics and converted Protestants (Romberg 2003a,b) in everyday parlance, dreams are accorded transcendental importance by the general public in Puerto Rico, not only among declared Spiritists. Dream narratives and their sharing have become, in a way, part of the Puerto Rican experience. Dreams, according to the Spiritist tradition, are not only our present memories of our previous lives, but also one of the ways in which the dead visit and communicate with the living.

In a lecture I attended at a centro espiritista on the outskirts of Bayamón one Sunday morning, the speaker, a female Spiritist and parapsychologist, was also a well-known pediatrician who worked in the obstetrics department of a hospital in San Juan. Further framing the educational and academic nature of the lecture series offered at this centro, the speaker spoke in a scholarly tone (initially odd for me due to the topic) about the moral and scientific aspects of reincarnation. Based on thousands of cases she had encountered in her practice, she explained the basic ideas behind reincarnation and the existence of a spiritual world, "especially manifest at the moment of birth," offering "empirical" examples to make her point:

> There are various forms of indirect evidence of previous lives: we can find them in birth marks, and in precocious children (assumed to be reincarnations of genial personalities such as Mozart's). Evidence of previous lives also appears in our dreams, in déjà vu experiences, and in certain manias and phobias. We carry [in our present lives] whatever we know from previous lives.[11]

Within societies that assume the spiritual continuity between the past and the present and between the invisible world of spirits and the everyday concrete world of humans, the previous discussion about the phenomenological gap between the dream experience and dream narrative becomes irrelevant. It is, indeed, foreign to the experience of dreaming (since such discontinuity between the dream and its telling is not assumed), as well as to the dilemmas arising from the linguistic modifications apparent in each retelling of the dream. Any formal analysis of dream narratives and their changes over time and space thereby betray the experience of dreaming as having been lived, for example, not only by espiritistas and brujos but also those raised within similar traditions of dreaming.

Colonizing the Imagery of the Beyond

Even though Western individualism, by and large, and Freudian dream interpretation theory in particular have anchored dreaming and its significance within discussions about the self, in other eras and places dreaming was a matter of institutional—not individual—import. Dream interpretation (and misinterpretation) provided important if subtle modes of control and management for medieval and colonial civilizing projects.

French anthropologist Marc Augé makes this point cogently in *The War of Dreams* (1999), drawing on the work of French medievalist Jacques Le Goff (1985) and his former student Jean-Claude Schmitt (1994). According to Le Goff, "the genre of oneiric autobiography" emerges historically during late antiquity out of a basic concern with death and its subsequent significance for the trajectory of the human soul; "the dominant theme of dreams recounted in this way is that of the journey into the beyond" (in Augé 1999:60). Schmitt, in his investigation of "autobiographical stories of revenants," shows the progressive link established "between representations of death and the dead, dream or vision, storytelling and the constitution of an autonomous subject." What Schmitt means by these is

> the story told of an encounter with one of the dead (who may well be "given the power of speech") by an individual, be it a monk or a cleric but equally, from the twelfth century on, an educated layman. The experiences which gave rise to this encounter and the source of the story are of three kinds: the feeling of a nearby presence (a feeling akin to the "disturbing strangeness," of the *Unheimlich* which Freud would be interested in), the waking vision of a dead person in a moment of ecstasy, and a sleeping dream. (Ibid.)

Throughout the first millennium CE, according to Schmitt, "only certain 'elite dreamers' (the expression is Jacques Le Goff's), essentially kings and saints [had] the capacity to experience visionary dreams inspired by God," while all other "average mortals were more likely to be regarded as an easy prey for 'diabolical illusions,' particularly while they slept" (in Augé 1999:59). Further evidence of the nature of dreamers and their transcendental relation to dreams appear throughout the High Middle Ages, when "the distinction between 'true' dreams and 'false' dreams was connected to whether their origin was divine (guaranteeing the truth of the apparition or prophecy) or diabolical (the diabolical dream, which was just as real as the other kind, prompts deceitful illusions which dragged the Christian dreamer to his downfall)" (ibid.). In *L'Imaginaire médiéval* (1985), Le Goff notes that when the "presence of the Devil" came under suspicion in the first millennium as a "counter-cultural system," false dreams were linked to "heretical components" (in Augé 1999:65). Conversely, Schmitt points out, "the stories of revenants, especially when they recounted a waking vision, were mobilized in the service of the reform of the Church" (ibid.). Augé asserts:

> It is because men are mortal . . . that dreams and visions are an opportunity for the Church to make everyone experience the uniqueness of a personal trajectory which after death is sanctioned by an individual judgment. Death plays an essential role here both because it is identified with the terrifying idea of that relentless judgment and because it is thereby the object of multiple testimonies which can assume the form of genuine narratives. (60)

Unlike dreams, which were considered personal, visions were the object of oral transmission and transcription, becoming a genuine "social object" (61–62). The experiences of dreamers-mediators of the Middle Ages show that "their relationship with the dead dictates their literary inspiration and singularizes their personality. The narrator's position is located at the junction of a social demand which is largely informed by the collective imagination and an imaginary experience which to some extent dictates individual memory and a personal relationship with death" (62).

Reflecting on the space of struggle over dream images in a historical perspective, Augé draws on Serge Gruzinski's *La Guerre des images* (1990) to address the war launched by the Catholic medieval Church in colonial Mexico over the dreams of Indians. According to Church doctrine, man, God, or the devil intervened in the production of dreams—a notion introduced by Gregory the Great in the sixth century. At different periods this basic correspondence—between categories of dreamers and the content of their dreams—was invoked to distinguish social status in terms of the dreamers' relation to the realms of God and evil.[12]

Crucial for the Church was its essential mistrust of the dreaming experience itself, given the lack of control of dreamers over its production and the self-assumed responsibility of the Church to oversee their souls. Following the often prophetic, ecstatic interpretative tradition of dreaming within the ecclesiastical realm, the dangers of misrecognition became an institutional threat in regard to the alleged source of dream production. Schmitt asserts (1994), "Waking visions, which were apparently frequent, were held to be less disturbing both because they were produced before witnesses and because they were instantly subject to the appraisal and interpretation of the religious authorities"—in contrast to "the ungovernable night of the individual" potentially driven by "the Devil and the indulgences of the body" (in Augé 1999:59).

Embodied Spirits

Why do I opt for such recourse to bygone worlds of meaning long buried beneath the effects of modernity? It is because those arcane personal relationships with the dead and with both benevolent and evil spirits also inform the dream accounts and visions of espiritistas and brujos in today's Puerto Rico. Even without direct evidence for the continuity from medieval to present-day worlds of meaning, spirits and saints do inhabit the space of brujos, generating their notions of manifestaciones (in this case, the visceral sense of the spirits' presence), as well as their waking visions of muertos during trance.

If considered as part of the collective imaginary, these experiential bonds show the long-lasting impact, since medieval times, of the Church's favorable attitude toward revelatory dreams about saints and the converse demonic threat of dreams in which evil spirits appear. Such impact is further enhanced by Spiritist attitudes toward the possibility of communication with the dead and especially with highly desirable "enlightened" spirits in human history. Constitutive of the popular tradition of dreaming experiences and narratives, dreaming of enlightened spirits or saints came to be interpreted as a clear signal that beneficial spirits claimed the dreamers as their protégées, guaranteeing continuous protection as the dreamers' guardian spirits.

Carmen, a teacher who came to consult with Haydée, had one such dream. At the time, she was experiencing serious work problems at the school where she taught as well as family tensions between her son and her husband. During divination Carmen told Haydée that she had a dream about La Milagrosa. "Buy a medal of her, and also light her a candle," Haydée immediately advised, adding, "You have her [figure] in a [household] niche, right?" Carmen replied, "Yes, we put her in a niche. My mother dreamt about a *jardinera* [a flowering plant], with its flowers, so we placed a few jardineras around her."

Today, as in medieval times, worshiping the saints and praying and making occasional offerings to them (especially when making pleas) are considered vital procedures for assuring their unflagging protection. A compact is thereby summoned between worshipers and their guardian spirits or saints that is similar to the one betokened by medieval *promesas* (ex-votos)—silver medallions left as offerings and as symbolic emblems of pleas made to the saints.

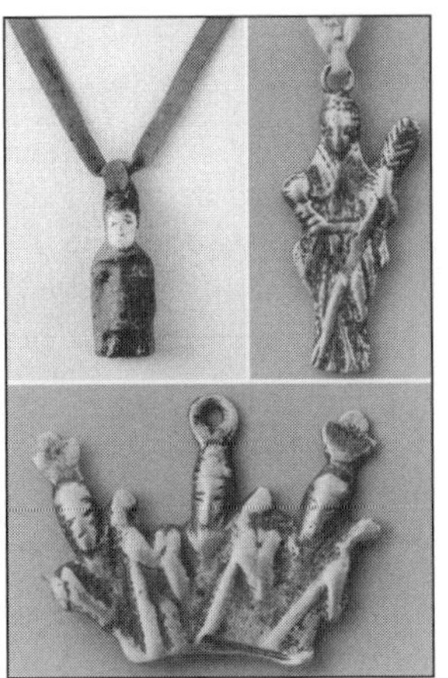

Puerto Rican *medida* (medallion) and silver ex-votos of San Blas (Vidal 1986).

Premonitory Dreams

Offering not only a transspatial vision of human affairs but also a transtemporal one, spirits may warn individuals through dreams of impending dangers to their well-being: an illness, accidents, misfortunes, perhaps a death in the family. Most importantly, when interpreted appropriately, these warnings can imply some form of advice on how to prevent the impending mishaps.

Basi, with whom I spent many hours talking about Spiritism at her botánica—the first I visited in Puerto Rico—and during my stay at her house, shared with me dreams she had while I was there as well as memorable, life-changing earlier ones. Once when she was telling me about her life struggles—first as an orphan, then as a single mother—she told me about a revelatory dream she had one night sometime in the mid-1950s, when she was still married. "In that dream I was shown exactly where my husband's lover lived. I woke up the next morning and as if guided by an invisible hand, I went directly to her house. As I was walking, I recognized the streets as I had seen them in my dream; I knew exactly the way to her house—my protecciones led me directly to her house." She did confirm her suspicions and with this distressing evidence in hand decided to divorce her husband.

Dreams such as Basi's are often interpreted as premonitions, or *revelaciones* (revelations). When I met Haydée for the first time, she explained the scope of her facultades, saying,

> I have revelaciones in my dreams; one day, one week passes by and the thing happens; it is seen. Already as a child I had revelaciones. I always felt I liked espiritismo; I was born for this. Already as a child I had fluídos. [The spirits] used to present me with situations, which I deciphered. Whenever I had dreams I felt the need to tell about them. And then I saw them happening: If [I dreamt that] an accident was going to happen, I didn't see it [happen] the same day or the next, but after some time, I did, the same way as I had seen it [in my dream]. Exactly as I had seen it, I used to see it happen. I always had to share it [my dream]. I used to tell my mother, and then my ex- mother-in-law and my children. When it was revealed to me that my eldest son was going to be killed, I told him. But he didn't listen to me: I gave him the medicine but he didn't buy it.

Although ultimate knowledge given from the beyond in the form of prophetic dreams may become a source of empowerment for those who have these dreams, such knowledge may also be the source of fear. An incident in Haydée's life four years earlier illustrates the double-edged nature of premonitory dreams:

> It was revealed to me that my ex-husband's daughter would be involved in a car accident. I saw her in the cemetery. I told her my dream. One has to be fearful of dreams. After a week she called me from the hospital; she had an accident! Sometimes we espiritistas sense when we are going to die. Once I had a dream that I was sick. I saw myself walking, and at the end of the path I saw my mother. I told her: "My time hasn't arrived yet."

Evidently, along with the empowering force of these dreams come no little psychic cost for brujos, especially due to their responsibility in passing along the messages given to them about those involved in prophetic dreams.

In a similar fashion, dreams are valued by Moroccan fellahin for their prognostic as well as directive powers—both of which have the potential of influencing the dreamer's future (Crapanzano 1992:242–243). One particular type of response is expected from "visitational dreams," which involve the appearance of saints, *jnun*, and other spiritual beings in the dream (244). These visitational dreams articulate a basic conflict of the dreamer, often unknown to him or her; offer a possible course of action, even if not entertained by the dreamer; and lastly present "a primary orientation point" (245) for the "articulation of experiences that are central to the individual's personal history" (257).

In this vein, Katherine Ewing shows (1990) that certain dreams recognized among Pakistani Muslims as "initiation dreams" have a culture-specific transformative power on the dreamers. The semiotic content and power of initiation dreams are culturally recognized (Ewing offers a Sufist template) and may become the source for a new self-representation (that of a Sufi disciple), which entails the search for a particular Sufi *pīr* (the one appearing in the dream) under whom the dreamer should undergo initiation.

Even if in Puerto Rico there are no equivalent culture-specific dream genres and prescriptive interpretations, members of a family believe it is crucial to inform one another if one of them has been the recipient of messages and omens. As noted many times by Haydée, dreamers have the moral obligation (following the Spiritist belief in free will) to share the content of their premonitory dreams with the person who appears in the dream and for whom the message was intended. One morning Haydée and I went to visit her sister, who told her that she had dreamed about Haydée and her ex-husband, Roberto. In the dream, Roberto was in Haydée's house, where there was a wedding. They interpreted this dream as a bad omen: "A wedding means death," Haydée and her sister explained to me. By telling Roberto of this dream, Haydée's sister may have been warning him and, in effect, offering him the possibility of amending something in his life and precluding this bad omen from materializing.

"I Gave Him the Medicine"

The fact that even years after they had particular dreams, people tell and retell the premonitions given to them in dreams suggests that dream telling is a narrative genre intimately bound to the numinous.[13] Not only among devout Catholics but especially among espiritistas and brujos, having premonitory dreams attests to and proves the spiritual devotion and power of the dreamer. Further, having these dreams confirmed by actual events shortly thereafter (what brujos call *confirmaciones*) indicates the dreamer's godly gift of mediumship. Repeated narrations of these confirmaciones by brujos who had premonitory dreams help them, as will become apparent below, advertise their own fame and unique gift to foresee events.

The following is a dream revelation Haydée had of a trabajo made against her to drive her lover, Julian, away from her; it was, she said, "rather a vision, a *transporte* (transfer, voyage) given to me in a dream":

> A man dressed in blue pants with his shirt tucked in arrives and stands up like this [shows me], and I am standing behind the curtains. He hands me a plant—more like a flower arrangement, but with a cellophane wrap on top of it—and some leaves fall off. "Who sent me this?" I ask. "I don't know," he says. "Read the card." But his eyes penetrate mine, and I am left puzzled. When [the man] says "read the card," Julian enters by that door [points to the side door].

Haydée gestures with a slight agitation as she makes an extraordinary effort to convey the unusual ways in which the man in the dream entered her home, not by the already open main door, but by a side door that always remains closed.

> He wears khaki pants, has a bag with food from the cantina, and asks, "Whose flowers are these?" "I don't know," I say. He looks at the card. I sit down and see outside a tall white woman. "As these flowers are alive, so also your [relationship] with Julian will be," the card reads. I sit down. The woman touches me like this [caresses her head] and says, "Don't worry, your thing with Julian will not end." And then I

> am told about the time, place, and day in which a trabajo was made for me—that's when Willie [Julian's friend] wakes me up.

Reflecting on this dream-vision, Haydée says, "Indeed, the flower arrangement was already given to me" a few days earlier, "and I didn't know who had sent it." Haydée thought the man in khaki pants that appeared in her dream was Julian. She saw him leave in a tunnel, which she interpreted as "death." Shifting from the dream narrative to her actual feelings that morning, she lamented not having seeing Julian for four days, since the previous Sunday. "I know he's been driven away from me. . . . I am seeing it clearly."

When Julian's friend Willie arrived that morning on his way to work, Haydée turned the dream she had the previous night into an omen meant for her lover, which she relayed to Willie:

> Tell him to be careful when he leaves his workshop, to be careful he's not killed, not to leave so late and with his back to the street. "Not everyone that laughs with him is his friend" [an aphorism]; and tell him he's been envied in Camero, and [some] prefer seeing him dead rather than alive. Willie, I don't want to be at his burial crying, because "whatever I say here you can date" [it's going to happen], because it's been three nights that am dreaming; that man that handed me the flowers with his profound gazc is the same Julian. He was dressed very smart, like Julian. And there's going to be a robbery. Remember that he made a lot of money these days, that he had been working a lot these nights; and it's going to be somebody from Camero. He always takes his money on himself . . . that tunnel that I went through with Julian when we looked at each other. . . . That tunnel is a tomb. . . . *¡Uy! ¡Carajo!* (Oh! Shit!). . . . He leaves us [dies]. [Haydée starts to cry.] He was very protected with me—that's why he's been driven away from me. [As a revelation given to her by the spirits:] His son isn't his. *¡Uy! ¡Uy!* He's been prevented from getting here [to me].

Haydée was so distressed that morning that she asked Reina, her assistant, to cast the cards for her. Reina said,

> You guessed what I was going to do for you. Haydée, when are you going to be the one you were? They [the spirits] say that the water is black. Why do you let yourself be fucked over [*te dejas joder*]? If you have more than what you imagine, how was that man driven away from your side? He was taken away—*that* you know. But They say that

> "this is until today" [*eso es hasta hoy*]. There's a *rompimiento* [breaking of the spell]; there's going to be happiness with that rompimiento; some money will arrive. If you don't set yourself right soon and continue like this, everything will fall. But They say, "This is until today."[14]

As the reading continues and the spirits reveal that Haydée had been the object of negative thoughts, of black magic, of spells against her, Reina begins to show signs of trance. The spirits then urge Haydée to be her usual self, to recompose herself, to gather all her forces. And as Haydée cleanses herself over the *fuente* (a spherical glass bowl filled with water), banging her hands over the table three times and raising her arms over it in circles, she falls into trance herself and delivers the following message in the language of *bozales* (unbaptized enslaved Africans):[15]

> Oh, you my good Madama, you telling me I be calm [with a sobbing tone]. You to know, today I be calm because I soon to see what I want see, because I be informed and see everything that possibly coming up. But They say, not let negative things touching me, may these tremblings passing me over. And you tell me I should not to work, I need leave this *cuadro* [spiritual power] because I not able to move with this foot, you know. And pray for me a few Our Fathers. *Que la Paz de Dios quede aquí, ahora y para siempre, amén* [May God's peace remain here now and forever, amen].

As Haydée recovers from the trance, she says, "I thank my good cuadro. Now I will have to cleanse myself."

No doubt Haydée took seriously her dream omen and dealt with it accordingly. The dream was circulated, told and retold, and then its warning taken to the test and further verified in divination. In order to prevent the omen from ever becoming a reality, Haydée's protecciones and cuadro were recruited and their cleansing invoked. I remember her telling me that dreams need to be taken seriously; it is not enough to be warned (as she had warned her son); one needs to do something about it. Many times I heard espiritistas insist that their role is limited because "one might reveal the medicine that someone should take, but that person has to swallow it," thereby placing the ultimate burden of responsibility on the afflicted person, not on the one who tries to help. It is not the reality of remedies given by the spirits through dreams that should be questioned if the expected results fail to materialize but the forcefulness of certain individuals to closely follow their advice. Especially when the premonitory nature of dreams is assumed, an interesting cross-genre hermeneutical affinity between divination and dreaming emerges. Both presume the reality of the warning and remedies given by the spirits, and thus the counsel offered in premonitory dreams needs to be taken no less seriously that that given in divination.

Disembodied Selves

It is as if the living spirit of the person in the dream wanders into it, very much like the incursions that spirits of the dead make into the dreams of their living kin. Although I never heard brujos articulate the beliefs upon which dreaming and dream interpretation are based, cross-cultural examples of similar dreaming traditions can help elucidate their significance in relation to notions of the self (Rouch 1978).

The anthropological literature on these issues is quite extensive. For example, among Moroccan fellahin, "the dream is generally believed to result from the wandering of the soul (*ruh*) during sleep. . . . Daydreams, too, result when the soul leaves the body but stays close to it" (Crapanzano 1992:241). Most notably, according to Nadel, the Nupe believe that the element of the personality that is part of but separate from a human being—"the *rayi*, the vital principle, the *life soul*, in Latin the *anima*—frees itself from the body's boundaries and goes wandering" during nighttime dreaming (in Augé 1999:26).

> [W]hat an individual sees in his or her dream is what the *rayi* sees in the course of its roaming around. But the *rayi* cannot travel alone; it is accompanied by the *fifingi*, which is the double and image of the individual body. It is the *fifingi* which is seen by those who dream about him through the intermediary of their *rayi*. The double is bound to the living body: it is the shadow it casts. It survives death and continues to make appearances in the dreams of the living, even though individual identity, be it of someone living or dead, corresponds to another entity: the *kuci*. It is to the *kuci* of someone recently dead or to that of an ancestor that sacrifices are made in order to ward off what is regarded as a bad dream, according to the Nupe key to dreams. (Nadel in Augé 1999:26–27)

Dichotomized into bodily and spiritual, human experience according to the Christian tradition appears as relatively simple when compared to other cosmologies, in which they branch off in multiple, overlapping degrees and spaces of existence. Instead of a dual notion of the self, a plurality of interlocking selves is assumed in some Asian, Latin American, and African traditions. For instance, among the Bambara, the Dogon, the Mossi, the Tallensi, the Songhay, the Ashanti, the Ewe, the Ibo, and the Yoruba of Africa, as well as among the practitioners of Santería (an African-based religion in the Americas), a plurality of selves is presumed. María Reinante, a santera whom I befriended in Puerto Rico and invited to speak together with her husband, Manolo, a Cuban babalawo, at the college where I was teaching at that time, explained as follows the various components of the self according to Santería:

> Human beings are composed of a material visible part, the *ara* or physical body that contains the spirit on earth, and an ethereal body, *ojiji* or shadow, both of which disappear at death. *Iye* and *ori* refer to the mind and intelligence, respectively, and are seated on the head; they drive our destiny by means of prudence and intelligence. *Emi*, the spirit or divine part of man, is supposed to influence in a very positive way the *okan* or soul. Okan is lodged in the heart, the seat of the soul and emotions, which should be managed through intelligence and reasoning. Each okan or emi belongs to a major family group of personal characteristics, which are possessed by individuals who belong to these familial groups. One's spirit is immortal, and since we believe in the resurrection of the spirit, it exists before one's birth, continues through life and after death. With death—the transition where we leave behind our material body—we retain our existence and the characteristics essential for maintaining our identity. In any desired moment, we can appear in a recognizable form to living beings.[16]

Espiritistas also assume the plurality of the self and the permanence of our spirit after death or disincarnation. Appearing in dreams and visions and materialized in trance and reincarnation, the complex spiritual components of selfhood assure continuity between the living and dead and between the past and the present. In this sense, the experienced "reality of the dream" attests to the many journeys that one of the composing selves has undertaken during the night, revealing "the continuity between waking life and the life of the dream" (Augé 1999:27). Dreaming under such conditions entails "a double movement, of exit and return" of one of the selves, which Augé then compares with a similar yet inverse type of "exit and return" during possession (27–43).[17] Assuming this "double movement" during dreaming, it is imperative that the vital parts of the personality of the dreamer indeed return, without which "the life of the dreamer is at stake" (27). This reminds me of what my father explained to me as a child about the Jewish prayer one has to perform before rising from bed in the morning for the purpose of thanking God for "returning our soul" after sleep.

During possession, ethnographies tell us, the spirit of the shaman leaves his or her body to let the gods inhabit it, with no small risk to the shaman upon his or her spirit's return, marked by coughing, inability to speak, and other sensual markers of confusion and disorientation, usually accompanied by signs of awakening from a deep sleep (Rouch 1971, 1978; Stoller 1989a). Imagining the relation between dreams and possession as "inverse rather than opposed phenomena," Augé then stresses the direction of this double movement as one of ascension and descent—of the spirits of shamans and of gods, respectively. In both dreams and possession this double movement is "defined by a single absence: the absence of their own bodies, both of the journeying shaman, which abandons it, and the possessed one, who is dispossessed and excluded from it" (Augé 1999:27–28). While dreams entail an "*enigma of presence* (of the dreamer towards his or her dream)," possession brings about an "*enigma of absence* (of the possessed person towards the possession whose object he or she is)" (30).

I often heard Puerto Rican brujos complain about the weariness of their materia that they regularly experienced as a sequel to both the nightly journeys of their spirits to help their clients resolve earthly problems and the perils of possession, especially when their bodies "catch" (*cogen*) the evil spirits pestering their clients (on this phenomenon also see Rouch 1971, 1978, and Stoller 1989a). In both cases brujos are left in a relatively risky state. When the spirit exits the body at night, its return is assured—even if the journey might tire the sleeping body. In possession, however, the perils are comparatively higher and thereby demand an attending assistant to ensure that the medium's body is not hurt and that the spirit returns safely to the body. This return is marked in a dramatic way by mediums, who appear disoriented, knowing neither where they are nor what had happened to them during possession, corresponding to the behavior of one recovering from the loss of consciousness.[18] This enactment is also similar to the momentary disorientation we may sense after awakening from an especially vivid dream in which we had felt transported to another space and time. But unlike possession, which entails forgetting what transpired while the inner self of the healer was away from his or her body to enable another entity to enter it, waking dreams and visions call for the recurrent reminiscing and retelling of the different, sacred reality experienced by the inner self while on journey elsewhere.

Nightly Journeys

During the night—especially toward dawn—is when most of the signs, visions, and omens are given to healers, and thus the boundary between dreams and visions gets blurred.[19] Often I heard brujos and santeros begin their accounts saying, in one way or another, "I had a dream; no, it was a vision." Why shortly before dawn? Apparently, as suggested above by Roger Ekirch (2001), that is when—following a few hours of sleep—the experiences of our waking, conscious life finally give way to other perceptions, which during the day remain paralyzed. Students of the mind might answer that it is when our conscious waking life gives way to our unconscious, while brujos and espiritistas might say that it is when the spirits of mediums travel to other worlds. Some would refer to them as paranormal experiences that emerge when our "channels are open"—as Doris, a medium I met at Basi's botánica, once described the unique state of mind achieved by those who develop mediumship abilities.

Especially during sleep, Doris has her "channels open." She *gets* many things in dreams:

> In dreams I am taken on trips, am given recipes of how to heal, for many people, even for the governor, but I don't call them. Sometimes the dangers are maddening, because there are things that don't have and won't have explanation. They gave me things in a dream for the instructor of *metafísica* [mediumship workshop she attends with Basi]; I called and told her she was a little ill (*malita*). When I went to see her she had been in bed for half a day already. I was given [in the dream] the *resguardo* (protective amulet) she had to wear and the novena [she had to say] to unravel who had put her in that state.

Maritza, a developing medium and santera I met at the home of Mauro (a Cuban babalawo I mentioned in the introduction), first realized she had mediumship abilities while working in a funerary, where she washed and prepared the dead for burial. For some inexplicable reason, she always knew the specific look they used to wear when they were alive and how they wanted to be groomed for the wake. She prepared them accordingly, to the utter astonishment of the mourners. Having realized this unique sensitivity to muertos—"They talk to me"—Maritza began her development as a medium among espiritistas. After a few years she was initiated into Santería, and by the time I left Puerto Rico, she was beginning her initiation into a secret society that specifically communicated, bonded, and worshipped the dead. Explaining the particular bond she had with muertos, she said, "My muertos wake me up at dawn, in the middle of a dream, and thus I need to wake up, open the Bible, pray, meditate, and then I know what will happen that day and try to modify it. I wash and get dressed."

Mauro referred to his spiritual learning and journeying as taking place mostly at night:

> I interpret the signs of Ifá [the most complex divination system of Santería] at night; when I go to bed I have my books with me and study the signs [the 256 configurations that relate to an equal number of *patakis* or myths, some of which have several versions]. I fall asleep at three and get up at six. Signs have to be interpreted. Orula [the divination orisha] gives me the signs, which I then interpret. When the coconuts [of the basic *obi* divination system] said "yes" to disaster, I saw Chernobyl. I study specific configurations and write them down in my notebook, which Lorena then transcribes into the computer. The sign [the particular configuration of the cowry shells] of the chain of shells, or the [configuration of] nuts tell you what will happen in the future, but in comparison to Hindus, in this religion you can modify [the outcomes]. The son of a babalawo was recently killed. Did you see it in the newspaper? I predicted it about two weeks ago and called him [the babalawo] to tell him. He promised to come [see me] but was too busy, and now his son has been murdered.[20]

It is during the eerie hours before dawn that all the movements of exit and return take place except those of possession.[21] Journeys to the world of the dead and to the dreams of others occur, and visits from the otherworld come about, communicating vital messages to the living. Predawn hours are the time of the uncanny detachment of the multiple selves of healers, whose experiences are then reconstituted during waking times in a kaleidoscopic form of being.

Healing Dreams

One reason the multiple selves of brujos exit their bodies, as suggested above, is to heal and help others; hence the mission, sacrifice, and charity they allude to in their discourse. Such is the case when healing recipes are given to them in dreams for themselves and especially for their clients. "Whenever I go to the hospital to visit a friend or a client, I come home sick. My spirit can't avoid helping people in dire need." With these words Armando, the espiritista santero from New York I met through Haydée, asserted his mission as a chosen healer. He told me about dreams he had that helped him heal his clients. He dreamed once about a man who was very sick in the hospital:

> After I had that dream, I took my santos and placed them [spiritually] inside the man's flesh. I had seen [in my dream] a snake devouring half of his body. The man left the hospital walking [on his own power]. I had seen all in my dream earlier, the night before, exactly as I then performed it [my healing work]. I had seen him in the corner of the [hospital] room with all the machines [hooked up to him] everywhere, and when I went to the hospital that is exactly as I saw him. The wife said she had hoped her husband would be moved out of intensive care before the weekend. I said, "I won't go until he's moved; there, I will work for him." That [which made the man sick] was a trabajo sent for him. I got the serpent in my stomach; I was there about an hour. "I can't take this" [I thought], feeling an unsupportable ache at the opening of my stomach; it was a cobra that was eating my stomach. *I* was feeling whatever was sent for him, whatever *he* was feeling.

Some healers describe their own spirits as antennae or light-sensitive photographic surfaces that detect and imprint ethereal messages from other living beings, from the various entities, and from the dead (at whatever stage of spiritual development they might be). Healers can also embody at a distance the type and intensity of pain felt by their clients. Are healers not, then, indeed surrogates—proxies—for other human beings? What selfless if cunning existence they have! I recall healers telling me about their *pruebas* (tests given to them by God in the form of personal misfortunes) and their endless sacrifice and charity. Elsewhere I have discussed the meaning and extent of their godly missions based on this kind of discourse (Romberg 2003b). But this sacrifice acquires another layer of meaning when one considers the phenomenology of the kaleidoscopic integrity of their multiple, detachable selves—it applies to each and all of those selves. Both when the spirits of healers exit and return during dreams and visions, as well as during possession, and when parts of the selves host and embody the pain directed to others, they act as stand-ins for other human beings and, in trance, for spirits as well—sacred forms of surrender, indeed. Even though this kind of surrender of the self is suspect as pathological within Western traditions, it encapsulates the ultimate significance of personal sacrifice on the part of healers.

On one occasion, Basi's adult daughter, Lisi, joined Basi and me for coffee in the early evening, as we usually did while I was living with Basi. We were sitting together in the small room adjacent to my room in the garage. Lisi told me she had a big statue of her patron saint, Santa Bárbara, in her apartment's balcony with its face turned toward the street to protect Lisi like a shield. "Once, at a time when I was having all sorts of problems," Lisi told me, "while I was in bed, probably half-asleep, I felt Santa Bárbara cleansing me, hovering over me in circles. Then I saw San Lázaro talking to me, moving his lips, but there was no sound." Since she was not completely asleep, Lisi suggested, she saw and felt the presence of Santa Bárbara and San Lázaro not in a real dream, but more in a vision or waking dream. She added, "Dreams *give* me things [visions, premonitions], especially what will happen." That information helps her help others as well as herself.

Further, dreams might themselves be healing events, revealing and initiating the healing process. This is what happened one morning on my way to work, as usual, with Haydée. The previous night she dreamed of her dead mother, who warned her about some negativity she saw lurking around her. In the dream, her mother gave Haydée a detailed recipe for a cleansing bath, which Haydée set out to prepare that very morning upon waking. But sensing the lingering presence of her dead mother (a problematic state for espiritistas, who make sure spirits return to their abodes) while in consultation with a client, Delia, for whom she was dictating a recipe for a trabajo, Haydée interjected her own dream account:

> Let me tell you the dream I had about my mother because, having not slept the whole night, now I have to strip this shadow off of me. While I cleanse you, I need to cleanse myself with oils as well. Listen to this: A tall man, whose face I couldn't see, comes and gives me $250 tied in a small bundle. I couldn't see his face, nor that of my mother, you know. Remember, the dead don't reveal their faces. And as he gave me the money, he showed me his back, and my car [license] plates appeared both straight [in sequence] and in reverse. I arrive at my house, and [the car] is not there. My mom, lying in bed, tells me, "Child, buy yourself a black dove, and tell your friend to cleanse you, so all that is black around you goes away."

"¡O cará!" Reina called aloud, recognizing the prophetic nature of the dream. Haydée repeated her mother's directive and continued,

> I see two bunches of guineo [plantains] on the fence, a country [homegrown] avocado, and a *guanábana* [soursop, *annona muricata*].

> And as I am about to open the [fence's] gate to enter the farm, I see my mother. She had the dove on her lap; I caressed it, picked it up, and kissed it as a baby, and [said] "You will shelter me, protect me, and free me of all that is black around me." I caressed the dove like this . . .

Interrupting her account and implying a transcendental significance for her action, Haydée ponders, "But why did I pick up [the statue of] La Caridad just now?"

Addressing Reina directly, Haydée said, "I don't know, but you will be in charge of this, because my mother said, 'your friend,' and my friend is you." Reina uttered "¡Uy!" as a sign that the spirits had inspired Haydée's words and therefore were expressing a command to her. Haydée continued with her dream narrative:

> I see the plantains, and they had two *maduros* (ripe plantains); I see fire flames and go into them. I open the gate, but the flames don't touch me. On the farm I take the plantains, two avocados, and as I am about to put them in a basket full of maize I say to myself, "*Caramba*, I won't put them in the basket. I will distribute them because, if I keep them in my house, they will get spoiled; and there are people that suffer from hunger, while I have [food] in excess." I thought to myself, "I will wrap the guanábana in aluminum foil because I'm going to eat this one and will cleanse myself with [another] guanábana after I cleanse myself with the dove—since this one is so ripe." I leave the farm and enter my mother's house.

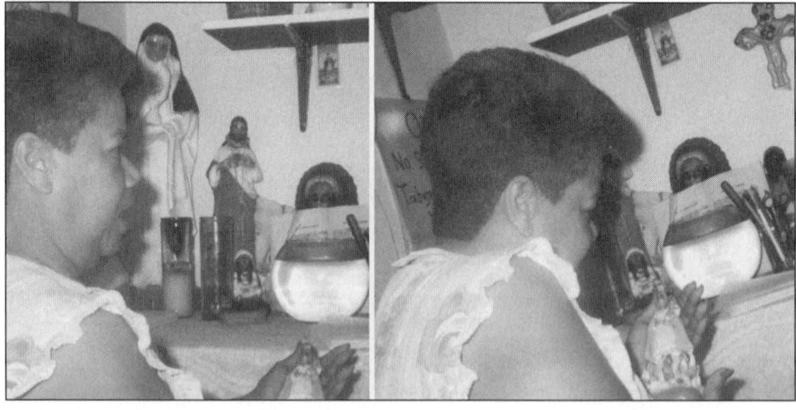

"Why did I pick up La Caridad just now?"

—[She tells her mother,] "I gathered everything from your farm,"—she was not looking at me, but she was talking to me—"and will distribute this."

—Child, you're always the same, giving what you have and what you don't. Here, underneath me, there's something that when I turn, it cries.

—You know, Mother, you know what it is. It's a doll.

—But, a doll, at this time of my life?

—It's a doll.

And that's when I woke up, without [the earlier] headache; my mother gave me the recipe. I talked to my Caridad: "You are going to help me." [She turns to Delia.] Now let me continue with your recipe.

After Haydée completes the recipe for Delia, another client came, a young woman; and in the middle of her consultation, too, Haydée retold parts of her dream, adding the following:

Look how my mother gave me this dream. They are telling me that I need to perform that recipe that my mother gave. [Addressing Reina she says,] You need to give me that *despojo* [cleansing], Reina, and take [the polluted cleansing solution] to the seashore. While I was praying [this morning] I saw some stars that passed by my eyes and my forehead. I need a black dove, two ripe plantains, very, very, very ripe, and a guanábana. I'll give you the money and you'll buy them, because my mom told me, as I was petting my dove, "Buy yourself a dove, and your friend should give you a despojo in order to drive all that is black around you away," because my mom didn't say "your sister"—she said "your friend."

Revelation Dreams

One morning, during the usual opening prayer Haydée performed in her altar before beginning her consultations, she mentioned a possible "seaquake." I had not heard anything about a seaquake in the news, so as soon as she finished the prayer I asked her what she meant by it. "I knew you would ask me," she said, explaining:

I know a seaquake is coming; I lived it [experienced it in a vision]. I saw myself on the road from Loíza to Piñones [bordering

> the sea]. I was passing and saw that sea when it recoiled. In the vision I had—it wasn't a dream—I was coming with my [dead] mother; I was driving a blue car. I told my mother, "When it comes it will take everything." She said, "You'll stay alive." And I was left on top of the rivers and the sea.

To call this experience a waking dream is probably misleading in terms of how the vision-revelation is experienced. But it might help in figuring out what these different sorts of visions or journeys—some while asleep, others while awake—mean to healers. Often the distinction between sleeping dream and waking dream is implied—not in these words, however—but by contextual clues or direct specifications made by the dreamer. This is particularly relevant when people refer to a dream that they take as actually having functioned as a vision. Augé makes this and related distinctions in reference to the work of shamans among the Pumé Yaruro, an indigenous group of Venezuela. For example, the waking dreams of shamans resemble their "traveling" at midnight when the gods come down to improve the shamans' singing. "This quasi possession, this vocal possession, parallels the journey, the waking dream of the shaman. But if the possession must be forgotten, the dream must be remembered" (1999:18).

Not only do revelatory dreams have to be remembered, they also must be retold as the testimony of a sacred encounter. Imprinted in her memory as a decisive, life-changing encounter, like those mentioned by Ewing (1990), Haydée insisted on showing me the exact place of an encounter she had with God as she saw it in a vision-revelation.

At mid-morning one day after Haydée had consulted a couple of clients, she, Reina, and I went, as planned the day before, to the place where Haydée had a revelation seven years earlier with Papá Dios. She saw him then as the Sacred Heart of Jesus. It had been a critical revelation for Haydée, a turning point in her life, one that would mark the beginning of her *obra espiritual* (spiritual work). Thus she wanted me to document it exactly as she had experienced it seven years before.

We drive through the town of Loíza and head toward the seashore to the exact place where she had "heard Papá Dios talk" to her. As we drive on a very narrow dirt road toward the shore, Haydée orders me to pull over and stop because she has just seen a magical plant growing at the edge of the road. Visibly satisfied with her find, she exclaims, "It's *higuereta*!" (castorbean, *ricinus comunis*). She breaks off a branch and returns to the car, ordering me to continue driving. But responding to her enthusiasm, I first take a picture of her holding it.

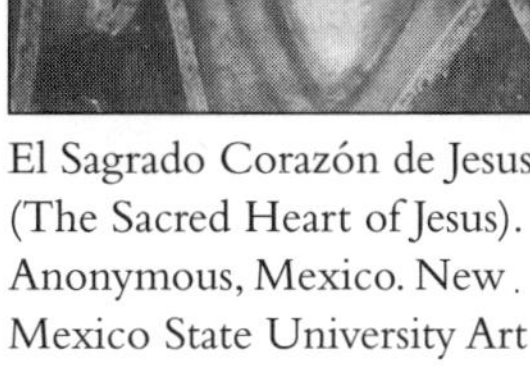

El Sagrado Corazón de Jesus (The Sacred Heart of Jesus). Anonymous, Mexico. New Mexico State University Art Gallery collection.

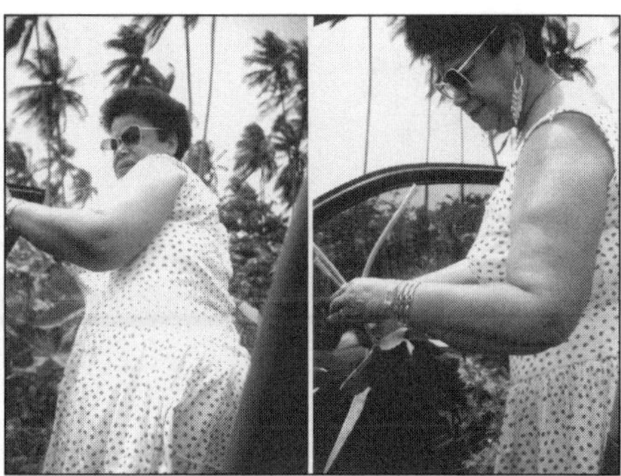

"It's higuereta!"

When we arrive at a deserted stretch of the shore, she carefully chooses the spot under a palm tree where she wants me to record her vision on tape. As she sits under the palm tree, she begins:

> This is the most precious place; one comes and can deposit one's tears in the sea. Imagine how many times my name was tossed [in a magic work] into the sea, because I know who has tossed my name with a stone many times into the sea. I know who had wanted to cause me harm, but they couldn't. I am very happy. I often come to places like this. I sit down quietly with Reina, and then we walk together and reflect.

Shifting to a more formal tone and posture, markers of the sacred nature of what is to follow, she begins the testimony of her revelation:

> This is how I spoke to Papá Dios, no, rather how He spoke to me in the vision, because I'm nobody to speak with God. This is a very moving event for me, because like this I was sitting under a palm tree when I had the encounter with Him when [my spirit] moved toward the *morro* [knoll]. In the vision I was above the water, and He was, too, with La Caridad del Cobre by His side. When He presented Himself to me He said,

Haydée's vision at the shore.

—I want you seated.

It was just like this, beneath a palm tree. And when I heard Him say, "I want you seated," I said,

—How is it that You want me seated? I work seated.

—I want you seated.

And as He said that, He began to walk above the waters. Then also La Caridad stood by His side, and He extended His arms to me. I extended my arms to Him, telling Him, "I want to reach you." But as I was approaching Him and thinking He would embrace me [*arroparme*] with His arms, He was getting farther from me. But all this time He was above the waters; He never stepped on the earth and neither did I. We walked and walked, and at the end of the journey we arrived at the morro. He then reclined on the morro's side and extended His arms to me; I tried to get closer to Him so He could embrace me—because my yearning in this vision was that He embrace me, but He never did. He [again] said,

—I want you seated.

—But I'm seated, I work seated . . .

> —It has to be right away!
>
> As He uttered "right away" He began to rise, and He rose, rose, rose; and I saw Him with a ray of light over Him. And then La Caridad stood near Him, and she said, "I also want you seated." He disappeared and I woke up.

Shifting again her tone, she interpreted the meaning of the revelation:

> Papá Dios left because He already performed His mission; He told me that He wanted me seated, and it had to be right away. And I didn't know what was going to develop from there. Also La Caridad disappeared. And I said, "My God, what does all this mean? What did He want from me? I do work seated, I work at the typewriter." I asked myself this question while I worked, "What does God want from me?" Two weeks later I get a bronchial asthma, so strong that the doctors ordered me not to bathe for a few days. "Hahahaha," I said to the doctors, "I cannot stop bathing!" Doctor Rodríguez said, "Trini [a nickname based on Haydée's last name, Trinidad], we'll give you an injection for the bronchitis." "Do I have tuberculosis?" "No, but don't take a bath for three days." But even as I followed the instructions I got a stronger case of bronchitis. So I said, "I need to go to the Fondo" [the government agency that handles work claims]. Right there, the Fondo sends me to the hospital to see a lung specialist. There I got an asthma attack, and as a result they told me to rest until I can go back to work. I remember it was November 3, 1989. I resumed working on March 29, 1990, and left work altogether on April 3, 1990, and never returned. The doctors decided to hospitalize me for a month; they thought the atmosphere—that is, the pollution—at work produced these attacks. But for me it was the *comprobación* [proof] of God, that I shouldn't stay seated there but elsewhere. During the hospitalization I was given cortisone, which affected my bones; my knees had to be operated on with the help of the Fondo. I saw myself in a wheelchair after the operation, but it was God's *misterio* [mystery]; it was what He wanted for me. As I was discharged from the hospital, I thought, "Haydée, you will return to be what you were before," because I was always dynamic, coquettish, hard-working, strong, never letting anyone dominate me—only God. And he had a misterio for me. "He and His santos—He will put them over me—only they would govern me." When I left the hospital and went home, the Fondo sent me Doctor Avila, who said,

> —Doña Haydée, you need to be hospitalized. You can't return to your job.
>
> —But my God, how will I neglect my studies, all that I've learned, my computer, my typewriter, and my office? (I was a supervisor in that department.)
>
> —You can't go back; you're disabled.
>
> I got 100 percent disability, which granted me $25,000 as compensation. They bought me my house; that is, La Caridad gave me that house so I could work [for her] there. And then I continued and continued and here I am seated in my altar, where He wanted me seated, forever in my altar, to be my own boss, because He and my santos are the ones who govern me from the sky, nobody else!

The vivid way in which Haydée narrated her conversation with God added to the experience itself, especially the impact God's message had for her. Inscribed in her memory, the waking dream (or, as she called it, the revelation) she had at the shore was rendered as a sensuous experience: heard, felt, and seen. The experience of her revelation was indeed an all-encompassing reality.

What comes to mind is the unquestionable reality we sense when we dream asleep, which reminds me again of the alter-reality that emerges when the lights in the movie theater go off and we are engulfed by the images on the screen, losing ourselves and the outside reality in the process. As I listened to Haydée's vision, there were moments when I lost myself and forgot the strong winds blowing at the shore—as during a film or when reading a good book—engulfed by her vision with all its shapes, textures, and colors. Only at the end of her account, as I began to put away my recording equipment did I realize it had become full of sand.

Some brujos and espiritistas I talked with described the visionary experiences that revealed their clients' problems during divination as very much like the images they would see projected in a movie. After a consultation for a woman, Haydée explained,

> Look, Raquel, all the things I told this woman, "You came for your husband but [the problem] is your business." It's not me. I sometimes wonder, how is it that things are given to me so clear; and I know it's not me—how then? I see things because they are presented to me [*me lo presentan*] as in a movie. That's why I tell you, Raquel, I don't need anything to work, no cards, no altar, I can work in my room

> without icons [*imágenes*] without the fuente or the cards, only with my Caridad because she's my santa.

Visions given as waking dreams are inherently different from those personal revelatory visions in which the healer is one of the characters, as in Haydée's revelation at the beach. Probably this is the best way I can characterize the difference—which might not be so evident outside the experiential worlds I am describing—between visions and revelations.

What is the role of the imaginary (both of the present and that inherited from the colonial past) in creating visionary experiences?[22] Think about the power, on the one hand, of images we see in our waking lives in shaping our individual dreams (the "residues of the day" mentioned by Freud) and, on the other, of icons (residues) left by proselytizing and civilizing projects of the colonial past. In *La Guerre des images* (1990) Gruzinski shows, for instance, the power of the Catholic Church in Mexico in shaping the collective imagination of the colonized. About the conditions in which this was produced, he explains that

> from the sixteenth century on, the mendicant orders, then the Jesuits, set out to colonise the Indian imagination in the very domain of visions. Indian visions were reproducing the pictography of the codexes. . . . On this basis a strategy connecting the image and the vision was organized. . . . [T]he teaching of painting and engraving and sculpture to the Indians and the diffusion of plays inspired by the medieval mysteries showed the status which the mendicant orders had accorded to the image in their evangelical campaigns, thus laying the ground for the visionary experience orchestrated by the Jesuits during the baroque period. (In Augé 1999:20)

The Jesuit colonization "takes place through the image," Augé adds, as "two powerful imaginations confront one another and come together. But they have their confrontation in the realm of practice" (ibid.). Often described as "syncretic," this confrontation, Taussig reminds us (1987, 1993, 1997), entails not just the folding of the underworld of the conquered society into the culture of the conqueror in an organic synthesis or "syncretism" but—as colonial Inquisitorial documents attest—a chamber of reflecting (distorting) mirrors, "conflating sorcery with sedition, if not in reality at least as a metaphor" (1987:218). From the colonized perspective, Catholic narratives and images are not merely received by the Indians, Augé finds, "through painting and sculpture, they undergo adaptation, are re-created and creatively re-made. There emerges a new Indian art which is not to be confused with that of the Spaniards" (Augé 1999:21).

Through such countless materializations in paintings and dream narratives various versions of God's and saints' apparitions were relentlessly reproduced and circulated for centuries in Latin America and further reinserted in modern state projects and popular worship (Taussig 1987, 1997). Did this impetus also inform Haydée's motivation to return to the exact place where she had experienced the vision with God, its reproduction in photographs and tapes serving as a durable testimony for years to come? I never had such revelatory experiences myself, but as I was listening to Haydée's account of these vivid images, I had flashbacks to similar depictions in paintings and drawings produced for the Catholic Church and exhibited in museums. These in turn triggered others, resonating with those I had seen as a child in an oversized children's book of selected Old Testament stories. I especially remember one picture that represented—through rays of various hues of yellow and orange—the presence of God behind the Burning Bush that stood in front of a kneeling Moses—related stories, remote images, all coming together at that beach.

Fieldwork Dreams: My Imagination Colonized?

I had many unusual dreams during my fieldwork—unusual for me in their content. I wrote in my field notes, "I am not sure what to make of them." Obviously I thought they meant something; I always felt the urge to jot them down, even if in shorthand on a piece of paper if I woke up in the middle of the night or in my field notebook upon waking up in the morning. Assuming the healers and mediums with whom I was working would help me decipher their meaning, I tried to share them. But I must confess that my attempts, unlike the quotidian easiness of my interactions with them, met with little success. Quite frustrated, I later recognized in my fieldwork that the unresponsiveness of brujos and mediums to my attempts were no different from that displayed toward their clients every time the clients were about to tell their dreams during divination.

And yet, I still wished for some answers. What did they mean? Was there any personal significance to them? Did they have any significance for my research? And if so what kind of understanding did they suggest? These questions occupied my mind—alongside my research.

After my first meeting with Mauro in June 1995, for example, I dreamed about my Argentinean past. I jotted it down in shorthand in the middle of the night. It was about my (dead) father, my mother, Aunt Clara, and cousins—Tili, Mimi (who was eating melted-cheese toast), and Eva (who was killed by the military regime). They were all happy to see me again. Only Tami—one of the young daughters of my cousin Judith—was sad because her birthday was not as lavish as that of her sister, Michelle. I thought, How strange it is to see them poor, not able to afford maids, because I knew in my dream that they were very wealthy in reality. I woke up with an eerie sensation that for some unknown reason I needed to remember that part of my past.

The following two nights I dreamed again of Eva, my cousin and best friend. In my dream she complained about having a sore throat. It was quite shocking to dream about her twice in a row—I never did for the twenty-three years since she was murdered by the military sometime in 1977, at the age of twenty-two, together with her husband. They were among the thousands of "disappeared" under the military dictatorship of the 1970s. I was no longer living in Argentina by the time she and her husband, as many other thousands of students, had been murdered. We have no physical place to go to mourn for Eva or her husband. When I woke up in the morning, I had an inexplicable sensation that Eva's spirit wanted me to do something—perhaps inquire about her death.

What was going on? The spirit of my best friend was communicating with me through dreams? Was I neglecting my Argentinean past? Like many other urban, middle-class Argentineans, I was raised within the Freudian interpretative tradition of dreams, and yet I was trying to decipher my dreams in Spiritist terms! Freudian theory no longer seemed relevant; I thought there must be another explanation for the ways I was thinking and (mostly) feeling about my dreams.

As I drive to Mauro's that morning, Eva's spirit is very much present in my thoughts. Mauro, I remember, told me before that his wife, Lorena, has a protective entity, Juana, who possesses her and helps her in divination. It occurs to me to ask Juana to help me figure out what had happened during the last days of Eva's life. I want to know who killed her and, most importantly, where she is buried. Finding that place is crucial. Can Juana help me? When I arrive at Mauro's, he tells me that Lorena has gone to the market. My earlier resolve to ask for Juana's help gradually melts as the impression of my dream fades into the ethnographic realities Mauro is sharing with me about his life as a babalawo. The thought of recruiting Juana to my aid seems more and more outrageous as the hours of waking life—and old certainties about dream interpretation, guilt, and unconscious wishes—sink back in: it is not spirits after all but our minds that play with us during dreaming. When Lorena finally arrives, she joins in the conversation with Mauro and begins to plan the ritual they would have that afternoon for one of their spiritual grandsons. Eva and Juana are by now far, far away from my worries.

On consecutive nights I dream about car "tools" (*herramientas*, also referred to as the sacred objects of orishas). I see myself rubbing them with a special liquid to prevent their oxidation, and I think in my dream, "Here's Ogún, the warrior orisha, owner of iron." Then I see a children's game board fully decorated with glitter and placed on the floor, and I think, "Here is Eleggua" (the child phase of the orisha). I then see a thunderstorm and dark clouds through a window and think, "This is Changó, the orisha owner of thunder and fire." At the end of the dream I see the head of a monkey, after which I wake up, quite agitated, in the middle of the night. It all makes sense to me, except the head of a dead monkey. In the dark, my eyes half open, I jot down: "I just dreamed about Ogún, Eleggua, and Changó, and a monkey's head." I fall asleep again wondering, *What does the monkey's head mean?* The names of various African orishas—*Ogún . . . Ochún . . . Olodumare . . . Olofi*—keep ringing in my head as I wake up and fall asleep again and again throughout the night. As these foreign words drift in my head, I sense they must be a sign, but of what? Mauro had told me his head was "owned" by Obatalá, the orisha characterized by analytical thinking and composure, the encompassing energy of all the orishas, and symbolized by the color white. I entertain the bewildering thought that perhaps this dream is a sign that Obatalá is claiming my head as well. But women, Mauro had also told me, cannot become babalawos within Santería (even though he knows of some women who went to Africa to get initiated). I tell myself, "I am good at deciphering signs, I am extremely patient, and I fancy white foodstuffs (like Obatalá does). Are these signs that I am Obatalá's child?" Should I pursue initiation in some way?

My thoughts then drift to my adored brother, Victor, who died at age twenty-three of cancer. He must have been the son of Changó and Eleggua—he was a true seducer, like Changó, irresistible to anyone interacting with him; and also very playful, like Eleggua. *Shall I tell all this to Mauro the next day?*

I make a record in my field notes about the possible coincidence between the bizarre nature of my dreams and the stories Mauro and Leonora tell me about divination, magic, healing, and the orishas. It is uncanny for me to dream about the orishas and even more to interpret these as cosmic signs given to me as messages by them. It is as if not only the images of Santería have entered (conquered) my imagination, and thus the iconic aspect of my dreams, but also their underlying myths and cosmology have utterly transformed my heretofore habitual ways of interpreting them. Dreams had acquired a reality for me that was intimately tied not to who I was but, more so it seems, to my everyday ethnographic experiences. Was that an extreme form of researcher empathy? Or was it just the result of the "residual" material of everyday life events that, as Freud suggested, tend to be elaborated in our dreams? Or were my previously closed channels finally opening up to the messages of the spirits and orishas as a result of my experiences with brujos?

I tried telling Mauro about my dream about the orishas and my interpretation, but to no avail. As I began telling him about my dream, he quickly shifted to another subject. And that was that.[23]

Just four days later, on June 30, 1995, I recorded in my field notes: "Just read that monkeys are the animals sacrificed for Orula." What an amazing coincidence! Now I understood. The head of the monkey at the end of my dream was definitely a sign that I should become a diviner. Orula is the owner of Ifá, the highest divination system of Santería. Why not, I thought. I could be a very good diviner—still unsure of what this unusual conclusion really might mean for me.

One of My Selves Journeying into Haydée's Dream

One morning as I arrived at Haydée's, she began telling me of her dream *about me* the night before. I was extremely curious, of course. A couple of weeks earlier she had an operation on her foot and had been feeling sad for not being able to consult regularly. That morning I was glad to find her in good spirits—much more energetic and optimistic than she had been since the operation. Also, the atmosphere was festive: she was planning a dinner party for me and Osvaldo, my husband, who had come to the island to celebrate our wedding anniversary. Haydée was preparing my favorite food: a traditional Puerto Rican roast leg of pig, accompanied with rice and beans and fried maduros. As we sat in her altar before her daily consultations, she told me about "the dream I had of you":

> You arrived at my place at exactly five o'clock in the morning, and since then I've been awake. You take my hands [she reaches for my hands] like this [I open my hands], no, like this [puts her hands inside mine], and you say, "With all that you know, it's not for you to be only on this planet: it's for you to be in the whole universe." There I open my eyes, got up, and didn't go back to bed. I got dressed, took a bath, and told Veronica [the housekeeper's daughter, who was staying with her after the operation], "Look for some clothes for me.

> I don't want my robe today, I don't want to stay in bed [recovering from the operation] today." And here I am, [coquettishly] beautiful as always [laughs].

She was in such good spirits that she decided to work, after more than ten days of convalescence following the operation. As she was consulting Hanny, a woman whose son was involved in a shooting and was now recovering in the hospital from an eye wound, she suddenly interrupted the prayer she was addressing for Hanny's son in order to tell her about her dream from the night before, the same dream she had told me before Hanny's arrival. This time, however, she quoted her and my words in the dream and added some information about my role in her altar:

> —Doña Haydée, with all the knowledge you have, you should not be on this planet; you should be in the universe.
>
> —But the universe is God's!
>
> I was awakening at five in the morning. She is Argentine, you know? [In a half-modest tone] I ask her all the time, "When are you going back home?" But she wants to stay with me!

She then continued with the consultation until her beeper sounded—it was Reina. Haydée retold the dream to Reina, using almost the exact same words, except that this time she added: "The dream scared me; the person who appeared wasn't [really] Raquel, but the Virgin—the Virgin Mary transformed in Raquel. I couldn't go back to sleep. And now Raquel just brought a box for me so I could lay my foot on it, because I had it hanging [with the cast]."

The circulation of this dream—three times in a couple of hours—seemed unusual, perhaps an indication that the message about her spiritual powers being cosmic had made a very strong—and in this particular case, healing—impression on her. Especially after the hard times she had after the operation—having to depend on others and not being able to go out and to consult as usual—this dream marks the beginning of her real recovery. Apparently, she experienced it as a healing dream of the Virgin Mary, embodied in my face and hands, which was later confirmed by the waking experience of my own nurturing act of placing a box under her foot. It seemed that my presence, which she jokingly referred to as "relentless," was perceived by Haydée as a positive one that publicly demonstrated her high status as a healer. Seldom, I thought, does an ethnographer receive such public recognition of the positive exchange that the fieldwork situation has for those who receive us and share their lives with us. It was a spiritual recognition, and I felt flattered and moved by it. Although Haydée had always expressed her appreciation for the small gifts I regularly surprised her with—her favorite foods, sweets, clothes, and jewelry—her dream asserted, most of all, her trust and appreciation of my presence. I was a *persona grata* at her altar.

But then, some might interpret the significance of Haydée's dream involving me in a totally different way. Following a biopsychological perspective, for example, her dream might reflect in oneiric form a change in her physical state, one of which she might have been unaware in the waking state—an idea inherited from Aristotle and later developed by Freud. During sleep, waking somatic sensations of the onset of illness or its cure can be converted into visual dream presentations (Stewart 1997:881). In Haydée's case (as well as in Stewart's ethnography), dreams might reflect a healing process that takes place during waking life. Even Aristotle, the great skeptic of all times on the prophetic value of dreams, could not avoid conceding some degree of veracity to dreams about immediate changes in health (Dodds 1973:20, mentioned in Stewart 1997:881).

Intersubjective Spirits

As I am working now on this chapter—in June 2006 on Ilha Grande, Brazil—I cannot avoid reflecting on the intense manner in which its contents are affecting me emotionally. As I did in 1995 at the beginning of my fieldwork in Puerto Rico, I have been dreaming for many consecutive nights about my family in Argentina. One night, for example, I dreamed about my uncles Zoltan and Alberto and about my father, each of whom died after I left Argentina. In my dream they looked very groomed and satisfied. And though in my dream I was aware that they were dead, I was extremely happy to see them coming back from death in such an optimistic mood. As I woke up, I felt a sense of bliss, of having been visited by them. In the morning, I could not resist lighting a candle for their souls. Surprised at my own reaction—I am quite sure this was not part of my Jewish upbringing—I had an inexplicable feeling that this was the natural thing for me to do, probably as a direct result of my experiences with espiritismo and the material I am working on. The candle's light and brightness were offerings—light being the best gift for the dead.

It is as if I have now remembered what I learned about the world of the dead during my fieldwork, which after many years I had forgotten. Considering my own upbringing in a cosmopolitan, Jewish, middle-class atmosphere, strongly influenced by a very active Argentine Freudian community, I knew I had been transformed during my fieldwork.

For instance, while in Puerto Rico I began to perceive—*imagine*, rather—the connections between various levels of reality as I experienced the daily lives of healers. Encouraged by a *curandera* (folk healer) who had made for me a concoction of natural herbs for asthma, I began to make it myself and to learn more about medicinal plants. I even went through an initiation into Reiki, a Japanese self-healing system, in the Yunque rain forest (as described in Chapter Six) and incorporated into my daily life some gestures and ways of perceiving my interactions with others in direct relation to espiritismo. The signs of this—what some might call New Age or yuppie—"conversion," I am quite embarrassed to reveal now, did not go unnoticed by those closest to me. When I would call home to speak with Osvaldo and my children, they perceived this change every time I suggested they pay attention to the spiritual consequences of the things they did, the words they uttered, and even the thoughts they entertained. "Where are these weird comments about paying attention to our aura and possible negativity surrounding us coming from?" they would ask in one way or another.

I found myself retaining some of the more blatant spiritual gestures upon my return to Philadelphia. My office desk at home began to look like a small altar; stones and branches that appealed to me found their place next to selected photos of family and friends in a spiritually significant arrangement, which kept changing according to events in my life—very much as altars do. Objects were never again "just" objects to be arranged aesthetically; each one in itself and in the configurations I created were kind of offerings meant to summon my dead, certain entities, or cosmic powers.

Even now, almost ten years after my fieldwork, I come back to these habits as I write this book, as if what I had learned about the workings and ethos of the spiritual world were intermittently coming back to me as sensuous, somatic memories triggered by a familiar smell or sound. Their nondiscursive, ethereal, yet concrete, effect remind me of Crapanzano's "imaginative horizons"—which I interpret as those unreflective hermeneutical frames that shape and mold how we experience and constitute reality.

Not quite sure that my evocation of Crapanzano's imaginative horizons fits his intentions, their suggestive yet elusive meanings speak poetically to me about the immaterial yet powerful (if transient) incursion of foreign horizons sometimes brought forth by emotionally engaging fieldwork. Especially when healing and magic are involved, these incursions raise skeptical questions among interlocutors in the academy and elsewhere about the researcher's involvement and belief in "those things." Rightly so, since witchcraft and magic (dictionaries and religious institutions tell us) stand in opposition to the commonsense knowledge that my interlocutors and I share about reality and everyday life; and yet, those fleeting, nontotalizing incursions of other imaginative horizons into our own commonsense logic afford those things an occasional, unexpected permeability and coexistence.

Fieldwork Dreams

Searching for answers to what I ingenuously assumed was my idiosyncratic attitude toward dreams in the field, I found among other works Iain Edgar's 2004 book on anthropological methodology and dreams and was gratified to read about other ethnographers who had recorded their dreams and made them public.[24] No doubt this collection encouraged me to reveal the notes about my dreams, which were written without the intention of making them public. Edgar's leading assumptions in this guide for researchers are that "dream imagery" is an ethnographical significant source of data and that "imaginal thinking" (quoting Kracke 1987:52) "in the form of myth, dream and art can be a valid form of knowledge" (Edgar 2004:120). Edgar himself kept a dream diary that he integrated with his field notes when researching a therapeutic community for disturbed adolescents in England using his dreams to measure the tension he attributed to the culture shock, disorientation, and anxiety he felt in doing fieldwork in that context. Also Nadia Serematakis kept a separate diary (1991) for her dreams while doing fieldwork in Inner Mani, Greece. She related how her dreams began to follow local, rural dream codes while she was doing field research there (232).

Other anthropologists mentioned by Edgar (2004:122) have commented on the influence of fieldwork on their personal dreaming (see Goulet and Young 1994:313–314). Among them, Jean-Guy Goulet describes (1994:23) how he began to dream and understand his dreams within the cultural idiom of South American Guajiro Indian society, as soon as he "maximized" his participation in their society. To reinforce the analytic importance of dreams (both of ethnographers and their research subjects), Edgar mentions the disparaging comment made by Barbara Tedlock (1991:166–167) on Malinowski's apparent lack of interest in the dreams of the Trobriand Islanders (as expressed in his diary), which she interprets as correlating with his apparent lack of respect for their culture. I would not take his lack of interest in dreams that far. Even though by now most agree (as would Malinowski, no doubt) that ethnographers are at least somehow transformed by their fieldwork, their seeming lack of interest in the dreams of the people they are researching should not be taken as a sign of disregard for the respective cultures but rather an indication of the particular research interests that guide their work.

Consider that Malinowski, working in the early decades of the twentieth century, was most likely trying to establish a separate social field of inquiry that stressed the impact of social institutions on the individual against the then-pervasive influence of Freudian psychoanalytic dream theory, which stresses the human mind, not social systems. Similarly, Elliot Oring (1993) points to the actual (albeit not recognized—repressed, if you wish) influence of Freud's writings on Victor Turner's work on ritual symbols. Showing that Turner himself failed to acknowledge this influence until his later writings, Oring demonstrates that the paradigm within which anthropologists work not only determines their research questions but most crucially also obscures their awareness of the extent to which pervasive ideas outside of their working paradigm might have influenced their choices. In Turner's case, as Oring painstakingly demonstrates (275–283), Freud's propositions about the semantic structure of symbols (especially in the 1909 and 1911 editions of *Interpretation of Dreams*) strongly influenced Turner's theories of ritual symbols (their multivocality, unification, condensation, and polarization) and their interpretation (following the exegetical, operational, and positional meaning of symbols). The point Oring makes is that although Turner belatedly and obliquely acknowledged Freud's influence on his writings "in matters of style more than content" (273), he was still evasive about it. Influencing Turner in much more direct ways than mere "style," Oring explains the "repression" of Freud's influence on his writings is the a result of (1) Turner's own theoretical biases as a follower of structural functionalism, which led him to focus on the social conflicts inherent in ritual at the expense of conflict and competition at the individual level; (2) his metaphysical assumptions about symbols, mainly in terms of their manifest, social content; and (3) the delegitimation of psychology within the discipline of anthropology in the early 1960s (285–289).

Following this trend of thought, I suggest that the ongoing debates of reflexive anthropology since the 1980s and the current re-valuation of the anthropology of experience, emotions, and the senses have facilitated and informed in a substantial way the above discussion of my own personal, revelatory dreams. Moreover, since the subject of dreams emerged from my fieldwork material, as evidenced by the dream narratives people spontaneously shared with me, it is only natural that I have chosen to address aspects of it, including its influence on my own dreaming—and sharing of those dreams. But as much as I did not obtain the answers I expected regarding my dream narratives, I suppose that healers, too, were somewhat perplexed by the indefinite answers I gave them, when—to my surprise—I was asked to interpret their dreams.[25]

How odd for an anthropologist to be confronted with the challenge of having to "answer" in appropriate ways to the questions posed by those who shared their knowledge with her. Rather than having to learn how to listen and "how to ask" (Briggs 1986) in order to surmount the obvious communicative gaps of fieldwork, I had to learn "how to answer," that is, to show my dexterity in speaking in the Spiritist language they introduced me to and which they assumed I was predestined to learn. Was I able to meet their expectations?

Chapter Three
DRAMA

"The Doors of My Heart Are Opened for You"

Miriam, a young woman in her late teens walks into Haydée's altar with some difficulty; one of her legs is in a cast from her toes to her thigh. The obvious heaviness of her pace is matched by the chubbiness of her physique and overall clumsiness of her clothes, as well as by her dull, inexpressive visage. Before opening the cards for her, Haydée makes a few unexpected general comments about this young, sad-looking client.

> —You fell down; your leg is swollen beneath that cast. When do you have it removed? Where's your mother?
>
> —At home.
>
> —Where's your boyfriend? You're alone. You have another one; if you don't love your boyfriend, don't destroy him. If you love him, make him happy. You need money; whom did you ask for it, Mami or Papi? Neither one of them, because you don't know how, and because of that money you'll shed tears. You have some friends that are not good; lately you've been hanging out with girls who are into doing bad things. You're smoking . . .

Suddenly Haydée sounds the bell (indicating the revealing words of the spirits) several times, bangs the table a few times, and asks forcefully,

> —Why do you need that money? If they don't give it to you, you'll get very angry; Mami never tells you No. You're spoiled; you're rebelling. What's the matter with you? You see preferential treatment [of your siblings] and you suffer. Your guy is OK with you; he doesn't want you to smoke, but you do it in secret. Miriam, did you feel like selling your body for money?
>
> —I once . . .
>
> —Don't do it! If you do it, you'll catch HIV. You slept with your boyfriend . . . with somebody. Look, you can't bullshit me; you can't cover up anything with me, because those who come with lies, I throw them out. Here, the bruja is I!

Adding to the unfolding drama, Haydée snaps her fingers up and down several times, proclaiming her vision: "¡Uy, carajo! They want to see you on the ground, like that, on the soil. Your enemies want to see you back and forth, back and forth, and up and down," Haydée says, using the vernacular expression for prostitutes that characterizes their lives as an endless going up and down the streets in search of clients and encapsulates an embedded warning for Miriam.

As if reading Miriam's mind, Haydée continues with her worrisome revelation:

> You made that comment [about selling your body] not long ago. But remember that the woman who sells her body is worth nothing. When one sleeps with a man, it has to be for love. Forgive me, Miriam, for telling you these things. I was given these things perhaps to open your eyes, to prevent you from falling into that error. Because a beautiful girl like you, young like you, has all her life ahead. You need to study and work, of course, when the cast is removed, because you can't do what you had in mind to do. You thought nobody would tell you this. He said he was going to marry you—victory for you! He's aware that you are not a *señorita* [virgin]? You want to get married in white, don't you?

Sensing Miriam's emotional state and asserting her own divinatory power once again by voicing Miriam's innermost past thoughts, Haydée finds a way to reach her in both a harsh and hopeful message:

> You want to cry. They are going to point at you. You want to go to the altar wearing white; nobody has to know about it. But I saw it here; you're not betraying anybody. You even wished to run away from home. You're rebelling. Where in hell were you going to go? You don't have a job. You're falling, or rather they [your enemies] are pulling your spirit down, and it's your own family. San Miguel always hides you, but you're [owned by] La Caridad or La Milagrosa. I see the blue mantle that shelters [*arropa*] you. How old are you?
>
> —I'll be eighteen in March.
>
> —You're not even legally an adult. You're a shitty girl to be thinking of selling your body. These are the trabajos that they [your enemies] make to see you crawl in sin and despair [*arrastrada*] in the quagmire. And how much money do you need, five hundred pesos? For what?
>
> —For a car.

> —And where are you going to get the money? Are you in a vocational school? When you want something you are ready to make sacrifices; for a car you would do it. But Mami has a car. She has to take you to school, given your condition. You're very stubborn. You're a *machúa* [tomboy]; you should have been born a *macho* [male]. What do you want to be, a nurse? I want to see you beautiful, all dressed in white.

Reflecting aloud on Miriam's character directly to her and addressing Reina and me, Haydée further assesses the girl's personality metaphorically:

> But this girl has no ring, no shackle, no wafer, no saints [is indomitable]. No *cabrón* [cuckold, idiot] would put up with her—ha, ha, ha! [To Miriam] The only thing I can tell you is don't sell your body. If you do, you'll catch HIV, and then [to me] the next time when you're back from Philadelphia, I'll be telling you, "Raquel, that girl with a cast died of AIDS" [now to Miriam] because that's what I see for you. *¡Uy!*, you'll get all that money, but you'll be infected. Thank God you arrived here. [She bangs forcefully on the table, indicating the spiritual nature of her statement.] You arrived just in time!

In a softened tone, realizing the girl needs urgent help and comfort, Haydée voices once again Miriam's depressing thoughts, but then counteracts her grim revelation with a hopeful vision and promise of support.

> Don't be embarrassed. I want to see you beautiful, a professional woman all dressed in white. I want to be able to tell [everybody], "There goes Miriam; [she's] in that hospital—she will help you." I don't want to learn that you died of AIDS. I'll give you a few little things, like a cleansing bath. Will you carry it out? Don't cry. I'll leave you *chavitos* [a little money]. Here's some money for that cleansing bath.

In a more practical tone, Haydée starts writing and dictating the recipe for a bath:

> I want a despojo of flowers; white lilies (that'll cost one peso); a despojo "Thirteen Rays of Sun" (also one peso); *alcoholado* [spiritual herbal cologne] "Caribbean Breezes" (that might cost you three pesos); and some cinnamon sticks. As soon as you have all this, bring it here. You come by bus, right?

Framing Miriam's hardships in a comprehensive spiritual and familial context, including those obstacles that almost prevented her from seeking help, Haydée presents her with a final diagnosis:

> You wanted to arrive [today], and whatever you were thinking about, I told you about it! Here, take ten pesos for the products. Your Mami cannot treat you the ways she does, but you leave that to me. They [the spirits] tell me to tell you that Haydée loves you very much. Not as much as your mom, but remember that if Mohammad doesn't go to the mountain, if Mami doesn't go to the mountain, if she stays negative, you will not approach her. You're like your Mami, stubborn [and] hard. [She addresses Reina and me.] You need to know how to deal with these youngsters with love. [Then to Miriam] Don't worry; I see you dressed as a nurse.

While Reina and I have been visibly moved, Miriam has sat in silence throughout most of this divination session, apparently absorbing the inspirational yet often harsh and revealing words of Haydée, whose message, based on her initial vision, was meant both as a warning of potential misfortune and a promise of salvation. Portrayed in vivid, practical ways, this troubled teenager's innermost thoughts were thus brought to light, evidencing a reality until then hidden and eliciting an empathic promise of unconditional love and help geared to solving Miriam's most mundane preoccupations, which obviously her parents had failed to do.

Offering to pay for the cleansing products (quite an unusual gesture), Haydée asserted in a basic, unquestionable way her total commitment to Miriam—a commitment that was elevated to a spiritual bond, articulated and sealed in the following closing prayer performed at the end of her consultation day:

> My God and celestial Father, at this moment I close this humble altar, which has been opened for the good and closed for the evil. If something has remained or been said that was not of your pleasing, my God, I plead for your forgiveness.
>
> Now I ask you to accompany me to my home, that you give me strength so I can refresh and cleanse my matter with fresh, pure water. I ask you to take me safely where I'm heading with Raquel, my reporter, and Reina, and return me safely to my home. Remember that while you walk with me, you're the driver of the car that takes

us. Remember, my Caridad, that I leave, but you stay in my home; I leave my enemies, those who are entangled with me, in your arms and hands and at your feet, so you can deal with them, not me. I plead that no hate will be sown in my heart, because in order to work this clean and pure cuadro as it should, I cannot harbor any hatred toward people.

All that is negative around me, drive it away, and leave all that is strong, positive, and courageous with me, to accompany me and to keep me standing like the trees. Don't let anything destroy me, anyone bring me down (*me tumbe*), govern me, mock me. Always keep my head high like you do, my God, because remember that I plead and you give, I plan and you break, we declare but you decide; you're the only one who governs, together with La Caridad, and I put everything in your hands. I beg you to give me strength to continue my obra espiritual, to help me to help others.

After this introductory plea, in which Haydée's total devotion to God and La Caridad was vividly portrayed, a direct plea for Miriam was made in front of her. Haydée's words and tone of voice poetically conveyed this message, which I even now can visualize following the spiritual energies she invoked (those that protect her in her daily activities and that she recruited to aid her client).

Now, look at this youngster I have near me to my right, my God. [Raising her voice] Take care of her! [In a trembling, sobbing voice] Accompany her! I plead with you for her as if she were my own daughter. Don't destroy her! Don't allow anyone to harm this poor soul. You know that she's at the beginning of her flowering youth, beginning her life. Put some love in her parents' hearts for her; remember that she feels lonely. She didn't tell me—but I know what she feels—that she doesn't have a single friend, that she feels there's no one to advise her.

I ask you that every time she feels destroyed in her heart, you bring her to the doors of this home . . . [sobbing] that I receive her in my heart, that I gather her in my arms as I would my own daughter. Always protect her body, her active mind, and her benevolent and happy soul. All the approaching negativity—drive it away! You know that the young man who is by her side is a good young man. Allow

> her to be with him, even before she finishes her studies. [Sobbing] Because, remember, that everybody belittles her, everybody humiliates her. [Crying] She didn't tell me, but I know it is so.
>
> Oh my God, why do you permit me to shed tears for this young woman who is not my daughter? I ask you to always stay inside me so I can help my loved ones, my neighbor as myself, and host all the troubled youth of Puerto Rico in my heart like my own children. Oh my God, I had my child and you took her away from me, and who knows, couldn't this be my daughter reincarnated, the one you took, the one I always saw as suffering, always felt my heart aching for?

At this point Reina and I are very emotional, shedding tears in utter identification as much with Haydée's pain as a mother who lost a child as with her sobbing portrayal of the suffering of Miriam. To my surprise, Miriam remains stoically seated, her face immutable all this time. (What I then interpreted as unresponsiveness may have been, instead, the signs of total disbelief, shock, awe.)

> But I know, my God, that from today on you will open your sky, your celestial mansions; you will shelter her with the mantle of your mother, La Milagrosa. You will not permit anyone to approach her to harm her. Oh my God, [I plead] that if somebody wants to harm her, my Christ, it will be me whom she sees as her savior, my arms that she sees as refuge, as protection, as consolation.
>
> My God, allow me to help her; don't ever let me say *no* to this being; keep my arms open for her. Instead of her giving to me, let me give to her. [Crying] Because I know, my God, that she needs a friendly hand, that she needs a mother's heart, I ask you to insert her in my heart even more than I now have her.
>
> I ask you to take care of her. Take care of her! [Whispering] I leave her in your arms, in your hands I leave everything in your name, in the name of the Son and the Sacred Spirit. My God, stay in my home, walk with me in the road. And now [raising her voice], go with this youngster! Don't abandon her! I know that every plea I make, I see [fulfilled]. I know that you're always alert to my needs; don't destroy her; walk with her, holding her hands. In your hands I leave everything. [She bangs the table.] Amen!

Only Miriam's emotions seem not to be heightened. I could sense it then but can hardly describe it now. The promised feeling of protection evoked by images of God holding Miriam's hand and of doors and hearts opening for her stand in stark contrast to her initial forlorn state.

Shifting her tone, Haydée addresses Miriam directly now, her hands gently embracing Miriam's temples as she offers motherly advice, marking it symbolically with a kiss on Miriam's forehead:

> Remember, for you, my doors are always open. Whenever you feel the need—all right?—I'll receive you as a mother. I don't know why I have to cry for you. You are insolent with your mother, but with me you're not machúa, you're not insolent with me. I am your mami, too; when your mami tells you something, think it is me who is speaking. My home will always be open to you, my dear. All the danger that comes toward you, refuse it, because I will take charge of you from today on, with my blessings. All right? [Kissing her on the forehead] May God look after you!

Talking directly to Miriam in a less ceremonious tone, she says:

> When is the cast coming off, my child? You're thinking of taking it off yourself and walk off. If that's your wish, La Milagrosa will make it happen and it will be all right—you still have screws there. You didn't ask to be born; your mami and papi brought you into this world. Tell Mami that I want to see her, agreed? Before [the age of] eighteen you are a minor, and I don't want to go on because I might open your eyes. . . . OK, let me go take a bath now. I wouldn't want to go out after this; we're all very charged.

Reina and I agree. We are still under the effects of the drama that unfolded in the tiny altar, moved equally by the gravity of the revelation, the tragic, defenseless presence of Miriam, and Haydée's visceral motherly response.

It was undoubtedly a staggering consultation. Knowing Haydée's history of multiple child loss, I was further moved by her words. Spiritually charged, this consultation was, indeed, unique both in its overall dramatic intensity and the degree of Haydée's personal involvement with a client. Reina and I were both witnesses and participants in Miriam's sponsored journey, marked—like the Via Crucis—by the gradual passage from a state of pollution and disgrace to one of purification and salvation.

Recognizing the cathartic (and, in Spiritist terms, cleansing) nature of her prayer, Haydée proposes we all hear it again. It is the first time she has made such a request. I quickly and eagerly rewind the tape, satisfied at my being able to fulfill such an impromptu, significant request. As the tape begins to replay, Haydée reflects aloud, "This is something to remember." (I could not have imagined that my Sony tape recorder would ever morph into a cleansing apparatus and reservoir of sacred memories.) Still mesmerized by the original, the four of us savor its replay emanating magically from the black box. Though only a minute or so had elapsed between that originating moment and its commemoration, an imperceptible phenomenological distance had been created during this interval: Miriam and Haydée had just become characters in a mythical encounter, a drama that might be relived again and again in the future (and which I myself relived when transcribing this tape). Befitting such a dramatic encounter, Haydée bids Miriam farewell: "May I fall before you do! You'll marry this young man and will study to be a nurse."

Miriam's passivity during the divination session had been overwhelming. It amazed me to see her as a sacrificial lamb, unreceptively absorbing whatever was being delivered about and for her. Neither rebelling against nor acknowledging the truth of the revelatory messages offered by the spirits, Miriam submissively accepted their verdict. She was "the perfect patient," patiently acting as an empty vessel ready to receive all the spiritual action—the harsh warnings and disparaging comments issued in her (ultimately) best interest.

Lack of will, passivity, and idleness are assumed in the case of those unfortunate individuals who (as a result of their weakness) fall victim to bewitchments (following cross-cultural witchcraft discourses) and those who fall prey to bad peer influences and dangerous antisocial situations (following sociological discourses of deviance). Miriam showed signs of being a victim in terms of both types of discourses.

Her defenseless inaction seemed to be a state of being similar to what Robert Desjarlais describes (1996) as the loss of the sense of presence or the loss of life force that characterizes some states of illness among the Yolmo, a Tibeto-Burman people. When a person suffers from "spirit loss"—when one of the vital components of the self, the *bla*, leaves the body—the person loses the volition to act and does not care to eat, talk, work, travel, or socialize. In fact, the person "loses the sense of kinesthetic attentiveness or 'presence' . . . that characterizes local states of health" (144–146).

Despite her apparent loss of "kinesthetic attentiveness," or perhaps because of it, Miriam had let herself wholeheartedly become the receptacle of salvation, transforming via the process of divination into an object of love, care, and blessings that in the future might help her develop into a productive social being. Notwithstanding their being achieved in the here and now, are these not in themselves, however, the desired future outcomes of a healing therapy achieved—as it was—during the very process of setting up that goal?

Lévi Strauss made a similar observation (1963a) when he contrasted the passivity of a Cuna patient in regard to the shaman attending her and the active role expected from patients of psychoanalysis vis-à-vis their analysts. In the latter case, is it not the expected responsibility of the patient to actively engineer the desired transformation expected from therapy? This is what is so different from nonmainstream therapeutic systems such as brujería. Maybe this is why divination (in Miriam's case also an exorcism) is a liberating, healing experience in itself, regardless of the content of the spirits' revelation and what the patient ends up doing as a result. What I am suggesting is that healing occurs regardless of actions taken after the ritual (and regardless of whether the spirits spoke the "truth" about the cause of the problem and its solution) because rituals "do" in the process of their performance. Here I am inspired (as many other anthropologists have been) by John L. Austin's (1975) proposed performative or illocutionary aspect of language, that is, the action embedded in propositions that "do" because they are rooted in certain legitimating institutions or social frameworks.[1] Applied to the field of healing rituals, Austin's performatives suggest that the effectiveness of these rituals should be searched in their very enactment, not so much outside of the ritual event.

Desjarlais (1996) seems to arrive at the same conclusion. Exploring the healing effects of somatic images, he describes how Yolmo shamans of north-central Nepal change the overall sensibility of a person during "spirit-callings" from a negative attitude—bound by loss, fatigue, and listlessness—to a positive one, marked by vitality, presence, and attentiveness. "A cacophony of music, taste, sight, touch, and kinesthesia activates the senses" makes a person "wake up" and alters "the sensory grounds of a spiritless body, and so change how a person feels." In sum, by means of "altering what it feels," Yolmo shamans change "how a body feels" (143). Focusing on the sensorial aspects of the healing ritual of spirit-calling, he writes that it is less "a mythic narrative, progressing from one stage to another, than an imagistic poem, evoking an array of tactile images which, through their cumulative effect, evoke a change of sensibility in the bodies of participants. . . . Seen in this light, it is more the poem's visceral impact than its metaphoric structure that effects change" (151). The patient's physiology is a key player, especially at the conclusion of the spirit-calling rite. When the acoustics of the rite (the drumbeats and shouts from the audience), the flickering of candles, the aroma of incense, and the tasting of foods finally converge, it renews a villager's felt participation in the world (159). The goal of this awakening ritual is to "prompt new sensibilities, and so reform the cognitive and perceptual faculties that, in large part, make up a person." In the words of one of the patients, "'When the spirit returns . . . it feels like a jolt of electricity to the body'" (159). In sum, the goal of these rituals is, in Desjarlais' apt expression, "to jumpstart a physiology" (160).

Indeed, certain gestures, words, and attitudes within the realm of ritual "do"—they effect immediate results beyond their functional materiality when performed within the framework of magic.[2] This is an idea suggested by anthropologist Jean Favret-Saada (1989), who conducted fieldwork among rural farmers in the French Bocage, where bewitchment and unbewitching practices still take place. She found that by performing the minute rituals of unbewitchment, prescribed for the bewitched head of the farm by the unbewitcher who had been consulted, his wife successfully unbewitched both her husband and their farm. By means of her minute acts of "indirect violence" and "aggressive defense" (50), such as cursing the assumed witch and preparing protective amulets and placing them in different parts of the farm and its livestock (tasks that men in Bocage believe are menial and thus "feminine"), the wife effected a drastic change from the previous inaction and failure of the farm instigated by witchcraft—without any participation of the husband, himself the object of the witchcraft. Empowered by and feeling the pleasurable effects of efficient action, the wife had promoted the beginning of the whole farm's recovery, eventually evidencing the truth of the unbewticher's diagnosis.

Perhaps the transformative, healing, and reconstitutive power of divination rituals resides in the drama being created in the process, which engages its participants in ways that extend beyond their individual wills. Actors are not really responsible for what happens. Brujos are vessels of their own ancestors and guardian spirits, lending their bodies as amplifiers of the spirits' messages. Occasionally, they also embody and host the evil forces that have attacked their clients in order to force them to stop pestering their victims, to expiate their evil deeds, to enlighten their spirits, and then to send them on their way to the celestial mansions. Clients, too, are receptacles—but of another kind, themselves the object of some negative forces now absorbing the divinatory and redressive enactments elicited on their behalf by brujos. Rituals have that power: even though they are believed to unfold according to the whims of spirits, not of humans, they modify human behavior.

In Miriam's case, the only active role she took the first time she consulted Haydée (which marked the beginning of her improvement) and in the following weeks was to seek help and present herself at the doorstep of Haydée's altar. Indeed, after a few days, having removed the cast by herself without the intervention of a medical doctor, Miriam came to see Haydée again. For a couple of weeks, Miriam joined in with the few habitués at Haydée's altar and home, receiving regular treatments for her recovering leg and all the nurturing and caring for her spirit.

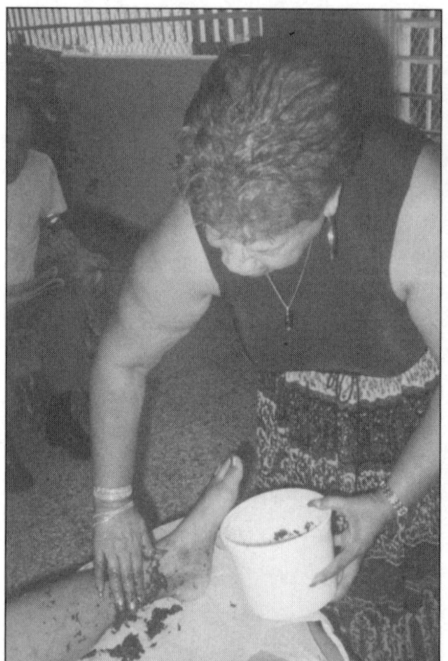

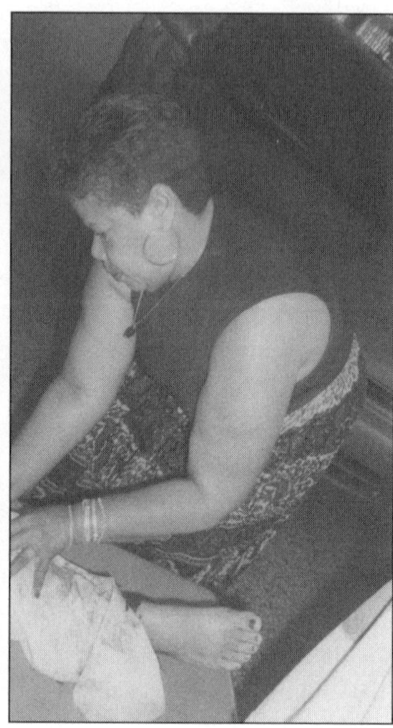

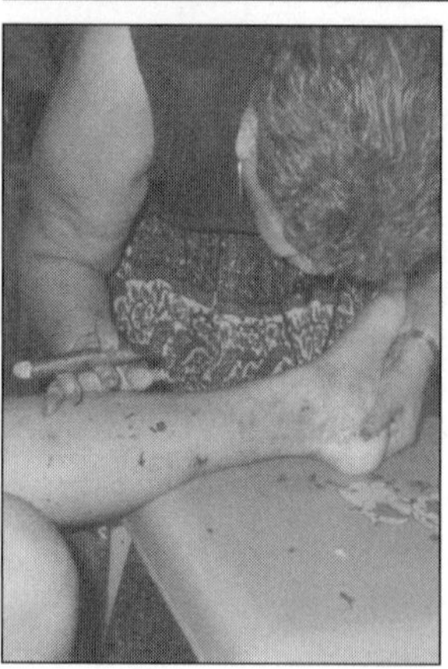

Haydée curing Miriam's leg.

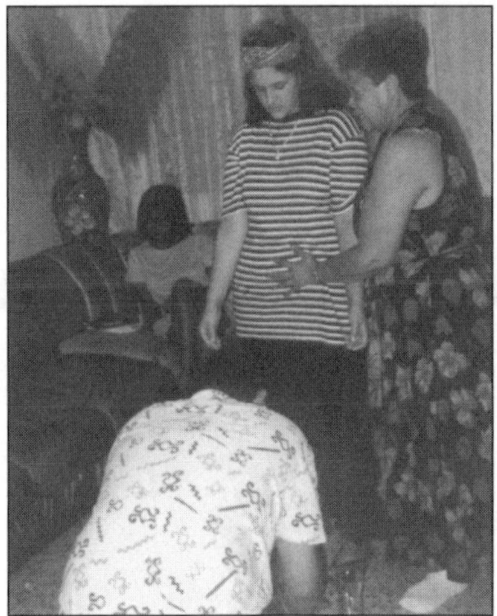

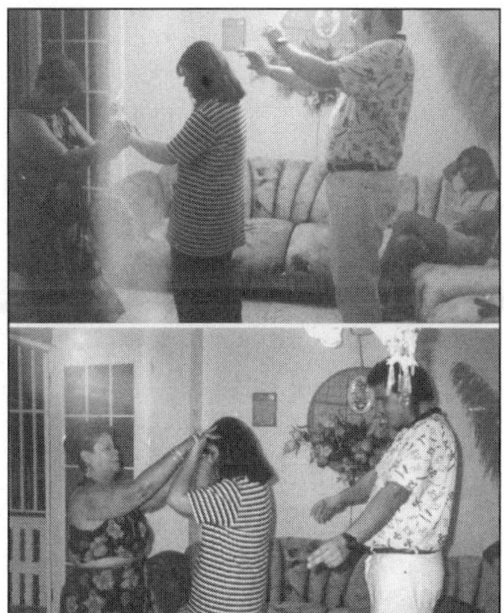

Miriam's exorcism.

Completely free of charge, Haydée applied herbal compresses regularly on Miriam's leg, infusing this sacred mixture with the healing powers of the Indio (an Amerindian spirit) by means of puffs of smoke from his cigar. Between treatments, Miriam participated in the daily routines at Haydée's as a surrogate daughter, partaking in meals with Eliseo (Haydée's son) and occasional guests. She just hung out all day at the house. Haydée called her *mi ahijada*—my godchild—and bestowed on her (as promised during the improvised prayer at the end of her first consultation) the intimacy and demands of a close family member.

After Miriam's leg was almost healed and she had recovered most her ability to walk, Haydée decided it was time to conduct a special cleansing ritual for her, which, due to the gravity of her case, was framed as an "exorcism." Recruiting Reina and Armando as assistants in this expectedly difficult exorcism, Haydée set up a whole afternoon free of clients for this event. We all gathered in her living room. Reina, Haydée, and Armando danced and sang to música santera, playing Yoruba and Catholic praise songs to the Afro-Cuban rhythms of rumba that celebrate and summon, one by one, the orishas/saints.

Haydée falls into trance, after which we all hear the poetic words of the spirits, supported by Armando's interjections.[3]

> H.—She needs a bit of love. But They tell me that she has a beautiful cuadro. Because what she has is a sad *arrastre* [drag, incarnated

negativity], which she doesn't have to carry by herself. Because she is not to blame for what happens to her. Because God will hear her sacred wish; God will give her what she needs.

A.—So be it.

H.—Love, Faith, Hope, and Charity!

A.—So be it.

H.—And [They] tell me that I'm leaving until the next occasion. May God's peace remain here with you. And may God enlighten me.

A.—So be it.

H.—Who's this "Alberto" [that the spirits are mentioning]? [To me] Are you recording, my dear?

A.—Cleansing . . . Sambia [the highest cosmic force of Palo] upward . . . Sambia downward . . .

H.—Give me that handkerchief to cleanse her with her Santa.

A.—Cleansing . . . Gathering . . . Throwing . . . Cleansing . . . Gathering . . . Throwing . . .

[In litany, two times]

"On the mountain Christ died,
God and true man,
He did not die for his sins,
He died for our sins."[4]

[In litany, two times]

"Stop fierce animal and drop your beard to the floor. Because before you were born,
The redeemer of the sky had been born,
Jesus, Mary, and Joseph."

A.—*¡O, cará!*[5]

H.—Bring some red flowers, for the Indio to cleanse her . . .

A.—Cleansing with your sacred wine. Light to the wine. Gathering, giving light . . .

H.—Light . . . Progress . . . Faith . . . Hope . . . Charity . . . and most of all Love!

There are those who need love and are rejected.
There are those who are sad and hopeless.
But there are those who extend their arms
And always find a smile of peace and harmony.

There are those who sob and are heard.
There are those who plead and are rewarded.

There are those who deserve because they speak up.
There are those that say "I'm sad,"
And their tears are wiped away.

But there are those who sob,
And their tears are wiped away by Papá Dios.
Because They tell me that in this moment
This girl is lacking everything—
Or *had been* lacking everything.

Because They say everything has arrived for her,
Especially light, love, peace, and happiness;
Because everything she'll ask for she'll be given,
Not only in material but also spiritual ways.

Because there are those who plead but are not heard.
There are those who knock, but doors close upon them.
There are those who implore and are turned down.
Because They tell me, God pleaded and was heard,
God spoke and was heard.
God sobbed and was consoled.
[Armando asks for ice for rubbing Miriam's face and neck.]

Because there are people who betray those creatures, daughters of God;
Because everything that God gives, he gives in abundance;
Everything that God asks for and everything he does, he does for goodness.

Say that this creature will be blessed, starting today,
Because she's a daughter of God.
Don't suffer. Don't cry. Don't agonize.
Because you found someone who will liberate you,
You found someone who will console you,
You found someone who will help you.

Because They say that those who rejoice with you
Enter the celestial kingdom,
Those who disparage you will be humiliated,
And those who are humiliated will rejoice.

Because, my Celestial Father in the Sky,
May the window of a home open to feed the beggar.
They say that those who open the door to cry with the one who cries will be blessed,
To laugh with those who laugh,
To plea and to give
Because those who plead will receive.

From now on you'll have a spiritual and a material mother.
Everything you'll desire you'll have.
In the name of the Father, the Celestial Father,
And in the name of the Virgin of Charity, you'll gather,
Because everything of yours will be deposited in the
bottom of the sea
From today on.

Because God says, "Ask and I will provide,"
"Search and you will find,"
Blessed of the Skies,
Because the doors will be open for the humble to gather.

Because from today, my girl, my virgin, my saint,
You are cleansed;
Because you are a saint,
You are not just a woman.

Because you came with a bewitchment,
But this [bewitchment] ended today
Because God freed you,
And then La Caridad in union with Santa Bárbara
(because they are the same, united).
Even if your father and mother have abandoned you,
I will gather you.

All this time Miriam is standing quietly, almost motionless, in the middle of the living room, where she is being anointed with flowers, her head and face wiped with a blue handkerchief, symbolizing La Milagrosa's touch and energies, her face and neck rubbed with ice cubes (to cool her negativity), and her lips wet with red wine (Christ's blood) mixed with the petals of red flowers. Perhaps this ritualistic use of colors, sounds, substances, and other sensory stimulants is what Victor Turner has identified as the merging of the ideological ("normative") and sensorial ("orectic") poles of ritual symbols (1974:55–56). It allows them to both deliver a message in discursive terms and cause a transformation at the sensorial, emotional level. In a ritual setting, certain colors, smells, shapes, and consistencies evoke desired individual and social attributes (the ideological pole), such as purity, clarity, sacrifice, and charity, and provoke sensorial and emotional reactions to them (the sensorial pole).

The poetic words of the spirits informing Haydée's sequence of prayers, invocations, and blessings guided and shaped the expected ritual transformation, both of cleansing and healing. All the tears she cried and the negativity Miriam had are now gone, dumped forever on the bottom of the sea, far away from her. From being a suffering, humiliated, destitute girl, she had been transformed into a "Santa," "a Virgin," and a desired child, protected and embraced by God, La Caridad, and the love of a new spiritual mother.

Haydée drew a parallel between Miriam's suffering and that of biblical figures who suffered until their humiliation was transformed into blessings and salvation—also assured to Miriam. By means of a multisensorial alchemy, Miriam was publicly transformed. She was now a santa: the doors of Haydée's heart were opened for her; La Milagrosa sheltered her; the purifying energies of flowers and wine fed her own energies; and from then on, the hands of God would accompany her wherever she went. Through the drama of exorcism that unfolded, Miriam was cleansed and healed via "the evocation of experiences with the sacred" (Csordas 1996).

A dramatic reenactment of the suffering and misery Miriam experienced before coming to seek help was necessary to expiate the pain right there, effecting the desired cleansing and healing. One could compare this with Hamlet, who is able to disclose his father's real murderer and thereby avenge his death only after he decides to put on a play of the regicide in front of his murderous uncle and mother. Why does Hamlet (or Shakespeare) choose a theatrical device to unravel the truth? Is it because discourse is more prone to deception and ambiguity? Or perhaps Hamlet understands that the concreteness of a play (as of dreams) spurs a visceral reaction to the drama represented. The play itself does that for the audience; the play within the play does it for the "audience" within.

The real-time spiritual trajectory dramatically engineered through sacred and poetic words and vivified in material symbols—the flowers, the wine, and a canopy of blue fabric—beckoned a parallel spiritual transformation from a marginal, beaten, polluting youngster into a santa. This spiritual journey is not unlike that aptly depicted by Victor Turner in his work on pilgrimages (1974). This is perhaps what Turner meant by the actual transformative power of the pilgrimage, in which the sacred is embodied in the very kinetic power of the pilgrimage. It is a movement that strips individuals of the ordinary—their everyday obligations and earthly roles and status. It has the capacity to remove them from one type of time (historical and social-structural time) and transport them to another (sacred, mythical). But unlike Turner's pilgrimages, Miriam's kinetically and sensuously engineered transformation did not emerge from her movement in space but from an internal progression within herself.[6]

But how is this internal progression achieved and directed? Other worlds of meaning and contexts come to mind in evoking the gradual development of Miriam's self as it was engineered during the exorcism. The one-by-one unfolding stages of her transformation parallel the patterned sequence of actions that drive the development of adolescent fictional heroes as suggested, for example, in Vladimir Propp's morphological study (1968 [1928]) of Russian fairy tales. With respect to historical religious heroes, Turner found (1974:37–42) similarly patterned sequences of actions exemplified in two historical dramas that produced the martyrdom and sainthood of Canterbury Archbishop Thomas Becket (1118–1170) and the patriotic heroism of parish priest Miguel Hidalgo in nineteenth-century revolutionary Mexico. Simply put, what is shared by fairy tales and historical dramas—those ending with, respectively, the triumph of a beaten adolescent and the establishment of a religious or political icon—is a parallel between the progression of the action (beginning with a conflict, followed by a magical intervention, leading to a resolution) and the development of the persona.

There are many ways to identify this progression and its various stages. Turner suggests, for example, four phases of public action for "social dramas" (1974:37–42): beginning with a "breach," moving to a "crisis," rising to a "redressive action," and ending with the "reintegration" of the main character, now transformed. In Miriam's case, the "breach" is her polluting, marginal state, vividly depicted as that of a girl whose cries are not heard and who is mocked and shunned even by those closest to her. Her marginality reappears in the "crisis" stage, marked by her willingness "to sell her body," which, if carried out, would put her health and probably her life at risk. The ritual then progresses to the third stage: the enactment of a "redressive action," in which all the insults and offenses Miriam had endured are set right and compensated by the magical aid of Haydée, including the promise of future protection and guidance by God and the saints. This leads to the fourth and final stage, "reintegration," in which Miriam emerges as a transformed (no longer "ordinary," but "sacred") self. Through an inspiring yet arduous journey sensuously driven by a progression of images—of closing doors, mocking eyes, and then of opening hearts, sheltering saints, and guiding hands—Miriam entered (at least for the duration of the ritual) the symbolic domain of a sacred existence, becoming—like pilgrims, Becket, and Hidalgo—a "total symbol," that is, a "symbol of totality" (208).

Was it through the redressive and reconstitutive compassion of Jesus that Mary Magdalene was similarly transformed? Has this parable also constituted in any way the form and content of Miriam's exorcism at Haydée's living room?

Images and Gestures That "Do"

Have Mary Magdalene, Becket, and Hidalgo become root metaphors and symbols, such that engender a wide range of future associations and motivations for action? Without such human tropes, how could we experience ritual, be transformed, or even *recognize* that transformation in ourselves or in others? Following a performative approach, the significance of religious and national root symbols (which speak to a wide range of socioreligious contexts) emerge, according to Turner (1974), in historically situated social action ("dramas") in particular situations ("arenas"), where conflicting ideologies and agendas ("fields") collide. Motivated by these agendas and via the concerted symbolic actions of individuals, or the "humanistic coefficient" (Znaniecki quoted in Turner 1974:17), social dramas (as in the theater) are played out after a series of conciliatory moves have been enacted, reaching a resolution or denouement. But regardless of how they originate, historically constituted religious and national root symbols tend to persist and engender new realities (even if in vastly different contexts from those in which they originated) as long as at least some groups continue to recognize their meaning and imbue them with renewed transformative power.

On a more general level, consider the powerfully social meaning that certain gestures and images carry (Boas 1888, 1944). For example, Gregory Bateson in his influential study on communicative frames (based on the observation of animal playful behavior) shows that animals recognize the difference—notwithstanding their formal similarity—between a "playful nip" and an "aggressive bite" (1972c:182). Similarly, Clifford Geertz (1973) points to our human interpretative abilities, which allow us to distinguish a mere, nonmeaningful eye twitch from meaningful eye behavior such as a wink, a mock wink, and a theatrical wink, even though the muscular movements producing them are the same. Further, when certain meaningful gestures encapsulate the ethos of a whole group, they become root symbols.

Bateson, in his "Metalogue: Why Do Frenchmen?" (1972a),[7] discusses—following a Socratic mode of conversation with his young daughter—a deceptively simple but actually complex question about gestures. In trying to answer his daughter's question "Daddy, why do Frenchmen wave their arms about" when they talk? Bateson offers a series of answers that raise new questions for the curious, innocently skeptical young daughter, all of which approach the communicative value of gestures (or of their lack) during speech: "I tell you—we have to start all over again from the beginning and assume that language is first and foremost a system of gestures" (13).

What is, in general, the meaning and effect of gestural root symbols? To get to the root of this question, Bateson seems to suggest, we need to think about the frames that inform their significance. The power of symbolic gestures within Spiritism is evidenced, for instance, in cleansing gestures. As "root" gestures they encapsulate the basic belief in the spiritual component of our "self" and its connection to other selves—past and present, living and dead—and to the cosmos. Thus the gestures performed in cleansing the body from evil influences, for instance, evoke in practitioners particular feelings and sensations with respect to freeing their spirits and minds from negative influences and thoughts, which of course remain obscure for outsiders (as the gestures made by the French for Bateson's daughter) who see nothing but hands moving up and down and around their bodies.

Illustrating the therapeutic application of symbolic actions in a different context in another part of the world, Lévi Strauss cites (1963a:200) the work of therapist M. A. Sechehaye, who applied in her clinical practice during the 1940s the idea of enacting concrete symbolic acts or gestures (such as maternally embracing her schizophrenic patient) in lieu of spoken words in order to reach the patient's unconscious mind.

Compare this with the spiritual effects of symbolic actions and images within brujería. When Haydée encircled Miriam's body—in the same manner I had seen her encircle her own body and that of others—with her arms tracing whirlpools of air from Miriam's head to her toes, she was marking off a trajectory along which harmful negative thoughts and feelings could be safely swished away. (Ken, for instance, whose socialization into Spiritism came via East Asian traditions, uses as part of his practice imaginary brooms to "sweep away" the negativity inside his clients' bodies.) When Haydée mentioned the sea and its saltiness as she was cleansing Miriam, she evoked the taste of Miriam's tears and her suffering. She also directed Miriam's tears far away from her by referencing the dark depth of the sea—the most remote location for depositing human suffering, from where there is no return. And the kiss Haydée placed on Miriam's forehead acquired a sacred significance, for it was not simply Haydée who was kissing Miriam in that ritual context. Centuries of religious iconographic traditions had ignited infinite associations, which transformed a simple earthly gesture into a godly gesture.

These images—embodied in narrative and iconic depictions of religious piety from previous eras—provide the content and associative chains pertinent to ritual elements in the present, imbuing them with a timeless magical significance.[8] As such, they linger between desires and outcomes in that ethereal space colonized by magic and shared by metaphors and riddles. Both magic and poetry rely on that insubstantiality even if they operate within substantively different degrees of naturalization. Although "metaphor is the trope of resemblance *par excellence*" (Ricoeur 1977:173), it also builds—according to Roman Jakobson's ingenious addition—on metonymic (specifically synecdochic) substitutions (Jakobson mentioned in Ricoeur 1977:174–175). Resemblance and substitution are thus both constitutive of magic, following Frazer, corresponding, respectively, to the idea of homeopathic magic—by similarity—and of contagious magic—by contiguity (Ricoeur 1977:178). The couched "being as if" that informs both operations (of similarity and substitution) remains obscure every time a connection of unrelated words is made via metaphor, and in every instance a relationship is established between separate objects via magic.

Within language this implicit "being as if" creates language games such as riddles, which also playfully exploit the idea of unrelated words (referents).[9] For example, by means of formulaically created confusion, riddles pose enigmatic questions about unrelated referents, asking us to provide the missing metaphor (Abrahams 1968:150, Black 1962). "Good riddles do, in general, provide us with satisfactory metaphors: for metaphors imply riddles, and therefore a good riddle can furnish a good metaphor," Aristotle notes in his *Rhetoric* (quoted in Sapir 1977:32). This kind of play with and socialization into naturalizing the phenomenological distance between the materiality of words and their referents undoubtedly erases its otherwise disabling awkwardness (were we to consciously think about it every time we uttered a word). Such games and other poetic use of language have naturalized that otherwise phenomenological awkwardness.

Within the rituals of institutionalized religions, the distance between certain objects and their magical effects has been effectively naturalized by means of hegemonic practices to the point that most Catholic worshipers, for example, would never question the transubstantiation during mass of the wafer and the wine into the body and blood of Christ. But outside of such contexts, the "as if materiality" of objects is not commonly accepted, except among shamans, brujos, sorcerers, children, and some artists. For it defies—at least from the Enlightenment onward—ingrained commonsensical inferences about how the material, sentient world really works in its spatial and temporal boundedness. And thus the ethereal distance between the materiality of objects manipulated by magic and their transspatial and transtemporal effects—between magic works and their targets (bridged by means of contagion or proximity and mimesis or similarity)—is not as easily naturalized.

But, strangely enough, objects represented in iconic or narrative forms are less bound by their physicality, as theorists of the "culture industry" may wish to suggest. It is as if we have learned to accept—as with commodities that have acquired a fetishistic meaning—their spirituality and transcendent effect on us. Consider the mysterious selective process by which only a select few of the world's mundane things and places become "representations," embedded with metaphoric, fetishistic significance. Once recognized as such, they transform our relationship to the objects and places represented, forever changing our somatic and emotional reactions to them. A phantasmagoric reality then creeps in, resulting in the incommensurable becoming, if only for a flash, commensurable and the unknown known.

Perhaps this kind of phantasmagoria explains why the abuses of power of the goddess Muu (Chapin 1976, 1983; Lévi Strauss 1963a; Sherzer 1983), which hindered the aching Cuna parturient from giving birth, were fought against by the shaman, whose words depicted the labor of his tutelary spirits, recruited to liberate the soul of the mother-to-be by means of their magical pointed hats and other such magical tools in order to clear the birth canal of the Cuna parturient. Or it can also elucidate for filmgoers why a camera zooming in on pearls from a broken string bouncing, one by one, on the floor or into a gutter might send a chill through our bodies as we imagine its owner simultaneously falling lifeless on the ground.[10]

Images have that power of filling in gaps between perception and reality, utopias and actual institutions, and representations and their magic—a realization interrogated by many through the centuries, from Plato to Durkheim and Benjamin. And yet these interstitial spaces remain ordinarily unacknowledged and mysterious. Probably, as with the power of "public secrets" Taussig so incisively articulates (1998, 1999), these interstitial spaces need to be left unrecognized as such in order for representations to keep their overpowering influence on us. He notes, for instance, that among the Selk'nam and the Yamana (of Isla Grande, Tierra del Fuego), during the several-months-long Big Hut's men initiation rituals, women are expected to pretend they do not know that it is, in reality, their husbands who hide under the masks of the "fearful spirits" and come to pester their communities. Upon seeing these spirits, then, the women are expected to run away in fear. And even more amazingly, the men know that the women know it is they who are inside the costumes, yet they also need to pretend they do not know that they know, in order to punish severely those women who defy their—the spirits'—menacing presence (1999:101–168). A kind of catch-22, indeed. Naturalized through public rituals, it becomes entangling only when we wish to decipher it and work it backward to the source of the originating "deception," a complexity that only becomes more surreal if we remember that in most cases images engender expected effects that stem from experiences we might never have had before, traceable only as part of a cumulative collective sensuous memory.

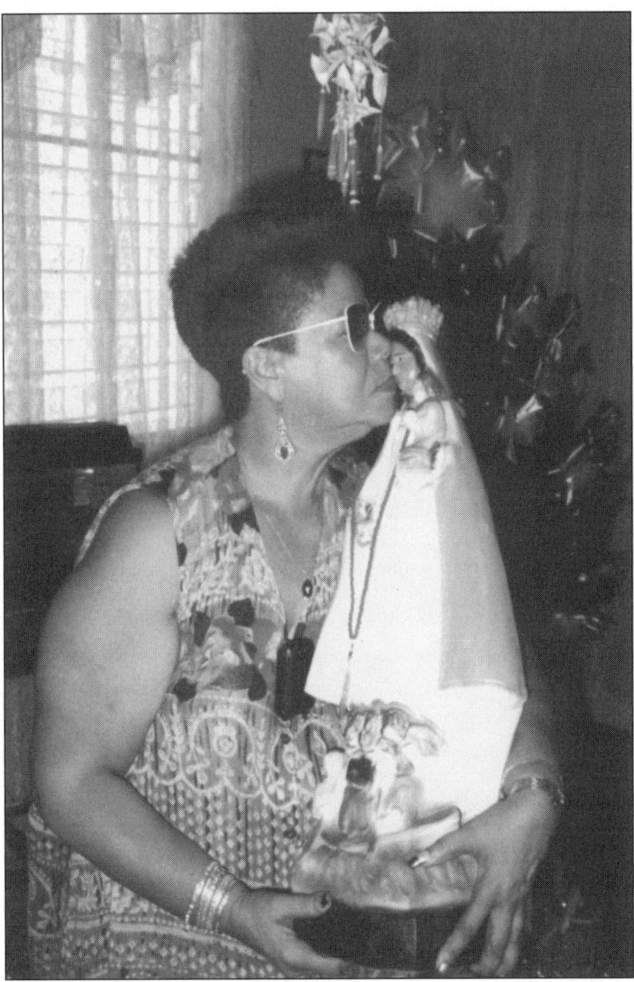

Haydée posing with her santa.

This explains why, during the time of my research, it was so important for Haydée to have her picture taken in specific self-choreographed poses. Whenever I followed her instructions—shooting pictures at her whim!—I felt I was contributing to her self-aggrandizement as a famous, not just an ordinary, bruja. And probably I was right. But I also learned in the course of my apprenticeship that it answered not just that agenda but a spiritual one also, a wish embodied in her stance and attitude.[11]

By means of certain frozen gestures carefully staged, brujos can magically summon a desired outcome, crossing that ethereal space that connects things to spiritual powers, recreating, in the present, religious images of their collective sensuous memory and refueling them with new meanings, thereby assuring their continuity. This is one of the practices that emerges from the basic Spiritist idea of manifestaciones (shared by other creole

Gestures that "do" (with fragments from *The Return of the Prodigal Son* by Rembrandt and *Christ and Rich Youth* by Bartolomeus Breenberg).

religions), by means of which spirits and their messages manifest themselves in things (such as famous apparitions), extraordinary events, dreams, and visions and through the bodies of mediums in trance.

Manifestaciones explain what brujos and santeros told me about the santos, other icons, and the ritual objects they exhibit and worship on their altars. What they worship are not the *icons* of saints or orishas, but their *manifestations* on earth. In a way, the idea of manifestaciones allows brujos and santeros to worship these entities in already consecrated objects and to summon them in new objects after they have been ritually prepared (cleansed, baptized, and empowered)—a process (often misunderstood by outsiders as guided by animism and syncretism) that also explains why enslaved Africans were able to "see" their orishas in the saints imposed on them by the Catholic Church.

As I now review the photos I took of Haydée, Reina, and Armando, I am drawn to those in which they pose as saints, their hands pressed together or blessing others; those in which they defiantly gaze at the camera while in trance, smoking cigars (like the Indio) or playing with sweets (like Eleggua); and those in which they lovingly embrace a statue of La Caridad del Cobre or Santa Bárbara.

I am again reminded of the significance of manifestaciones, for there is an implied spirituality summoned (*referenced*, if you wish) by these gestures:

The power of "root" gestures (with a fragment from *The Blind of Jericho* by Nicolas Poussin).

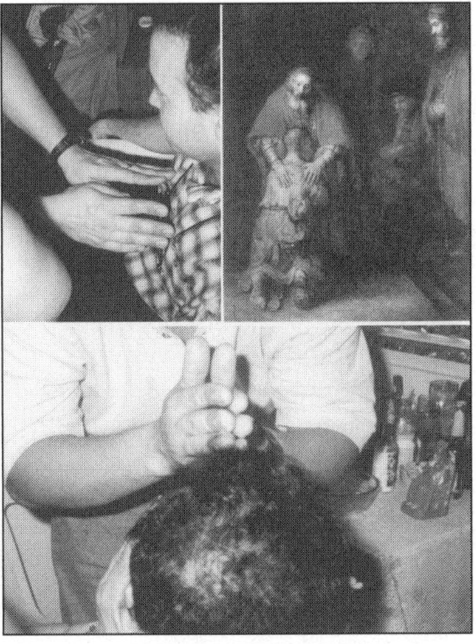

Images of the past in the present (with a fragment from *The Return of the Prodigal Son* by Rembrandt).

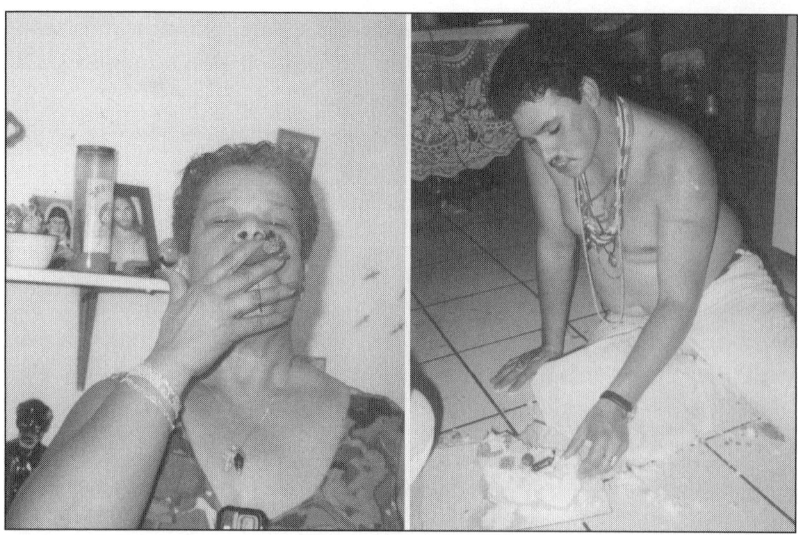

El Indio and Eleggua manifested.

they objectify and imitate a desired moral attitude as well as reference previous such enactments, depicted in numerous religious icons.

Extending the idea of manifestaciones to the context of Western philosophies, one can easily identify its correlation with the idea of objectification, which Karl Marx defined in contrast to Feuerbach's idealist materialism, in his transitional writings (1844–1847), as an essential, universal creative motivation of human beings to materialize their species-specific will. This practical engagement with surrounding reality, which human beings fashion at their will, in turn fashions them. Marx writes, "The whole character of a species—its species-character—is contained in the character of its life activity; and free conscious activity is the species-character of man. Life itself appears only as a *means* to life" (1983:139). One can also identify this basic will to objectification, discussed in other philosophical debates on power and history, in what was subsequently characterized as "the will to power" by Nietzsche (1967 [1887]) and "the will to knowledge" by Foucault (1980).

Manifestaciones thus can be interpreted both as the objectification of some existent reality (a spiritual entity or creative desire) and as the materialization of a spiritual or creative wish yet to be fulfilled. Following Taussig's evocative discussion (1993) of the magic of the fetish, manifestaciones suggest (like the fetish) the socially constituted "thinghood" of spirituality and the spirituality of things. The enactment of a wish thereby creates a link to (or summons) its effect. Although brujos are no way near to drawing on Marx, Nietzsche, and Foucault, this basic idea of materialization lies at the core of what they do, from their hermeneutical frameworks for dreams, visions, trance, and divination to the operative logic behind their magic works in general and the actual performance of cleansing, healing, and retaliation trabajos in particular.

Perhaps this is why Haydée took so much care in reviewing the photos I took of her posing in significant ways as she did in posing for them in the first place. It was as if her reliving of every detail that connected a desire and its effect had the magical purpose of further assuring that connection.

Once, while reviewing the pictures I had taken a few days earlier (when she was sick and able to conduct only a few urgent consultations as she lay in bed), she commented, with an understandable measure of preoccupation, "Look at this one, how I am reading . . . I look like I'm dead, as if I were the object of a wake; but I'm not going to die just as yet." It is as if that image of her in her nightgown and with her eyes closed had the power not only of evoking but also magically effecting that result, in this case, an unwarranted "wake" for her.

Likewise when brujos tell their clients how they "saw" them in a dream or a vision during divination, they mean that their gaze should be treated with awe, for they not only foretell (and forewarn) but also can, in specific cases, make that which was seen happen. Their gaze can "do." When Haydée told one of her young clients, Luis, *Te vi en un cajón* (I saw you in a casket), she was warning him of an impending danger to his life, that what she saw would occur if he did not modify his behavior.

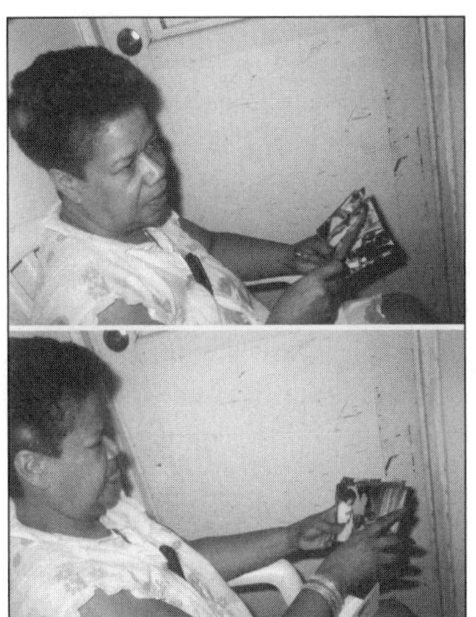

Haydée reviewing the photos I took of her.

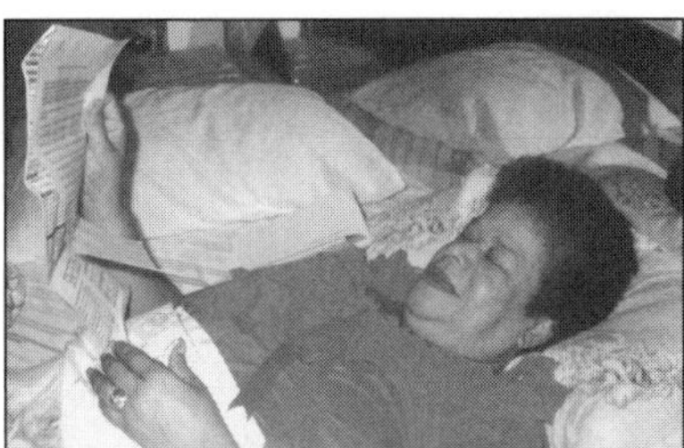

"Look at this one. . . . I look like I'm dead."

Manifestaciones can also occur in more dramatic ways, when they are embodied, for instance, in unexpected encounters or gestures or unusual occurrences in nature. Sometimes plants that should have died flourish when placed at a particular spot in the altar; in these cases it is often interpreted as a manifestación. *¡Cómo paren las cosas acá en el altar!* (How things flourish here in the altar!), said Haydée upon seeing that a piece of *tuna* (prickly pear, *opuntia rubescens*) that had been left by itself near the Buddha a few days earlier was developing new sprouts. Brujos are alert to such occurrences, for when things happen out of the ordinary, they might be manifestaciones, which require interpretation.

Patricia, a thirty-year-old single woman who used to come quite regularly to consult Haydée, was entangled in a conflictive relationship with a man named Garry, who was, among other activities, engaged in some illegal dealings. On one occasion, after the divination was over, Haydée kissed Patricia farewell not one or two times, as customarily done in Puerto Rico, but four times (two alternately on each cheek). Haydée, more so than Patricia, was surprised at the awkwardness of this. But then Haydée quickly deciphered it saying, *Te besé cuatro veces, porque cuatro tiros le van a dar a Garry* (I kissed you four times because four gunshots will be fired at Garry). Of course, this last-minute manifestación triggered a whole new chapter in Patricia's ordeals with this man, which from then on had to include—the spirits commanded—her commitment to shelter Garry and bring him for a consultation before he got killed.

"Think Strongly!"

During rituals and the performance of trabajos, one's gaze also has the power "to do." Haydée was adamant that every time she performed a trabajo the client should be present and witness the entire procedure, which would assure its having the desired effect. Step by step, as each configuration of distinct elements is gradually and precisely assembled and all its elements—candles, carpenter nails, powders, potions, plants, colored ribbons—sequentially introduced, the final trabajo emerges in front of the client's eyes. "Look how beautiful this trabajo is!" expresses both the satisfaction achieved at seeing the completed trabajo and at having summoned its expected effects. In other words, by means of their concerted gaze, clients together with brujos actively take part in promoting (as if igniting) the success of the trabajo made on the clients' behalf. Involving both clients and brujos, this performative aspect of the making of trabajos highlights the present-oriented dramatic nature of this process at the expense (I would venture) of the expected future effects of the trabajos made.

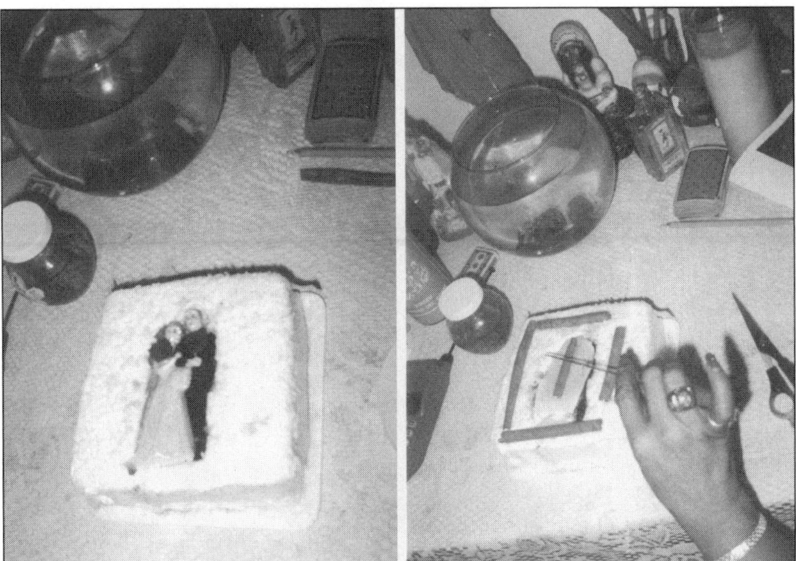

"Look how beautiful this trabajo is!"

This orientation to the present emerges as a consequence of the deliberate redundancy and repetition involving the making of trabajos, as evidenced by the care brujos take in meticulously describing every step of their procedures as they mix, tie, pin, or dress the various ingredients with clients witnessing the procedures. Further, brujos recite the ingredients of the trabajos they perform, uttering each word with conviction—with their thoughts in it—in order to start its effect. Stating aloud the correspondences that connect the surrogates with the victims and the actions involved in assembling the trabajo with the targeted outcomes, spells and prayers accompany the making of trabajos: "As this mercury [*azogue*] runs aimlessly,[12] so will the soul of so-and-so"; or "I'm not tying two wax dolls, I'm tying the souls of so-and-so together forever"; or "As this calf's tongue is tied with strings, so will your prosecutor's speech be." But why is this semantic oral and visual redundancy needed at all? Does the gaze of the client need to be directed by means of descriptive spells to assure the desired effect, connecting the gap between *this* object of magic and *that* effect? Might these spells define for the client a different spell, in which commonsense notions about the boundedness of objects and the semantic nature of words are wishfully suspended?

In preparing a trabajo at the shore for Bruna, whose mother-in-law was pestering her, the dove that would stand as the surrogate for this woman was painstakingly dressed with a series of powders of different colors and

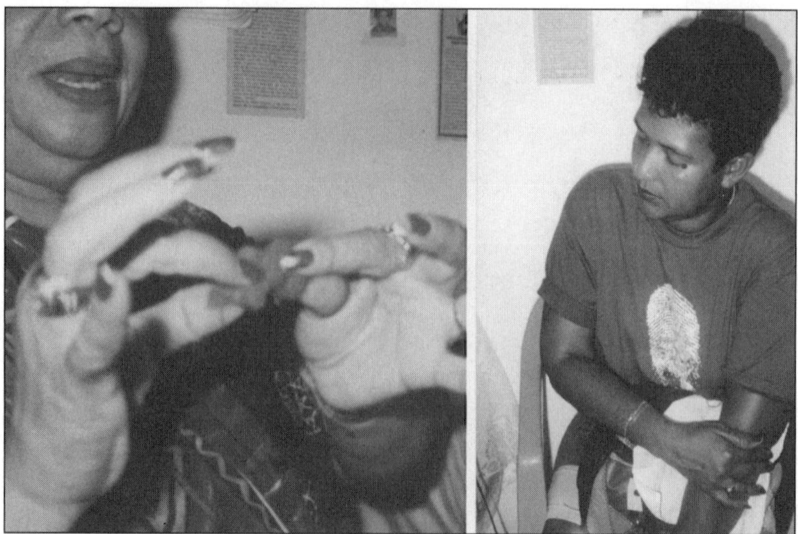

"As these two pieces of magnet attract each other . . ."

textures, each having a specific magic effect, to make sure that when the dove was later released at the seashore, so would also the threat upon Bruna be released. At each stage, the accompanying spells were uttered as Bruna's gaze carefully sealed the gradual transformation of this wretched dove—a transformation initiated when Bruna was asked by Haydée to "think strongly" about the name of her mother-in-law when buying the dove at a livestock store. At the end of the preparation, what Bruna held in her hands was not just an insignificant dove she had bought a few hours earlier at the store, but the pestering soul of her mother-in-law, embodied now in that dove. The connection between that person and this dove had been carefully drawn, step by step, configuration by configuration, and spell by spell, until the complete transformation was concretized. Had the dove finally become the "metaphor" for Bruna's mother-in-law? Do not metaphors substitute one term for another (Ricoeur 1977)? When the dove/mother-in-law was finally released at the shore, flying away until it became an imperceptible dot in the sky, Bruna sighed in relief. The dramatic flight had succeeded in lifting her worries, apparently providing the answer to her magic riddle, "What could connect a dove with her enemy?"

One afternoon Bárbara, a young married woman, came to Haydée to solve pressing economic and legal problems she was having with her aunt, who claimed ownership of the house Bárbara was living in, a house Bárbara had inherited from her father. After the divination session that brought to light this conflict, Haydée and her protecciones suggested that a retaliatory

Preparing Bruna's "dove" and letting it fly away.

magical procedure should be performed. To free Bárbara from the aunt's seemingly unwarranted and dangerous claims on the house and to prevent an imminent court case, the aunt would be symbolically ignited and, as a projectile, propelled far away from Bárbara's life.[13]

On the stipulated day, Bárbara returns to the altar, bringing a plastic shopping bag filled with an array of magical powders and carrying an iron cauldron she bought at a nearby botánica, wrapped in a brown bag. Haydée instructs her to write the name of the aunt—while she "thinks hard" about her—on a piece of paper torn from the brown bag. (Nowadays this ordinary material is used for making black magic works, substituting for the harder-to-get, expensive animal hide used traditionally.) Folded carefully a few times until the paper looks like a small square token, it embodies the soul and body of Bárbara's enemy—her name (metonymically related to her being) stands magically for the whole. Haydée places it (rather, "her") in the bottom of the cauldron. One by one the magical colored powders—dark pink, violet, and green—are poured over "her":

> "Polvo de Zorra," so that *cabrona* [bitch] will be pricked all over; "Polvo Volador," so she will fly away from Puerto Rico and leave for

> the faraway land of New York and then fly directly to hell; "Polvo San Alejo," so that she will withdraw forever; "Polvo Guerrero," so she will quarrel with everybody.

To stress the magical connection among the powders, their names, and their effects, the small thorns of the *zorra* plant are summoned to prick their victim, and the phonetic similarity of *alejo* (in San Alejo) and *alejar* (to create distance) is meant to assure the desired action of distancing. Likewise, the semantic meanings of Volador (flying) and Guerrero (warrior) aim at directing the actions and motivations of the victim, making her feel an inexplicable urge to *fly* away—to depart Puerto Rico—and to *fight* with her loved ones, creating conflict around her, which would further prompt her to leave everything and everybody.

When all the powders are poured, Haydée lights a match and throws it in the middle of the cauldron, setting the edges of the paper and the powders on fire. Asserting again the connection between the name written on that piece of paper and the person it names, she ceremoniously pronounces, "I'm burning here an SOB, an aunt who pesters her niece, that cabrona! Remember, Bárbara, she burned you alive by putting a demand on your house. Look now, look how she's burning, that cabrona." We are all entranced, watching the gradually burning edges of the paper-packet enemy begin to turn yellow, red, blue, and then black. "Are these powders flammable?" I wonder aloud. "Yes, they are," Haydée confirms. "They contain sulfur."

But as we all wait for big flames to take over and chat about various mundane topics, we disappointedly see how the initial combustion dwindles, leaving only black, incinerated bits still hanging from the packet. What an anticlimactic moment! Upset about this, Haydée quickly states the spiritual meaning corresponding to the abortive physical burning of Bárbara's enemy:

> She doesn't want to burn, that SOB! But she will burn, even if I have to take this outside and pour a whole bottle of benzene on it!

I have heard from *paleros* (creole sorcerers who follow Palo, the Angola-Congo practice of worshipping and summoning the dead) that in "hiring" the services of a muerto to perform trabajos for them, gunpowder (*fula*) is spread in small mounds around the *nganga* (also called *prenda*), or cauldron, that holds the muerto they own (for analysis of Afro-Cuban ritual see López Valdés 1985:106–115). Through a series of explosions of fula (also called, for some curious reason among insiders, *café inglés*, English coffee) the muerto seals a pact with the palero—the owner of the nganga—to be his "slave" and thereby to unwaveringly carry out whatever the palero has ordered it to do (Cabrera 1979:141, 145).[14] Often fula is used as a divination system aimed at revealing (by means of the number of mounds exploding) whether a desired trabajo will succeed.

Are the powders (fula) in Haydée's cauldron—her makeshift nganga—"speaking" to her, revealing perhaps that something is missing for the trabajo to ignite, to succeed?

Indeed, determined to ignite the trabajo (and the aunt's flight), Haydée takes the cauldron and places it on the floor of the garage, just outside the altar. Of course Reina, Bárbara, and I move as well to the garage, sitting about two feet from the cauldron. After pouring a generous amount of the extremely flammable benzene, Haydée strikes a match and tosses it into the cauldron, quickly jumping back a few steps. What a flame! Could it be that now, as in the depiction of one of Cabrera's informants, the *füirí* (the muerto owned by a palero or brujo) released in the flaring of the benzene "shoots out to perform its mission" (1979:145–146)? The women react with high-pitched shouting: "Ay, ay, ay, ay" and a series of "¡Uy, carajo!" Haydée adds, "Look how beautiful this trabajo is! Now she's burning, that motherfucker—*puñeta* [damn her]!—now she'll remain quiet!"

My thoughts drift. I am enthralled by the orange and yellow flames bursting from the cauldron. Images of agonizing sinners burning in hell come to mind, images that resemble those depicted in narrative and painting in medieval Catholic representations. The power of this drama unfolding in front of my eyes, the smell of smoke, and the expectation of punishment of Bárbara's kin for her antisocial behavior with such a violent retaliatory act drive my senses away from my commonsense assumptions of everyday life. One might say that I was "seeing" how the evil soul of a young woman's enemy was slowly burning in an iron cauldron, shaped like those I had surely seen as a child in fairy-tale books and later, as an adult, in art museums. The bright, billowing flames smelling of sulfur and eating up Bárbara's enemy ignited also my memory of Dante's *Inferno* and Hieronymus Bosch's *Hell*.

As Haydée, Reina, Bárbara, and I are gazing at the flames in the cauldron burning the substitute of Bárbara's enemy, a tape of *merengue* is playing in the living room.[15] Its tunes and words elicit a lively informal conversation between Haydée and Reina, who start humming and singing in litany. Stressing phrases such as *se fué, se fué* (he left, he left), and *que no vuelva nunca más* (may he never come back)—meant to convey the vengeful feelings of a disenchanted lover—they semantically matched the lyrics of these

"Now she's burning . . . now she'll remain quiet!"

songs to the purpose of the trabajo made for Bárbara—of sending her enemy away. This informal, quasiparodic reaction—odd as it may seem—only reinforces the seriousness and power of the trabajo being made. It reinforces the "indirect violence" and "aggressive defense" (Favret-Saada 1989:50) intended by means of playful (vocal and semantic) repetition and redundancy: *Se fué hace rato. . . . Lo que no conviene se deja, se deja* (He left a while ago. . . . Whatever is not convenient one leaves, one leaves). They half-jokingly mess up the lyrics, singing, *Se fué a volar hace rato. . . . Lo que no conviene se jode se jode, ha, ha, ha* (He/she left flying a while ago. . . . Whatever is not convenient one fucks over, ha, ha, ha). Haydée clarifies for me: "I'm singing, but I know what I'm doing."

Regardless of the women's actual, profane behavior, it was as if the popular song lyrics, when worded "strongly" by them, acted magically to reinforce the desired effects of the trabajo—to assure that the pestering aunt would "never come back." The drama of rituals and magic has that capacity. Not even the usually relaxed, ordinary atmosphere in the background (popular songs being sung and joked about, TV sets beaming, shopping lists being composed, unexpected requests from neighbors being met) can stop the forces unleashed by the homeopathic and contagious principles of magic.

When the voices of the spirits and the dead become manifest during divination and trance, their spiritual power is sensed, their sacredness is materialized. This is when the spirits reveal to the living the true source of afflictions, and their solutions, in a totalizing, emotional event that involves all the senses and when the body and the mind are treated jointly; in sum, this is when healing begins.

¡Aché! So Be It!

Comprobaciones, the corroboration of visions and divination, add another aspect to the idea of manifestaciones. When Marina came to consult, she heard Haydée conclude her vision with a message about her boyfriend: "José is going to be killed; he's going to be persecuted with a revolver. I see him walking in a monte, that is, among trees; and the road is always wet because the sun never hits it. ¡Uy! . . . and he will be persecuted with a gun, my dear."

> H.—Why do you smile?
> M.—Because he had been persecuted.
> H.—I'm seeing it.
> M.—He was caught and imprisoned in the Zarsal [penitentiary].
> H.—And so . . . he was persecuted and caught, and the road [there] is always wet. *Aché* [So be it, Power, or Amen] for you!

This was a comprobación of Haydée's vision, of the accuracy of the messages given to her by the spirits, which always produces an excited reaction in brujos, sometimes marked by their banging on the table followed by *Aché*. By and large, such comprobaciones corroborate the beliefs held by espiritistas and brujos, the irrevocable truth of their messages, and the efficacy of their work. While Haydée was applying herbal compresses to one of Manuel's ulcerated legs (this client came several times for this treatment), she told him that his health problems stemmed from his neglect of his mother. Indeed, he confirmed, he had not seen her in years. Haydée insisted that he needed to visit his mother before she died. As a way to make him understand that he should take her advice seriously, Haydée mentioned a recent comprobación she had:

> Tonio sent me a client of his because Tonio and I have the same spiritual faculties—except mine are stronger now (he's ninety and I'm fifty). This woman came to see me because of a big problem with her spouse. But I told her. "What the cards reveal is that you need to get ready because your mother, though she's a very young person and shouldn't die, will die." One morning—you, Raquel, are witness—as I'm passing through the waiting room to begin my consultations, this woman tells me, "My mother just died." Of course, she was destroyed, but she told me that thanks to my warning she at least had the chance to spend some time with her and, in a way, bid her farewell. Think about this, Manuel.

In this case the rightful disclosure of a misdeed in time—the neglect of a mother before she dies—allowed for a remedial behavior, which albeit not changing the final outcome, ameliorated its consequences for the living. Comprobaciones remind clients that they should pay full attention to what brujos reveal to them.

For people who doubt the efficacy and truth of the work of brujos even as they seek help—the infamous *buscones*, nosy, distrusting clients who *buscan* (search) for a spiritual solution to their problems—brujos have an answer and a warning: Not always are corroborations seen immediately, and your doubts will be disclosed sooner or later.

Imagine how a woman waiting for a consultation (mentioned in the introduction) must have felt when one day Haydée suddenly stormed out of the altar (leaving behind María, the woman consulting with her in the altar) and, approaching her directly, singled her out from among the seven or eight clients sitting in the waiting room, shouting, "You! Why are you here? You don't believe! What are you searching for? Are you just being nosy?" As I ran after Haydée to the waiting room, I caught a glimpse of the astonished María, sitting in the altar and pondering the significance of the abrupt way in which Haydée—and then I—had walked out on her, interrupting her consultation. I was as astonished as this poor woman was and also felt sorry for the other, frightened one in the waiting room whose skepticism was disclosed in such a public, violent way—a comprobación of Haydée's mediumship powers. Embarrassed, the woman acknowledged indeed having these doubts. Haydée dramatically disclosed to all those gathered in the waiting room that while consulting María in the altar she had sensed this woman's negativity: against her will, this woman's doubts manifested in another space and body.

Still shaken by this experience, I hoped that Haydée would never react like that to me, hoped my occasional doubts and analytical skepticism—which readers may well have sensed by now—would never be so strong or so pervasive that they would manifest themselves, would never be sensed by the brujos I worked with. Manifestaciones and comprobaciones can happen at any time, I learned, for they express a basic objectifying principle of a "so be it," or a potential energy that might burst—as a capricious genie might—as a result of any word and thought we utter, any image and gesture we enact, and any object we manipulate.

Chapter Four
SPIRITUAL TIME

The word "sense," as any thesaurus shows, is synonymous with (a) meaning, significance, logic; (b) intelligence, wisdom, common sense; and (c) feeling, sensation, awareness. It is the same word, yet it carries very different, even opposing, meanings. Characterizing the history of anthropological theory as a quest for finding the sense of the behaviors of fellow human beings, Michael Herzfeld argues (2001) that theories were engaged first in "making sense" of the behaviors of "exotic others"; then in studying the "common sense" or taken-for-granted realities of different groups within a society (including those of the anthropologist); and now are focusing on the "senses," or the realm of the "sensorium."[1] Even if reality—and, in this case, the periodization of a discipline—hardly fits so neatly into such an aesthetically harmonious semantic play of words, Herzfeld's categorization makes sense to me as an apt, "sensical" (following his lead) characterization of a phenomenology of the ethnographic enterprise. As with proverbs, succinct typifications often just "feel" right in capturing essential (if selective) attributes of otherwise fuzzy processes, such as the ones I encountered at various points in my own ethnographic trajectory.

In the summer of 1995, a few weeks after my arrival in Puerto Rico for the start of my fieldwork, a client at Basi's botánica, upon learning about my research, gave me the phone number of Mauro. Prior to meeting him for the first time, I was extremely apprehensive; I had never interacted with a babalawo before. Language was not really a barrier; but I wondered how I should approach him and what I should tell him.

I arrive at Mauro's home-temple on the outskirts of San Juan just before ten o'clock in the morning, and as I am shutting the door of my car, he appears at the decorated wooden gate of his house, where I can barely make out "Aleke" in the carved inscription. A very slender man of about seventy, Mauro is dressed in tight, youthful-looking white jeans and a blue shirt. On his left wrist he wears a luxurious gold watch and a green-and-yellow-beaded armband (the colors of Orula). He greets me, and we enter the house through a garage converted to a waiting room and office. I am immediately engrossed by a large desk with all sorts of ritual objects on it:

a small piece of zebra hide, an attractive scepter that looks like a barber's brush with its long, shiny, black bristles, and a long necklace made from halved pits of some kind of fruit intertwined with various kinds of beads. He asks,

> —How can I help you?
> —I wish to learn about Santería. That is why your godson, Willie, put me in contact with you.

Apparently unsatisfied with my strategically concise answer, he seeks clarification of my intentions.

> —Why are you here? Are you a journalist?
> —No, I come from the University of Pennsylvania. . . . I'm doing my Ph.D.
> —The BBC made a film about me. . . . What are you looking for? . . . Where are you from?

Because I heard him making bigoted passing remarks a few minutes earlier as we walked into the house about Jews, blacks, and Puerto Ricans, I purposely offer candid yet vague bits of personal information, judging that they are neutral enough in this context.[2]

> —I'm from Philadelphia and Argentina . . .
> —[He cuts me off.] I work with Ifá, the most complex divining system of the Religion of the Orishas. Espiritismo entails a prior level of mediumship. . . . So you've never been to a Spiritist consultation, or one with a babalawo, before? How is that possible?
> —As I say, I am a novice in these matters. I want to learn about the religion, about its unwritten history.

Trying to engage him about Santería, I point to the long necklace lying on his desk. Picking it up, he explains,

> —You toss it during divination. . . . You don't know what this is for?

I gather this is as strange an experience for him as it is for me; he is obviously used to having people come for consultations, not simply for information about the religion.

In no time he begins telling me about his life and work as a healer. But as he explains who he is and gives some details of his life as a babalawo, I feel awkward about my inability to make sense of large parts of his narrative. He speaks in a very low tone of voice—I wonder if on purpose—and since he is missing his lower teeth, the pronunciation of his words is not clear. I can hardly hear him, let alone make sense of much of what he is telling me. Further, he talks with his face strangely to the side, giving his words an aloof, evasive tone. Although I understand, literally, most of the individual words he utters, their stream of meaning eludes me—what am I missing?

Naturally, I follow routinely the order of words, the prosody (rhythm, pauses), the paralinguistic modifiers (gestures, tone of voice, body posture), and all other framing devices, trying to make a mental map—a kind of visual map, since stories elicit images—of the stories I am being told. Disconcerted, I realize, however, that what I deemed to be the subject of the story vanishes in a mesh of other seemingly unrelated but possible subjects; places I managed to locate and imagine as the background for the action end up being the subject, not the context of the narrative. In sum, all those unconscious, unspoken connections we usually make in deciphering the speech of others are useless to me in this first effort to comprehend Mauro's stories. Not only large chunks of his life and deeds as a babalawo are simply not accessible to me, but even more broadly the overall manner of his discourse makes little sense to me.

Indeed, the situation at the beginning between the two of us is stiff. For my part, perhaps as a result of the initial awe I feel toward him, I do not want to say anything that might interrupt (and annoy) him and possibly abort our first encounter; I wish to stretch it out as long as I can.

> So, Raquel, what are you looking for? You should speak with Lorena; we've been working together for fifteen years. She knows a lot—she helped me write many books and . . . [I am lost here. *Books?*] . . . she helps me because she knows how to communicate very well. She gives lectures, uses the computer and the fax.

Mauro continues his show-and-tell, pointing to the *tabla*, a circular, elaborately carved wooden board lying on his desk. I manage to discern the stylized shapes of various animal figures intertwined in a continuous border with abstract arabesques in bas-relief. He is surprised at my question,

> —What is this for?
>
> —[Testing me, he asks,] Do you know Robert Thompson and William Bascom?

—Of course, they are two pioneer American anthropologists who researched and wrote about African religions and art around the 1950s; but I can't remember reading anything about tablas—my research interest in Santería has emerged just recently, quite by coincidence.

Realizing that my question is consistent with my previously exposed intention to learn, he continues,

> William Bascom claimed he was initiated in the religion in Africa, but when he was tested at a meeting we had in Cuba, he couldn't respond. He is a trickster [*pícaro*], not a babalawo! This tabla is used in divination. There shouldn't be any empty space on its circular carved rim. I had this one made in Egypt. This religion originated in Atlantis, the city that submerged and disappeared, and from there it moved to Africa—to Ethiopia—and then to the Yoruba.

I had never before heard this version of the origin of Santería; but I realized later that it was consistent with his aversion to the current Africanization—or rather, Yorubanization—of the religion. He sees this latter reinterpretation of the origins of Santería as a result of the recent politicization of this religion following its appropriation by identity politics–minded practitioners and interpreters (who obviously exclude "white" babalawos like him). Instead, he sees Santería today as an upshot of an ancient mystical school, with strong ties to various European theosophical movements—its African trajectory just the latest one, not its origin: "Catholic paraphernalia such as the papal scepter—if you look at it—has clear Egyptian references." What people recognize today as the syncretism of Catholic saints and the African orishas in the religion is, I gather, just a later, added system of correspondences. If any exists, he seems to suggest in his particular roundabout rhetoric, it was the Catholic Church that syncretized the mysticism of the Egyptians and, later, other Africans. He then mentions the Vatican and its alleged secret libraries, with which mysteriously he seems to be familiar. Ancient books on magic, occultism, and alchemy that were saved from the infamous and mysterious burning of the library at Alexandria (circa 3 CE) are stored there, he tells me, away from the scholar no less than the general public.

Conspiracy, secret knowledge, persecution of mystical brotherhoods, ancient documents on magic purposely hidden: all of these are recurrent themes that gradually aid me in deciphering his discourse and my otherwise inconclusive field-note entries about Mauro's historical account of Santería's origins. As a revisionist version, it transports me to the fantastic, parallel conspiratory worlds—inhabited by Millenarians, Knights Templar, Rosicrucians, Gnostics, Freemasons, Jesuits, Cabalists, Alchemists, Hermetic zealots, and monastic Demonologists—I had once read about. These conspiratory wars, documented in the research of medievalists and fictionalized in accounts of the semiotician Umberto Eco—*The Name of the Rose* (1983) and *Foucault's Pendulum* (1989)—become eerily present through Mauro's discourse.

Initially, for this reason, I am amazed by Mauro's independent research of these secret, deadly wars—launched between competing branches of the Catholic Church, its brotherhoods, and various mystical sects. But then when he offers this research as proof of his own knowledge and practice of magic and healing as a babalawo, it all begins to make sense. He is tying his professional genealogy not just to Cuba but much earlier to the fantastic and unresolved puzzles of ancient and medieval mysticism.[3]

Out of the blue, he interrupts his eschatological lesson, saying, "I charge money for consultations, you know." Taken aback a bit but in a reassuring tone I respond, "Of course. I will pay." Exchange rules are fundamental not solely between humans but also, as I would learn later, between them and spirits. Reciprocity of some kind must operate as much in magic and healing practices as in fieldwork relations.[4]

Always aware that our interview might come to an end at any point during the first two hours of our conversation, I remain seated even when he suddenly stands up. To my relief, after a few minutes he comes back with a lit cigarette, and we continue our conversation. Through an open door I see a girl of about twelve—his godchild, I later learn—carrying some bottled water onto the balcony. She came to live with Mauro and Lorena several months earlier following some conflict between her mother and stepfather. The bottled water, I learn, is for a ritual scheduled to take place later that day. The clacking sound of chickens and roosters in the backyard is very loud and, added to the noise of the television, makes what Mauro is saying to me even more difficult to follow.

Again I am afraid that if I ask him to repeat any part of his stories or to speak louder and slower, he will get annoyed. So, I wait and see. I do manage to grasp, this time, details of his personal stories, which, I have to confess, seem quite unreal: for example, he claims to have divined for Italian, English, and American heads of state; for counts and Interpol agents; for famous entertainers; and for multimillionaire international industrialists.

But the essence of Mauro's rhetoric is not completely lost on me: he is (and should be) respected and feared by both older and younger babalawos because of his comparatively stronger magical prowess:

> My godfather was one of the famous Tatas [godfathers of younger babalawos] in one of the many Cabildos [ethnically defined, Church-sponsored fraternities] that used to exist in Cuba; I am already fifty years initiated as a babalawo! . . . I communicate with the spirits of my *padrinos* [spiritual godparents] who died only thirty years ago and thus are in a state of *pachamama* [spiritual bliss and enlightenment], unlike those who died three hundred years ago and have already reincarnated (that's why they sometimes make mistakes). . . .
>
> I help the rich and powerful get richer and more powerful. . . . I predicted the revolution in Iran . . . helped one of Panama's presidents rescue his illegitimate son from kidnappers and took him to New Jersey with Lorena, registered him in an American school, bought him clothes—not just any, the best—and after a year and half, when the danger had passed, called the boy's father and told him he could come pick up his son. But since the boy was staying illegally in the United States, I sent the Jewish Interpol—they are the fiercest—to fetch him and bring him back to Panama.

Laced with mundane commonsense details about schools and uniforms, stories of heads of state, multimillionaires, and spies may appear quite plausible if improbable. This particular story, then, rendered here only partially due to my lack of understanding of the whole plot, may sound clear to readers now as a result of my editing, in contrast to the rendition I heard for the first time. William Labov and Joshua Waletzky analyze (1967) formal and semantic components of narrative structures as well as the shared interpretative expectations of narrative genres among storytellers and their audiences. They note that narrative clauses, for example, are minimal narrative units that state the course of an action and are then connected by time indicators (such as "then" or "so") to create a temporal sequence. Yet, even when Mauro's stories follow this formal structure, their overall integrity and meaning are not at all transparent. In fact, it would take me many months of participation in rituals and hanging out in his home-temple before I would realize that his everyday narratives were no less esoteric than his incantations and sacred speech: they too needed to be decoded according to other than standard rules of composition.

Mauro continues:

> Every time I help state officials find people or things or foretell the future, I leave immediately after, because I don't want to have anything to do with whatever happens as a consequence. Also, in order to prevent enemies of the state, for example, from eliminating

> me, I never tell state officials in advance when I will be arriving, even though they pay for all my expenses.

I can imagine this happening only in films. But I hold on to my disbelief, which is matched by his:

> —You've never seen the energy emanating from people? You've never seen a shadow?
>
> —No.
>
> —Once I saw one sent by my enemies—eight babalawos who wished me dead. [Gesturing] I took a new dagger and pierced [the magical proxies of the babalawos] several times. One by one something happened to them after I had left them without power . . . after I poured wine over [these magical proxies] at night, that was it: one broke his leg, another [died? unclear to me]. It's a wine that I have that can kill.

Was he pulling my leg? And yet, I couldn't dismiss the feasibility of these fantastic deeds. After all, extraordinary deeds like the ones I hear Mauro narrate now (and subsequently on other occasions) are supposedly what healers and sorcerers actually perform.

Indeed, his stories and work do not belong to my commonsense world. I have never before encountered anyone telling me, as Mauro does, "I can leave my body and transmute. Lorena once saw me disengaging from my body, leaving my tendons and veins, until only my very little bones were left. . . . My forces are those of the cosmos. I change matter. Science and religion run parallel to each other [nowadays], but once they were united."

When I think about the now almost century-old anthropological fieldwork wisdom about the necessity of learning the native languages of those whose worlds we seek to study, I wonder how much more we need to learn in order to really be able to make sense of the worlds of "exotic others." For example, drawing again on Charles Briggs' work (1986), fieldworkers must not only know the language of their interviewees but also be competent in their discursive rules, such as those that guide what one can ask and how to ask it. Furthermore, he notes, "Statements nearly always relate to two or more features of the communicative situation, such as distinct interactional goals, at the same time" (103). How to better assess these distinct interactional goals is especially difficult during the initial stages of fieldwork encounters, when both interlocutors are still strangers to each other (as Mauro and I were), and the dialogic nature of such encounters is highly dependent on frail intersubjective understandings of the situation itself. In addition to Briggs' main thesis, aptly titled *Learning How to Ask* (1986), a no less important issue I raised earlier is learning how to answer, which increases exponentially the emergent nature of these types of encounters and the risks of their failing at any moment.

After about three hours, Mauro takes me into another office, which is unlike the public one I visited earlier; this is his "private study." It looks nothing like I had expected. Its space is crowded with books piled on the floor and on bookshelves, a cluttered desk, and several chairs—none without stacks of papers or books. Manuscript pages are scattered all around, partially covering a computer and printer. In this room he keeps all the hundreds of religious documents he collected and managed to smuggle out of Cuba upon leaving for the United States in the late 1970s. He also keeps his private *libretas*, notebooks, where he records his work as a babalawo—the names of all the clients he has seen in consultation and the prescriptions he has given them.

Mauro reaches toward one of the shelves and takes out an oversized manuscript. It is the text of Ifá (a divination system practiced only by babalawos),[5] informally translated into Spanish and printed on computer paper—the files saved on Mauro's computer. In addition to text, some pages have schemas composed of two symbols—"I" and "O"—lined up in various configurations, with African terms under them. I am only able to make sense of a few paragraphs of the text and to identify some topics, among them the creation of botánicas and certain taboos for using metal silverware. Though the text is in Spanish and therefore completely readable, I cannot understand the significance of what I am reading: these are sacred, esoteric texts composed of myths and prescriptions, all of which need to be decoded during divination according to the specific needs of each client. Like Mauro's life stories, the meaning of these texts remains obscure to me. Notwithstanding, I tell Mauro, I am utterly impressed: given what is known about the practices and myths of Santería, assumed to be exclusively based on oral forms of transmission, I had never imagined that practitioners use written sources as ways of documenting, safekeeping, and transmitting their knowledge, practices, and myths.

About noon on that first morning at Mauro's, a young yuppie couple comes by with two children about six and eight years of age and a baby in a carriage. Chris, the husband, is a Coca-Cola executive, and Lynnette, the wife, is an artist and kung fu aficionado from Italy. They live in New York and lead a cosmopolitan life, traveling often to Europe and Latin

America. This time they have come to Puerto Rico just to visit their godfather, Mauro, and undergo some cleansing and initiation rituals. They have many important decisions to make, and thus it is imperative that they get the orishas' support and direction. I remember Mauro telling me that he helps the rich get richer and that those with talent and power make the best of any future opportunity they may encounter after having consulted with him—lending support that the stories he has been telling me are not entirely fantastic.

Having to prepare for the rituals, Mauro interrupts our conversation, expecting that I will leave. But somehow I get involved in a friendly conversation with the couple, and so Mauro invites me to stay for the rituals—if I would not mind "catching something" (a spirit?). I gladly accept the alleged risk, of course, for I cannot resist the opportunity to participate in my first Santería ritual. Not knowing whether to stand, sit, or follow him around, I await his cues.

Quite uneventfully, the family den (part of the covered balcony) transforms into a ritual space, where the cleansing ritual for Lynnette will take place. Chris, dressed all in white and wearing a white cap and colorful beaded necklaces, prostrates himself on a bamboo mat stretched out on the balcony's floor. Mauro then places his hands over Chris' back. Standing up, they embrace two times, touching each side of their bodies in a ritual greeting typical of godfathers and their initiates. Mauro leaves for a few minutes and comes back wearing a white cap rimmed with gold embroidery. In the meantime the two older children, sitting at a dining table in the adjacent room in front of a TV set, are occupied drawing while their baby brother, seated in his carriage conveniently positioned in front of a ventilator—the temperature at noon is rising into the nineties—sleeps contently.

At this point Mauro asks Lorena to break open a green coconut. She goes to the kitchen, pours the coconut water in some cups, and returns with the cups to the balcony. On the side of one of two entrances to the balcony, there is a small table with goblets arranged in concentric rows, encircling a bigger goblet in the center, where offerings of all sorts—flowers and some plates of food—are placed. This is a *bóveda*, an altar for the dead, following Spiritist practice. On the floor are a tureen and a small Eleggua (in this case an abstract head made of cement with two cowry shells for eyes). Next to the Eleggua, Lynnette places an oblong white object (carefully extracted from her white purse), a special protective amulet Mauro made for her out of a goat's left horn, which he had previously filled with special herbs and blessed objects, the mixture sealed inside and topped with links of tiny colored beads. A black cauldron filled with Ogún's instruments (stones and all sorts of iron tools, nails, and so on) is placed at one edge of the bamboo mat, as Ogún's name is invoked (Lynnette is a daughter of Ogún), together with one of the glasses filled with coconut water. In front of these items is another group of objects: a divining tabla, a plate with bits of coconut, a stone, and small objects that appear to be tiny amulets.

Just outside the opening to the backyard I notice a burlap sack with something turning and tossing inside it. I soon learn that it is a rooster that was to be prepared in the backyard for the ritual—fed grains and anointed with special herbs. From the noises I hear, I gather that other birds and animals are also kept in the backyard, though I am not invited to accompany Mauro and Chris to the backyard, where Mauro picks up the bag and returns with it to the balcony.

Mauro takes the rooster out of the sack and brings it to the center of the balcony by the mat Lynnette is standing on. I remain seated on a chair on one side of the room. Lorena takes the rooster, cleanses it with some of the coconut water, then swirls it around and over Lynnette's head and body, passing it near her back and knees, while the restless rooster frantically beats its wings, slightly buffeting Lynnette's hair and clothes and making her eyes and face twitch in obvious disgust.

In the meantime, Mauro, with no apparent purpose, has gone several times in and out of the balcony and backyard, making it impossible for me to know when the ritual will begin, if indeed it has not already begun. Between his comings and goings he sits by my side, which disorients me a bit, as I am expecting him to be fully engaged in the ritual, and tells me still more stories about his experiences and feats as a babalawo: "I was able to predict ecological disasters of all sorts over the world—earthquakes, seaquakes, hurricanes, and typhoons; also international political and security crises, such as Chernobyl." (I am again skeptical about what he is telling me, but I go along.) Even after it is evident that the ritual cleansing of Lynnette is under way, Mauro comes at intervals and sits by my side, explaining to me what is going on—opportunities I use to ask him about the specific significance of the various ritual objects placed on the floor. I dare not touch anything; and so I point, for example, to a coconut shell filled with black nuts. He picks it up.

> —I gave this one to William Bascom to reproduce in his book, didn't you see it in his book?
>
> —[Feeling tested again, I respond.] The truth is, I might have seen it, but I can't remember everything I read. I might have read about ritual objects, but I guess I didn't really understand what they meant. Now through this experience I am beginning to have a deeper

> understanding, a feeling, of what all this means. It is now engraved in my body. I'm sure I will never forget it.

Contrary to my expectations, the atmosphere is very informal for a ritual. In addition to Mauro chatting with me and sustaining an everyday casualness, Lynnette, at the center of the ritual, often breaks the ritual actions with her constant expressions of worry about her children in the living room, especially her preoccupation about whether they are keeping away from the balcony. Even though Chris is in charge of taking care of them and feeding them lunch while Lynnette undergoes this ritual, she is still attending to what is going on out there. As a result of my previous understandings of anthropological depictions of rituals, I wonder why she is not in a state of complete spiritual awe, fully focused on the ritual. How can this ritual be at all effective with so many distractions?

With the same matter-of-factness reigning so far in this ritual, Mauro grabs the squawking rooster by the neck, then holds it over the empty plate next to the Eleggua. Turning it on its side with little effort, he gradually releases his grip on the rooster, which by now has stopped moving, seemingly paralyzed. It rests there on the plate, legs outstretched, as Mauro instructs Lynnette, who has hitherto been left with her own thoughts, to now make her pleas silently, thinking carefully and thoroughly about what she wishes.

Stunned at seeing the rooster so suddenly and unnaturally motionless, I use this short break to ask Mauro how this had happened. "I can hypnotize any animal, even a four-legged, larger one. I can render a goat like that, too. Once I left one like that and covered it with a piece of cloth; when the cloth was lifted, the goat was dead. This is my magic; let's see if any of these younger babalawos can do it!" I had no idea what to make of this. I found it just as hard to remain incredulous as to embrace his account uncritically.

After ten minutes or so, everybody gathers again around Lynnette, who had been pleading and meditating in communion with her guardian spirits. Mauro takes the still-paralyzed rooster and, lowering its head, makes a few short incisions in its throat with a narrow-bladed knife. It takes about ten seconds for the first drop of blood to ooze out. "It seems this rooster doesn't have any blood," he says to Lorena. But soon the blood starts to surge, and he pours it alternately over the Eleggua and Lynnette's amulet while Lorena and Mauro, nearly whispering, invoke the orishas and their spiritual ancestral lineages in what sounds to me like a long list of repeated, unintelligible foreign words—probably Yoruba. Without any warning, drawn by the dull sound of a quick, dry snap, I realize that Mauro has just finished decapitating the rooster with his bare hands. After dipping the base of the severed head into one of the cups with the coconut water several times, he finally places it beside the plate. The headless body lies shuddering on the cement floor next to the mat. All at once, the ritual action comes to an inexplicable halt.

Lorena goes to the kitchen. Lynnette sits down and begins chatting with me. Mauro and Chris go to the backyard. But the ritual is clearly unfinished, I gather from Lynnette's look of expectation that Lorena, Mauro, and Chris will soon come back. Lorena remains busy in the kitchen and does not come back. But when Mauro and Chris return, each holding an animated burlap sack, we gather that the ritual is about to resume. Mauro extracts two black roosters and quickly decapitates the pair by means of a single wrenching of their necks. Their blood is made to flow over the coconut shells with the black seeds and the stones in them, and Mauro again invokes the orishas and his ancestors. Kneeling by Lynnette, he asks her to hold each of the roosters, one at a time, and to present them (as offerings) in front of each of the different ritual objects and plates placed on the ground. He then picks up four coconut quarters from their receptacles on the floor, breaks off tiny bits and pieces with his fingers, and tosses them on the floor, all the while murmuring secret pleas. His head lowered introspectively, he asks the orisha owner of this divination system to empower the coconut quarters, which he would use in a while, in order to have an efficacious divination. He then tosses into the air in front of him several times the four reshaped quarters of coconut. They fall to the ground, some pieces dark side up and some white side up, constituting specific messages according to the proportion of dark versus white pieces in the configuration. The final toss reveals the *letra* (letter, the divination key) that in this Yoruba divination tradition contains (in mythical form) the answer to the question at hand. The oracle has answered: They may buy the new house they have been considering.

Kneeling on the bamboo mat, Chris bends to kiss the floor while Mauro and Lynnette kiss the mat. Mauro hands the body of a rooster to each of them, instructing them to pull out some feathers and place them inside each of the coconut receptacles while they make special pleas to the orishas. Chris suggests to his wife that she make specific pleas related to their current concerns. Once the feathers cover the various ritual receptacles and sacred objects, which have already been bathed in blood, Mauro pours honey over the feathers as a form of offering, causing them to further stick to each other.

Surely recognizing that I have not been registering everything, Mauro checks again with me:

> —What do you think about what I'm doing? Did you understand what was going on?
>
> —I'm not sure, but the beauty of this religion deeply moves me, impresses me. Reading about the religion is nothing like living it, experiencing it. I won't ever forget this. I understand it not through my mind but through my emotions. I sense it; I feel it.
>
> —[He is obviously satisfied with my response.] You can be sure you'll get your text [dissertation] from here.[6]

The end of the ritual is uneventful, and as informal, relaxed and slow-paced as its performance (except for my own visceral reaction to the roosters!).

Several times interrupted, the course of the ritual paradoxically seemed to unfold successfully regardless of what participants did on the side. When a baby chick walked uninvited from the backyard onto the balcony at the height of the ritual, Chris jokingly said, "Go 'way, you can't come in yet." We all laughed, and the ritual continued unaffected. (Apparently, ordinary events of the day that occasionally creep into ritual performances do not affect their overall efficacy.) The unleashed communion between humans and orishas—achieved through the mediation of the babalawo's spiritual power, the feeding (offering) of the orishas by humans, and the orishas' confirmation of their acceptance of human pleas—emerged as an indisputable reality that persisted beyond any minor human distraction. Lynnette and Chris—rather than being amazed at their having gone through a transcendental experience (as I expected, following my anthropological readings on ritual)—appeared quite nonchalant about it. They went through the prescribed motions of the ritual in the same natural way they attended to the needs of their children.

At the end of our first encounter and contrary to his previous statement, Mauro refuses to charge me any money, even though I insist. When he then offers me a *cafecito*, a small cup of the strong, black coffee that is served in Latin America, I sense that the terms of our initial exchange have just changed. Indeed, during our subsequent encounters I become his protégée. He introduces me as his (spiritual) godchild every time I participate in the various rituals he either officiates or attends as a guest of honor. Our bond gradually strengthens. After they learn that I love to eat shrimp, Mauro and Lorena organize a dinner party in my honor, invite the godchild who introduced me to them, and cook a special Cuban dish with tons of shrimp. I have become so unconditionally welcome in their home that I sense I can always call on his and Lorena's protection and guidance whenever I might need it.

To this day, ten years after I met Mauro, I reminisce about him—his voice, his bony, worked-out, long fingers, his penetrating eyes, and his sarcastic looks and winks at the behaviors of people he considered dumb, pompous, good for nothing, and stupid—and the strong emotions I felt during rituals in his company. The various pungent sweet-burning earthy smells—mixtures of sacrificial blood, fruits, herbs, and candles—and the heat and heavy air pressure during rituals and offerings remain inscribed in my senses. Inebriating and slightly nauseating, they perhaps remain as a sensorial experience of the sacred, initiated at that first ritual when I knew almost nothing about orishas, their foods, drumbeats, *fundamentos* (the symbols, tools, and stones, that embody the aché of the orishas), and their patakis. Ruminations about the meaning of all the fantastic, improbable accounts I heard take over my thoughts only after these emotions gradually gave way to another form of knowing: the analytical (the weaker form, according to my healer friends), which I along with other anthropologists (such as Stoller, Taussig, Crapanzano, Desjarlais, and Jackson) find inadequate for fully appreciating the power of rituals. After so many years, I am still overwhelmed with chills and tears when I am confronted with the drumbeats, gestures, and smells that announce the ritual presence of the orishas.

What has become clear to me is that in some cases, cultural competence needs to be assessed beyond the discursive to encompass sensorial competence as well. Dell Hymes, in his widely cited "Breakthrough into Performance" (1975), makes a point about assessing cultural performative competence at three levels, according to the ability of a member: (a) to replicate certain codes of behavior (after having internalized them in some profound ways and being able to emulate them); (b) to adequately interpret and make sense of the codes typical to a particular genre; and (c) to report about them in an understandable way.[7] These three dimensions characterize different measures of cultural competency but leave another important area, that of sensorial competency (developed recently by the anthropologists mentioned above), which addresses forms of knowing through the senses (Classen, Howes, and Synnott 1994; Desjarlais 1992, 1996; Howes 1991; Stoller 1989b, 1997). An area of competency that is hardly visible and resists interpretation, report, and even conscious emulation, it is nonetheless based as much on cultural competency as any of the other three dimensions. For, as my interactions with Mauro suggest, perceived lack of discursive transparency might nonetheless elicit sensuous, somatic effects that are profoundly transformative.

Sensorial knowledge is not only (paradoxically) more ethereal than discursive knowledge but also limited by its having to be experienced—an obvious challenge for conveying such realms in writing, particularly within academic genres.

At least in their current use, "knowledge" and "feeling" evoke two contrasting semantic fields that in a pre-logocentric time might have been related. Before the Enlightenment highjacked "knowledge" away from "feeling," Giambattista Vico, for example, proposed a scientific theory (1991 [1744]) of the origin of language that placed emotions—rather than rationality—as the mediating force between things and the formation of words (a mediation characterized by abstract and random relations, according to modern linguists such as de Saussure). With recourse to Vico, might "knowing" something about the word occur when one is "feeling" that it is the right word for a particular situation? Perhaps the three semantic fields of "sense" mentioned at the beginning of this chapter uncover the genealogical traces of the connecting branches among "logic," "wisdom," and "feeling." They all might be the result of a shared root experience of, say, a realization embodied in the experience of "Aha!"

Though Mauro's "fantastic" personal-experience narratives appeared clouded (and thus, perhaps, unjustly implausible) to me, their initial lack of transparency became commonsensical once I had become familiar with the ritual experiences that inform such narratives. They did not make sense to me, in terms of logic, because they assumed premises (and experiences) that were outside my own commonsense world.[8] Narratives must assume shared beliefs with respect to referents and structures (particularly a linear progression); but rituals, inasmuch as their components might be cryptic and mind-boggling, have a reality and internal logic that is to be sensed (felt) if not "understood." Bateson, for example, addresses this issue (1972b) within artistic contexts when he distinguishes between discursive (digital) and iconic (analogical) signs, suggesting the prevalently conscious interpretative process typical of the former and the overwhelmingly unconscious decoding process entailed in the latter. The realm of ritual operates primarily, if not exclusively, at the iconic, somatic level, ruled by visceral, participatory, nondiscursive kinds of meaning, which as Bateson notes in reference to artistic performances cannot be expressed in words.

Visceral Words

And yet, words can also elicit somatic reactions. Sociolinguists, folklorists, and anthropologists have noted the power of words in marking and authenticating social status and personal transformation and of establishing new social realities and legitimizing them publicly. Further, ethnomethodologists Harold Garfinkel (1967), Aaron V. Cicourel (1974), and various ethnographers of conversation (such as Harvey Sacks and Emanuel Schegloff) assume speech as the basic means through which social relations and meanings are intersubjectively constituted and communicated. This assumption is also prevalent in works by Mikhail Bakhtin (1981, 1986), Vincent Crapanzano (1992), and Paul Ricoeur (1991) that stress the dialogic aspects of speech and their role in constituting not only the meaning of speech events but most importantly the speaking selves.

The ritual power of words and the constitutive power of speech in ritual settings have been explored by many, among them Malinowski (1935), Austin (1975), Tambiah (1968, 1985a,b), and tested in cross-cultural settings by ethnographers of speech (Bauman and Sherzer 1989). Austin has noted, "Speaking generally, it is always necessary that the circumstances in which the words are uttered should be in some way, or ways, appropriate, and it is very commonly necessary that either the speaker himself or other persons should also perform certain other actions, whether 'physical' or 'mental' actions or even acts of uttering further words" (1975:8). Thus it is not the utterance alone that defines its status as either a "constative" (a proposition about the world) or a "performative" (a statement that performs an action) but the appropriate circumstances in which they are uttered. Folklorist Roger D. Abrahams (1977, 1981) and ethnographers of speech Joel Sherzer (1989), Michael Foster (1989), and Garry H. Gossen (1989), for example, found that folk taxonomies correlate a range of appropriate circumstances (speech events) with certain ways of speaking (speech genres), each defined by different degrees of referential and performative (illocutionary) functions as well as by their expected effects on the audience (the perlocutionary function).

Recognizing the special circumstances of ritual processes, particularly of magic or incantation speech, Roman Jakobson (1964:354–355) saw the need to adjust Bühler's traditional triadic model of language—based on three functions of language that correlate the "emotive" function with a first-person addresser, the "conative" function with an orientation to a second-person addressee (as in imperatives), and the "referential" with a third person (someone or something being spoken of). Jakobson noted that the "magic incantatory function is chiefly some kind of conversion of an absent or inanimate 'third person' into an addressee of a conative message" and offered a northern Russian incantation to illustrate this implicit conversion: "Water, queen river daybreak! Send grief beyond the blue sea, to the sea bottom, like a gray stone never to rise from the sea bottom, may grief never come to burden the light heart of God's servant, may grief be removed and sink away" (355).

What kinds of conversion are implied when spirits (through mediums' voices) assert a certain denouement for the misfortunes of clients? Remember that La Caridad, the Virgin of Charity, through the voice of Haydée, promised Miriam (the unfortunate adolescent with her leg in a cast) that her tears and grief would be deposited in the bottom of the sea, saying, "In the name of the Father, the Celestial Father, and in the name of the Virgin of Charity, you'll gather because everything of yours will be deposited in the bottom of the sea. From today on."

The performative or illocutionary force of ritual speech stems from the situation itself. Following Austin, one can argue that certain utterances achieve a change of state by virtue of being enacted under the appropriate conditions. But these conditions often emerge during (rather than exist prior to) divination and magic rituals. For instance, the power of words to "do" emerges as the status of speakers and addressees shifts in the course of rituals. The particular ontological identity of the sender of a message and of the addressee determines the degree of legitimacy and responsibility for the message uttered. When healers and spirits enter into ritual communication on behalf of clients (during divination, trance, and healing rituals) the utterer of the words might not be their actual author, and the addressee of the healer's words might not only be the client but also a spirit.[9] Conversely, although a healer might be the one uttering the words, the actual speaker might be a spirit who legitimizes and is responsible for the message.[10] For observers, one of the most puzzling effects of possession is the break in normative (standard) speech, based on the natural agreement (or unity) between the physical actor who utters speech and the force that motivates it—an assumption that is disregarded in (orally) quoted speech. During possession, an effacement of the speech-actor occurs, exposing a transcendental force that speaks not only to but through humans, yet it does so outside of standard rules of human speech. Indeed, in trance speaking "the utterer of the shifter pronoun (the speaking subject) is 'speaking involuntarily or nonintentionally—and thus, paradoxically, in another sense is not 'speaking,' if we understand by this acting as a responsible speech actor" (Alton Becker, quoted in Du Bois 1993:53).

When I saw Samuel Beckett's one-man play *Krapp's Last Tape* on a stage in New York (off-off-Broadway) a few years ago, I was taken by the drama emerging from the enactment of conflicting selves of the same person at different periods of his lifetime. Krapp (played by a real-life ex-convict) appears as an aging, solitary, rusty man (dressed, I thought, as a writer), sitting at a heavy, wooden writing desk in a dimly lit den. He sets an old reel-to-reel recorder on the desk and begins listening to a tape. Until this moment the audience has not heard Krapp's voice, but now we hear it as recorded on the tape he is playing. Krapp reacts to his own thoughts recorded when he was younger and full of illusions with jerky grimaces of impatience, pleasure, or anger—depending on what he is hearing. Is he reacting emotionally to his own taped discourse (at times pompous, at times poetic) or to the content of the experiences he is recounting or to both? All the "action" in this play builds upon and ends with this minimalist yet loaded situation. His own words, thoughts, and perceptions of the world as rendered on tape years ago seem strange to him in the present; he is estranged from his own words (and apparently his very being). Hardly recognizing his own words, Krapp is incredulous of the things he once said, thought, and experienced, and he engages in an eerie dialogue (via gestures and comments) with his other, split-in-time, celluloid self, returning to him via the magic of technology.

This situation resembles, in its creepiness, the confrontational dialogue that emerges between the various spirits—good and evil—that voice their messages through the same person during exorcisms, for instance. But as an existentialist, not a healer, Krapp realizes the pathos of the splitting sense of himself. This is dramatized on the stage when he impatiently fumbles in his desk drawers for a certain reel he wishes to hear again and by his angry disposing of some others he wishes to forget. Brooding, cursing, laughing, he listens attentively to bits and pieces of a few of the many reels numbered and archived in the drawers of his desk. Back and forward, back and forward he winds reels impatiently to recapture again or to avoid dwelling on words he once said, thoughts he had expressed, and situations in which he had been engaged thirty years earlier. Annoyed at times, he utters a "Pah!" Interrupting his conversation with his celluloid self, he then fumbles in his pockets and finds a banana, puts it down on the desk, stands up, and goes backstage, from where we hear the sound of a bottle opening and liquid pouring into a glass. Krapp returns, locks and unlocks one of the drawers containing the reels, takes out a new reel and listens. Obsessively, he winds this particular reel backward and forward, listening again and again to the same passage. He reflects for a few minutes. There's one of the passages that he relishes in particular:

> She lay stretched out on the floorboards with her hands under her head and her eyes closed. Sun blazing down, bit of breeze, water nice and lively. I noticed a scratch on her thigh and asked her how she came by it. Picking gooseberries, she said. I said again I thought it was hopeless and no good going on and she agreed, without opening her eyes. [. . .] I bent over her to get them in the shadow and they opened. (*Pause. Low.*) Let me in. (*Pause.*) We drifted in among the flags and stuck. The way they went down, sighing, before the stem! (*Pause.*) I lay down across her with my face in her breasts and hand on her. We lay there without moving. But under us all moved, and moved us, gently, up and down, and from side to side. . . . [*T*]*akes reel off the machine* [. . .] *loads virgin reel on machine* [. . .] *clears his throat and begins to record.* Just been listening to that stupid bastard I took myself for thirty years ago, hard to believe I was ever as bad as that. Thank God that's all done with anyway. (*Pause.*) The eyes she had! (Quotes and stage notes in Beckett 1965 [1959]:16–18)

This passage from his past motivates him to record his present thoughts. At the end of his long monologue, which he only intermittently records, Krapp suddenly stops recording, wrenches the reel off the tape recorder, throws it away, puts on the other one back on, winds it to the passage he wants, hits play, relishing again his own words recorded when he was much younger and naïve.

This drama of contemporaneous speaking selves—confronting past and present experiences and connecting distant and near places—reminds me of the intertextual, timeless drama sensuously created by the intersubjective layering of shifting voices in magic and healing rituals.

Spiritual Time

Divination, magic, and healing draw heavily on discursive elements in constructing a totalizing experience where the past, the present, and the future—as well as distant places and events—converge. Although discursive, the immediate effects of the words uttered during divination and healing surpass the order of discourse: they are meant to be sensed, not just listened to; they are meant to be embodied, not just understood. The complexities of magic, divination, and healing rituals encompass the mergings of various speaking voices and registers, shifting speech genres,[11] and nonlinguistic sounds produced by clapping, banging, and bell ringing, which altogether create a unique spiritual experience that promotes the sensing of a "spiritual time" as an alternative to everyday life with all its conventional forms of communication, perception, and feeling.[12]

In addition to uncovering what afflicts the client, the divination process becomes an alternative reality, where worldly, personal afflictions are reframed, acquiring a cosmological, impersonal status. Regardless of the practical outcomes of the consultation, participation in the enactment of this unique spiritual time often becomes, in itself, a healing experience for the afflicted. Contrasting the discursive rules (and worldviews) of everyday life, a timeless morality emerges during consultations in which humans are responsible for their actions in the past, present, and future. This spiritual morality emerges out of the polyphony of voices heard during consultations—each coming from distinct spatiotemporal experiential worlds, not unlike those recaptured by Krapp—coalescing in the Spiritist notion of "spiritual time." According to the Spiritist ethos, if a misfortune in the present has been caused by a past misdeed (committed by the self or by someone close to the self), it will continue to haunt the lives of kin in the future if not appropriately amended. By the same token, fidelity to the ethical tenets of Spiritism multiplies geometrically the rewards for any material and spiritual sacrifices made in the process, assuring a sense of cosmic justice ruled by a totalizing cosmic order that surpasses the limitations of human (earthly) experience.

And yet, what clients initially experience during consultations is confusion and communicative opacity. Breaches of standard discourses, shifts in speaking subjects and verb tenses, and a mix of discursive genres create an initial opacity that, I insist, not only precedes the process of healing and restoration but is itself intrinsically part of that process. Paradoxical as it may seem, apparent disorientation precedes and constitutes the drama of divination and trance, when the voices of the spirits coming from a distant elsewhere join in with the medium's messages and explanations, engineering a unified interpretation of the causes for one's afflictions. Thus achieved, an authoritative spiritual discourse—a cosmically encoded message—appears as truthful and irrefutable, promoting the potentially transformative processes that will bring about comfort instead of affliction and hope instead of despair.

For clients the overall purpose of consultations is to restore their general (lost) well-being, as mentioned earlier, a goal expressed broadly and succinctly when they say, *Vengo a resolver* (I come to resolve). They know that consultations might involve revelations through the reading of cards, messages reflected in the water and glass of the fuente, or information revealed in trance, tending to end with some form of recommendation for a future healing, cleansing, or magic work. But the whole procedure of divination never follows a close script; clients can hardly expect a usual course of action: the spiritual world has its own logic and modes of working. Expectations are therefore almost always upset, turning the consultation into an open-ended, often anxiety-producing event for clients.

The ethos of Spiritism, based on a quintessential timeless and spaceless notion of spiritual life and its relation to a cosmic order, is ruled by a set of spiritual laws: the Law of Cause and Effect, the Law of Love, and the Law of Reincarnation, which entail, respectively, that every action has its effect (in this or subsequent lives), that our actions should be motivated by love (following the model set by Jesus), and that reincarnation gives us subsequent opportunities to improve our karma through the exercise of our free will. In a nutshell: If a misfortune in the present is thought to have its cause in the recent or remote misdeeds of an ancestor or of oneself in a previous life, we can amend such past misdeeds in the present through a correcting action inspired by our indisputable free will and thus have an active role in determining how our future will be played out.

This spiritual ethos is enacted in various ways in every consultation. It informs the perception of social realities of followers of brujería (as well as Spiritism and Santería) in general and the practices of divination and magic rituals in particular, setting the limits of the interpretation of the discourse of divination and magic. As a folk causal theory, the moral time-space conceptions of brujería, embodied in the Spiritist Laws mentioned above, are extralinguistic premises that generate the discourse of divination, healing, and magic rituals. And as Greg Urban suggests (1991:26), extralinguistic premises set up the interpretive limits of these discourses as well as determine their circulation and value, in this case among a community of practitioners and clients.

Brujería consultations, which are private and secret, usually begin with a divination session. Haydée, for instance, reads the Spanish cards, sometimes a *clave* (automatic writing on a page), or the fuente. Clients arrive early in the morning—usually without an appointment—and wait their turn in the order in which they arrive to be consulted in the altar, sitting and often chatting among themselves in the waiting room. I always liked to check the waiting room (sometimes at Haydée's request, when she wanted to know how many remained to be seen) because these incursions afforded me impromptu opportunities to "gossip" with her clients, who, relatively secure in the anonymity of the waiting room, tended to be candid—beyond my expectations—in their conversations.

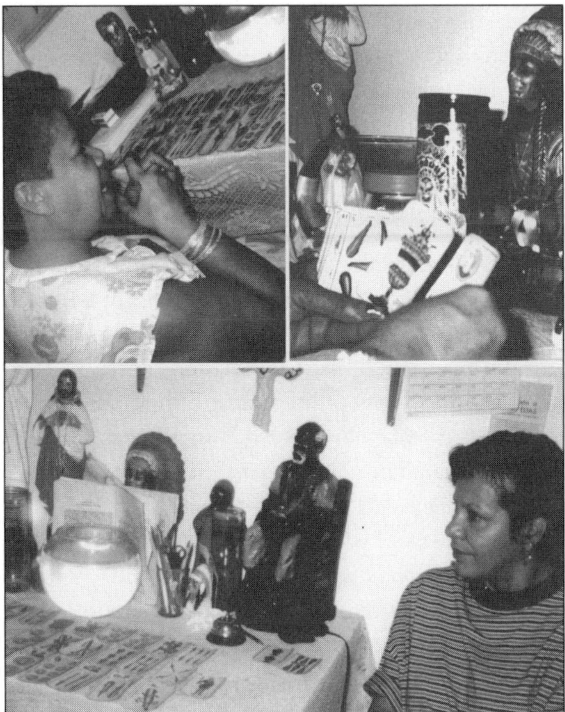

Haydée reading the cards.

León, a handsome man in his thirties, comes to consult Haydée for the fist time. He sits at the side of Haydée's working table, facing her at an angle (I am sitting behind her). She hands him a deck of cards, which he is asked to cut several times. She begins the reading following the particular configurations of the cards and the messages given to her about them by the spirits. León hears statements about aspects of his life that refer, for instance, to luck, love, a job, health, neighbors, and family members. Unlike standard discourse, these statements are disconnected statements—they do not follow any logic (semantic or temporal); they respond only to the path León initiated by his intervention with the cards (which espiritistas and brujos see not as coincidence but as rife with spiritual purpose). Without warning, the divining process takes a decisive turn when Haydée forcefully declares, "That woman belongs to another man. She loves you, and you wonder why she is distant. Her mother bewitched her. She does it with the Bible. She is a fervent churchgoer, but she does it [bewitches you] by inserting her magic work inside the Bible. Your wife looks at that other man and despises you without reason. It's her mother, that bitch, who never has accepted you." León remains mute. After a few minutes, during which I thought the man would have fallen into complete despair after receiving such a grim message, Haydée, now in a completely different tone and pronunciation, says, "Her family not want you. They thinks you not deserves her, that she are better off without you, and, oh, you cries tears of blood, you thinks of revenge." This was the voice of the Congo spirit, speaking in the tenseless language of bozales. Unannounced, the primordial and savvy voice of this warrior spirit is authoritative, disclosing unequivocally and without any embellishment the feelings and thoughts León might have had but probably until then had never articulated. Hate, betrayal, conspiracy, and suspicion—pulsating through people in close relationship to León—are suddenly made present via the voices of Haydée and the spirits in the altar. Haydée reveals more information about León's ungrateful wife: she was made pregnant by another man before León married her, and now she lives honorably and in luxury thanks to his hard-working habits. Under the spell of her mother, who thinks León is not good enough for her daughter, his wife despises him and plays with his feelings. In stark contrast to his quiet and confident demeanor at the beginning of the session, once he learns about the apparent deceiving and abusive relationships he is in and the injustice of it all, León is overwhelmed by a mix of shame and anger—as was I, troubled to a lesser degree, just from witnessing this tragic spiritual drama unfolding before my eyes.

Note the different levels of information León receives and the various registers in which it is delivered. In the tenseless language of bozales, an atavistic- and cryptic-sounding voice from a distant, heroic past discloses (in a metaphoric condensed way, such as "tears of blood") the painful nature and cause of León's misfortune, as well as his innermost (unspoken) emotional states of mind. As with poets, the words of the spirits thus spoken through mediums have the capacity of moving the living.

At the end of the consultation, León was given a number of instructions, among them to have an amulet made and a cleansing ritual performed for him in order to recuperate his spirit and thereby restore his confidence and ability to deal with his estranged wife. These trabajos aimed at restoring the overall self-reliance he had lost as a consequence of the trabajo malo performed against him by his mother-in-law. As he left, Haydée revealed to me that she saw an impending tragic outcome for León, *un crimen pasional* (a crime of passion) unless he acted upon the recommendations he was given by the spirits. As a matter of fact, to prevent the situation from further escalation and out of sheer caution and responsibility on her part, Haydée kept from León the additional damaging information she had received from the spirits. If he had known more at that time, before being given a protective amulet and a cleansing ritual, León might have done something irreversible based on what she had "seen" in the cards.

Imagine the initial disorientation of clients—even those who are experienced in consultations—when hearing, often without any external signal, the speech uttered by the same person yet spoken by two or more speaking subjects. One voice might be the voice of the medium transmitting the visions she has received for the client, another might be the voice of the spirits voicing their words directly though the medium, and still another the voice of the medium as a person summarizing all the various revelations given to the client. Carrying separate authoritative values and coded in essentially different ways, these discrete voices convey not one but several, if complementary, kinds of information, each adding its slightly different point of view and emotional register to the content of the messages conveyed. The multiplicity of voices thus intermeshed fashions a unique drama during divination, reminiscent of the drama created in *Krapp's Last Tape* by the shifting voices of his own self.

Often the drama created by a polyphony of alternative authoritative voices during divination is enhanced when a spirit or entity makes itself present through the body of the medium. Eva's consultation was remarkable for these reasons. When she came to Haydée one morning, she had just arrived from Chicago. She flew to the island to help her mother solve some family and inheritance problems. Just as many Puerto Ricans living in the continental United States seek the help of brujos when on the island, so did Eva. She had come from Chicago to Puerto Rico to help her mother get a loan to pay for her house, but she had recently been encountering all kinds of problems with her ex-husband and, consequently, was feeling physically very weak upon her arrival late in the day. When she woke up the next morning, her arms seemed almost paralyzed. Immediately she decided to consult with a bruja. Upon her mother's advice, she came to Haydée, who of course did not know what had brought her to Puerto Rico the day before.

As usual, the divination process scanned several points of her life, presenting a kind of general matrix about her friends, work, money, health, love, and so forth. To her surprise, Eva then heard Haydée voice her own innermost feelings and state of mind: "Why do you say, 'I'm not happy, I have never been happy, I was born to suffer and be miserable'?" Hearing her own thoughts voiced by Haydée, Eva became very emotional, her whole body trembling, her face and eyes distraught.

Continuing the divination process, Haydée, now quoting the spirits, said, "They say, 'Trees die standing.'" Reported words of the spirits are given special care, for these often cryptic messages (in the form of aphorisms, for instance) encode the general message of the divination session and as such embody a breakthrough in the divination ritual. As a key to the problem at hand, brujos therefore reiterate the essence of the message in their own words, rephrasing it several times, as Haydée went on to do in this case, bringing to light the different angles of the words spoken by the spirits, making them intelligible to Eva:

> You are strong and will endure whatever is happening to you. Trust yourself. You have a very nice future, you know? You have your own spiritual powers—you know that, don't you? They say: "Don't worry." They say, "San Miguel Arcángel will not let whatever they [your enemies] put back to back, heads down [created animosity, misfortune] to stay that way." They say, "You will ask for something besides solving your mother's problem [with the house]. You will tell Junior"—Who's Junior? [The client answers.] Ah, your ex-husband—"that he shouldn't fuck with you [bother you] any more, he should go to hell and leave you in peace, that if he divorced you, why is he mortifying you? That you don't want him meddling in your problems, and that he should let you be happy."

Every time Haydée quoted the words of the spirits (as they were given to her by them), the tone of her voice grew assertive and sharp, leaving no doubt that these words were meant to be understood as cosmic truths. Only when there was doubt about whom the spirits were talking about—in this case, who Junior was—did Haydée herself pose a question, for the spirits never indicate whom they are talking about. They just deliver their messages as blatantly and economically as possible, leaving it to the brujos to decipher them, to make sense of them for their clients.

A slight difference in authorship arises as a result of the various shifts of register—between the direct words of the spirits and the quotations or paraphrases of their words. When quoting, brujos are acting as the deliverers of spirits' messages; when paraphrasing, they are acting as translators; and when possessed, they function as loudspeakers for the spirits. The formulaic opening sentence "They tell me that" or "They tell me to tell you that" signals that what follows is a rewording of the spirits' message, which brujos deliver in their own voices. But when one hears "They say" or "They tell me" followed by poetic messages encoded in proverbs or metaphors, it is an indication that these are the direct words of the spirits.[13] In this and other cases when spirits talk directly, brujos often need to reiterate the essence of the message, rephrasing it and rendering different angles of it to make it intelligible to their clients. Although the spirits' voices inspire the messages and are responsible for their veracity, brujos are the ones who take responsibility for interpreting and transmitting the messages to mortals.

Sometimes the key to the divination process is expressed in the form of admonitions. "You neglect your elderly mother" was revealed to Manuel when he came to consult with Haydée after a series of misfortunes had hit him. One of his legs kept getting infected in spite of repeated visits to the doctor and applications of the medicine prescribed for the condition. Haydée's matter-of-fact admonition to Manuel conveyed the generalized belief within the Spiritist ethos that neglect of loved ones is a cosmic offense that can transcend generations, which in this case was interpreted as the source of a spiritual debt that had to be paid in order for Manuel to regain the protection of the spirits and a state of well-being. For Spiritists, the admonition encapsulates both the cause of ill fortune and the revelation of its implicit remedy.

Besides carrying a moral message, aphorisms may also convey a forecast for the client in terms of a forthcoming solution or resolution to a problem, and as such they provide a key message of encouragement and support, not just a warning.[14] For example, "A nail draws another nail out" was offered once by a medium to a desolate woman who came to consult after her husband had abandoned her. This was a condensed solution for her suffering. Meant as a forecast, the aphorism reassured her that another man would soon appear, love her, and make her forget the love and pain of "that other man." A prospective relationship—even if she had not yet met the person—was predicted by the spirits. The "loss" that she felt would eventually be mended by a forthcoming relationship in her life; it was only a matter of time. In this case, instead of encapsulating a normative message, the aphorism offered, in its condensed way, the foreseen solution to her situation.

Similarly, two aphorisms—"The river swells but returns to its level—the water becomes clear on its own" (*El río crece pero vuelve a su nivel—el agua se aclara sola*) and "Whatever you won't drink, let it flow" (*Agua que no has de beber déjala correr*)—were conveyed by the spirits as advice to a pair of clients who were desperate about their problems: the message was that their problems would be solved by themselves, without much intervention, requiring just their own patience and disengagement.

But at other times an aphorism might encapsulate a warning of a possible future misfortune if a certain recommendation by the spirits is not followed (Peek 1991, Winkelman and Peek 2004). "Whatever is wrongly taken won't shine" was the message delivered by the spirits to Teresa, a client who had some legal problems with a tenant. Having won a court case already in her favor, she was going to collect past-due rent money plus interest from her tenant, an unmarried mother on welfare. During divination, Haydée stated in her own voice that the judge's ruling had been "immoral" (according to the Spiritist ethos) due to the economic straits of the tenant and urged her client to consider a fairer deal. Sealed by "Whatever is wrongly taken won't shine," her previous pronouncement attained the status of a cosmic ruling given directly by the spirits' words. Here is where free will is crucial. If the woman followed this cosmic ruling instead of following the judge's ruling, she could avoid breaking the cosmic Law of Love (following the exemplary life of Jesus) and thereby the castigation of the spirits, which Haydée must have "foreseen" during divination when she told her,

> Remember, "Whatever is wrongly taken won't shine." [In a casual tone she asks,] How much does she owe you [just for the rent]? Because for me, "What's not mine I don't want." You have to decide what is yours . . . what you are asking for. . . . You're not taking what is not yours, you're asking for what is yours. The lawyer is demanding far more than he should—or what is not yours. But you'll pay . . . the lawyer knows how to [trick the law]. . . . But remember, "The cord breaks at its weakest point" [you are going to suffer, not the lawyer]. . . . If that girl takes you to Treasury or she takes you to DACO [the Department for Consumer Protection]. . . . You didn't think about that, ah? . . . They say again, They tell me to tell you that "Whatever is wrongly taken won't shine." And [They tell me], "It's not you." They say again, "It's not you, it's the lawyer." . . .
>
> I understand, "Money wants money." You see, here I have no food [no shopping today], Teresa, none at all, and [referring to me] she knows it; and the car is broken in the garage. But I . . . nothing [don't worry]; I'm happy. "What's not mine I don't want." If you and your husband have Social Security . . . If you have that, why take the money from those that need it? But greed for money—that's terrible: "The more you have, the more you want." That woman doesn't have even a place to fall dead. . . .
>
> I could charge [here] whatever I want, because whatever I do here you see the results. I bring back husbands. People will pay anything. But I don't profit from nobody because I know the kinds of sacrifice they have to make to pay $200 to me. Maybe they are left without food in their house for it. I don't take away from nobody. I prefer not to have food in my house myself before leaving you without your food, because I earn more. Look how I speak to you!

The aphorism "What is wrongly taken won't shine" creates a temporal coherence in the divination ritual, integrating all the different discursive elements of divination, each following a distinct pragmatic goal and style of speech, such as warnings in the form of aphorisms and exemplars of personal experience. When brujos add stories of their personal experience as exemplars, connecting them semantically and authoritatively to the aphorisms spoken by the spirits, they assert the applicability and reality of moral, universalizing statements about human nature to specific cases (similarly to the interpretation of proverbs within Ifá divination practices). In Teresa's case, the essence of Haydée's personal life narratives reinforces the diagnosis "What is wrongly taken won't shine." Her own life experiences serve as models for emulation: "What's not mine I don't want" and "I don't take away from nobody," spoken directly to the problem revealed during divination by the pronouncement of the spirits. The key diagnosis is further explicated by a generalization about human nature (assumed as the basic motivation guiding Teresa's greed) and the basis of the offense, "Money wants money" and "The more you have, the more you want." Their significance to Teresa's impending cause of misfortune is somehow lessened by another sort of greed: "It's not you, it's the lawyer." Further, the more personal statement made by Haydée, "What's not mine I don't want," precedes an impending threat, "The cord breaks at its weakest point," which is offered as a serious warning that if the advice of the spirits (to be charitable to those in need) is not followed by Teresa, she—not the lawyer—will pay the consequences.

Adding to the seriousness of the message and threat given during divination, Haydée asserts the legitimacy and power of her own speech in a reflexive tone: "I tell you this because They are giving it to me, you know. I'm not inventing it." Prompting Teresa to do the same by way of moral identification with her, Haydée makes a last appeal to her humanity: "Look how I speak to you!"

In spite of the various discontinuities in the discourse—marked by shifts in speaking subjects as well as by shifts in speech genres—how is the phenomenological coherence in the divination ritual accomplished? Suggesting a timeless and spaceless morality, aphorisms and proverbs conveyed (directly or indirectly) by the spirits help forge a spiritual time in which past, present, and future converge. As cosmic tokens of truth and wisdom, they acquire through the interpretation of brujos an immanence aimed at addressing directly their clients' experiences and, thereby, at being sensed as timeless, visceral truths.

Thomas Csordas makes some insightful comments in his discussion (1997) of the intersubjective unity (with respect to participants) and intertextual

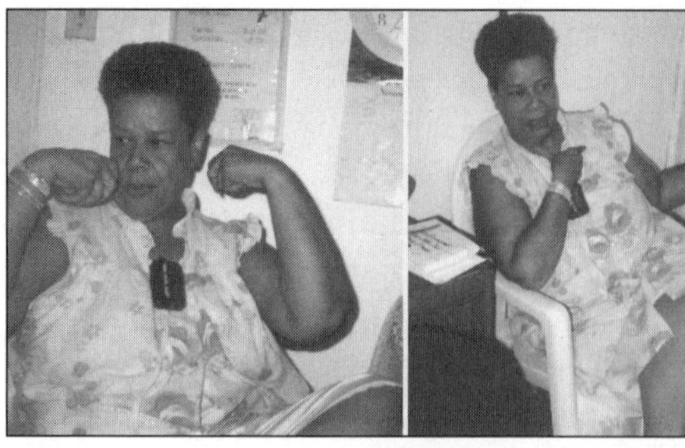

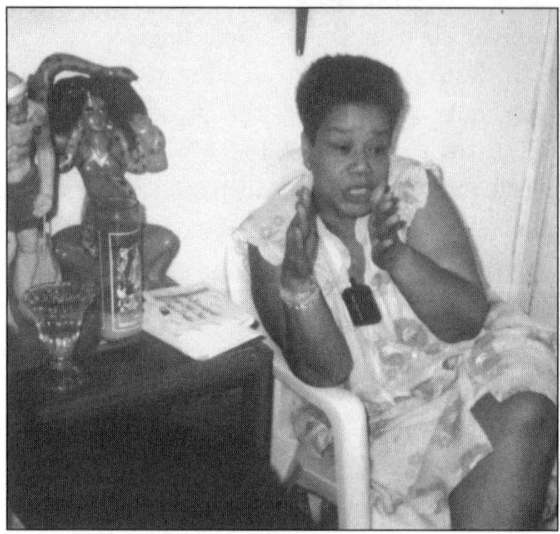

"Look how I speak to you!"

unity (with respect to other texts) achieved through the performance of metaphor in Christian prophecies—also significant for divination discourses within brujería. Aphorisms and proverbs uttered during divination operate at both the intersubjective and intertextual levels, creating a unity of meaning in spite of, and connecting, the various discontinuities and shifts in discourse (of speaking subjects, genres, and temporal references). One level of coherence is obtained by means of an intersubjective reality that emerges as the temporal selves of clients and brujos coalesce—at least for a flash—with the timeless presence of the spirits into an "inchoate 'we'" (327). On another level, aphorisms are semantic keys encompassing the essence of the spiritual message and affording opportunities for intertextual connections (based on content) with other types of texts or statements (personal narratives, Bible stories, and so on) delivered in the same divining session.

Although aphorisms express normative messages that suggest universal, timeless truths, each time an aphorism is uttered during the divination process, it creates associative chains of meaning in successive utterances, thus constructing a semantic/moral and temporal continuity of spiritual discourse. No less importantly, this continuity serves as a form of confirmation of the power of the divination session itself, which is a fundamental precondition for the legitimation that establishes and eventually boosts the ensuing healing process. As the emergent connection created between collective moralizing truths and the particular case being divined is gradually revealed to the client, the encoded spiritual message is thereby decoded and reinforced.

It is somewhat puzzling that the discourse of spiritual time would include aphorisms and proverbs. If, as suggested by folklorists Wolfgang Mieder and Alan Dundes (1994 [1981]), proverbs encapsulate "the wit of one and the wisdom of many," should we say anything less of the wit and wisdom of spirits?

At certain times the divination session changes its mode from a predominantly discursive to a dramatic event. This is what happened to Eva, the client who came from Chicago, during the second part of her divining session. After Eva heard the spirits reveal the cause of her misfortunes—her ex-mother-in-law cast a bewitchment on her—Haydée unexpectedly changed her body posture.

Although still seated at her table, Haydée bends forward, lowers her head (nearly touching the table), and lifts her arms to form a circle about her head. The words she utters are no longer hers; instead, the tenseless speech of bozales, mixed with unintelligible guttural syllables, begins to be heard:

Haydée "catching" the bewitchment of Eva.

> ¡Uy! ¡O, cará! And why you says that wi, wi, win, wings cu, cu, cut, ttttt, cluck, cluckkkk, cuut that chick, chicken? [Checking the pronunciation, she asks,] That is how you says chicken? And why cut chicken wings, so no fly? Why? Why? [imitating the clucking sounds of a chicken] Cluck . . . cuck, cuck-uck-uck . . . cluck-uck . . . uck, kkk.

The sounds continue for a few minutes, mixed with some stuttered guttural words in a crescendo, while we observe Haydée flailing her arms intermittently, mimicking the quivering flapping movements of a chicken. She then falters, shakes her head, slowly rolls her eyes—and gradually recovers, asking (as if she had just woken from a dream), "What happened? . . . Where am I?"

Not remembering what transpired during possession is a common, well-documented reaction found among those in various religious traditions who become possessed. It is a signal that spirits have taken over the consciousness of the medium and that only the medium's body is present, relegating to the spirits the responsibility for whatever transpires and is said during the period of possession.

In Eva's case, Haydée's possession publicly reinforced the success of the divination ritual, for not only did Eva hear the spirits' message, she was also confronted with an enactment of the exact moment in which she had been bewitched by means of a trabajo that entailed the severing of the wings of a chicken. A bewitchment that had transpired at a different time and place, and which was the main cause of Eva's misfortunes, was made present, brought to light in an eerie manner right there in the altar.

After Haydée recovers for a few minutes, she continues with the divination, explaining that she has just had a vision of the black chicken that had been used to bewitch Eva. The vision's content tells the story of her bewitchment, which was reenacted just a few minutes earlier in Haydée's small altar in front of Reina's, Eva's, and my own bewildered eyes. Through the vision we all now realize that the possession replicated the exact instant and procedure in which another bruja had performed black magic against Eva by cutting off the wings of a black chicken.

Unlike the first part of Eva's divination session, when she was warned about the bewitchment cast on her, during Haydée's possession the voice of a bozal entity transported us to the exact moment, the exact procedure that magically connected—through a mimetic performance—the evil wish and animosity of her mother-in-law with Eva's misfortunes, particularly her lost energies. Eva's own energies (wings) were cut when the wings of that black chicken were cut off. The words spoken were not Haydée's, and neither was the body; it was Eva's bewitched body that was enacted in the altar—as it had been invoked in the black-magic work and embodied in a black chicken (a proxy for Eva) some time earlier—bridging mimetically that moment of victimization with this impersonation.

Throughout this reenactment, while Haydée was visibly possessed by the evil spirit that ostensibly had carried out the bewitchment against Eva, Reina was protecting Haydée's body from injury, which often occurs while mediums are in trance.[15] After Haydée came out of trance, Reina entered into a "dialogue" with the evil spirit, urging it "to speak out, to come clear," and—following the edifying ethos of Spiritism—demanding that it "repent, search the light, and leave the living" and "return" from where it had come. Reina also invoked the help of Haydée's "spirits of light" and "guardian angels," beseeching them to rescue Haydée from the negative powers of evil that might have lingered in her body (from having acted as a surrogate for Eva) after possession.

Following this compressed version of an exorcism (as it is performed among brujos and espiritistas), Haydée voiced the emotional state of the client, interpreting and rephrasing the message of the spirits for Eva: "They tell me that you want to cry. Cry, cry, Señora, cry—it's good for you to cry." Shifting to her own voice, she continued, "No, stand up and cleanse yourself with this water [from the fuente]; it's clean" (without bad spirits). And while Eva cleansed herself with splashes of water scooped with her hands from the bowl, Haydée and Reina started praying in litany the Lord's Prayer and Hail Mary, commending this exorcism and cleansing ritual to the Catholic spirits of light.

What we experienced in this later part of the consultation was a drastic, qualitative change of interpretative frameworks: from narrative to drama and from semantic-referential to indexical frameworks. Rather than learning about the cause of Eva's misfortunes, we "experienced" the bewitchment of Eva and "saw" the quivering and clucking of the black chicken (that stood for Eva) when its wings were cut off during the black magic performed against her. And Eva was able to sense (both know and feel) and vicariously experience the vernacular saying *Le cortaron las alas* (Her wings were cut) used as a trabajo. This was the somatic trope of the general lack of energy, particularly in her arms, that she had been feeling in her body lately, every morning upon waking up. Imagine the cathartic power of this mimetic drama.

Modern psychodrama experts recognize the cathartic power of drama, especially its therapeutic possibilities for bypassing the entanglements of discourse, which might hide repressed events and thoughts more easily than actions. As mentioned earlier, this realization (via ancient Greek tragedy and contemporary folk theater) may have inspired Shakespeare's devising a play within a play in *Hamlet*. Although Hamlet had already been warned by his father in a vision about the truth of the murder, he puts on a play—*The Murder of Gonzago* (in his words, *The Mousetrap*)—in order to trap his uncle Claudius into revealing his guilt and avenge his father's death. Unlike verbal accusations, this theatrical representation becomes a trap that exposes the distraught Claudius, who leaves the play before it is over.

A different type of trap or dramatic catharsis ensued when Haydée voiced the unspoken (unconscious) feelings of Eva, as given to her by the spirits ("They tell me that you want to cry. Cry, cry, Señora, cry—it's good for you to cry," and "Why do you say, 'I'm not happy, I have never been happy, I was born to suffer and be miserable'?"). It is easy to imagine how powerful these words must have been for Eva. These might have been the exact words she was thinking at the moment or had been thinking lately. Having her state of mind and mood mimetically revealed in such visceral ways allowed Eva, who had felt paralyzed until then, to begin the process of healing or of opening her "entangled paths."

Anthropologists and folklorists agree in considering mirroring and mimesis as constitutive of various types of individual and group experiences, from basic personal socialization into a group, the development of a sense of self, the ability to control unknown situations, the management of felt disempowerment, to the acquisition of all sorts of knowledge (Cantwell 1993, Jackson 1998, Taussig 1993). Within consultations, the mirroring drama seems to affect clients directly by putting them into a state of emotional openness that promotes the initiation of a healing process during the consultation itself. Emerging out of an initial vision, brujos mirror their clients' overall state in words and actions in front of them (Is it a reverse transference?), making it possible for clients to see themselves objectified, distanced from their own pain. As brujos mimic their clients' bewitched bodies—and occasionally the evil spirits that had caused them misfortune—unspoken and painful feelings have a chance to surge, making visible (literally) the pain clients feel—and its causes. This mirroring drama is powerful enough to motivate even the most bewitched client (that is, one who has lost even the willpower to heal) to stop being passive and, instead, to engage in some recommended proactive, mending action, such as the performance of a cleansing ritual or retaliatory magic work.

Indeed, marking the end of a consultation, some practical form of action is suggested or prescribed after a client has heard the spirits disclose the nature and cause of the misfortune, mimic the client's own emotional state, represent the exact moment when social transgressions were made, and offer possible solutions to the problems. Divination is usually not complete until a series of recipes for cleansing and propitiatory rituals and magic works are carefully dictated and interpreted. While a past and present orientation defines the first sections of a divination session, the last part—when trabajos are dictated (or performed, during a follow-up consultation)—is oriented toward the future.

Notably, writing down the ingredients of a trabajo is not enough. The ingredients are recited and at the same time written down in the order they are dictated to brujos via some sort of vision or revelation. I have many times heard brujos stressing that they do not know ahead of time what the ingredients will be or what the trabajo will look like until they receive the spirits' visions. This combined reciting and writing thus serves the tripartite purpose of documenting a one-of-a-kind recipe, of explaining the effects expected from its ingredients, and of serving as a practical reminder of the list of ingredients clients need to purchase.

Sounding very much like a cooking recipe, the dictation of trabajos offers a quotidian, hands-on atmosphere where a real solution is designed, in contrast to those sacrosanct (and at times feared) moments when brujos make revelations and deliver premonitions and warnings. It is a time that bridges spiritual and mundane moments and allows for the occasional exchange of banal information, such as which market or botánica sells a certain product, how to get a photo of a loved one secretly, or what can be substituted for an ingredient the client cannot find.

What could be more at odds with a ritual discourse than one that addresses everyday necessities? I have seen Haydée and other healers nonchalantly interrupt consultations (assumed to be serious and sacred) with unrelated, often banal directives and observations and even jokes. After a while I began to make sense of these unexpected shifts of register. Haydée once realized during a consultation that she was out of milk; she called her housekeeper to the altar and asked her to go buy some milk and on the way back to pick up her dry cleaning for her. At another time, when her car needed to be fixed, she paged a mechanic in the middle of a consultation. When he beeped her back, she interrupted the consultation and told us all about this mechanic, who was one of her spiritual godchildren, and how he and other ahijados are always there to help her, proving once again that the blessings she gives to her clients "always come back multiplied in unexpected ways." As on other occasions, she resumed the divination session as if nothing had happened, with an implicit self-assurance that indeed nothing can perturb the aura of spiritual time. This confidence in the immutability of the sacred space and time established during rituals is similar to what I had experienced at Mauro's house-temple. Once in a while, Haydée would interject a playful comment in the midst of dictating a magical recipe. Aiming to help a woman get a divorce, for example, she had begun dictating the ingredients needed for the planned trabajo:

> I need a photograph of the husband, oil of rosemary, three leaves of *tártago* [*euphorbia characias*]—when you buy all these [ingredients], buy them in the name of that bitch [the lover]; a small locket; Water of Sunflower; a small can of sardines—you'll be surprised, but it's for divorce—[mischievously] and bring me one—they sell three [cans] for a peso—of those oval ones, so I can eat one with white rice. [Laughs.][16]

The change of voices that occurs during divination—back and forth from an ordinary to a nonordinary speaking self and from human to spiritual selves—creates an atmosphere at once unassumingly familiar and frighteningly unreal. Ordinary time and spiritual time mesh intermittently,

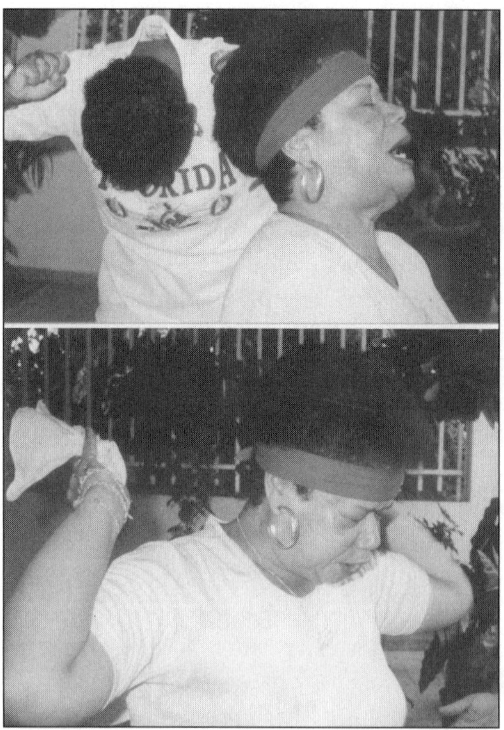

El Indio delivering messages in the waiting room.

challenging any assumed expectations about the fixity of consultations. Unlike in public divination sessions, where in-trance speech is expected at certain climactic moments, during private consultations in-trance speech may either occur or not; and if it occurs, it can happen spontaneously at any time, unexpectedly shifting standard communication rules. Rather than being an orderly, sequential process—in which, for example, the discursive "I" of the ordinary self is followed by the "I" of the nonordinary self (Urban 1989)—as most studies of ritual imply, private divination and magic rituals proceed in quite disorganized ways. Unannounced breaks and shifts during divination are disconcerting to whoever is part of the event. Probably, against the expectations of outsiders, the ease with which spiritually heightened moments might be interrupted and then resumed surmounts (experientially, at least) the assumed duality between sacred and profane realities.[17] Each time the quotidian creeps into the extraordinary, and vice-versa, it is a reminder that, above all, the order of ritual cannot ever be governed by humans nor be free from the whims of the spirits.

"The Santos Talk Bad"

Sometimes profane language indicates that what clients are hearing during consultation may be the direct words of the spirits, since spirits often talk in coarse, blunt, often obscene terms (as discussed in Chapter One) to unveil often-denied embarrassing but vital facts about clients whose future well-being depends on this disclosure. When this occurs, brujos explain that it is not they who are speaking that way—"It's the spirits." This is not said as an apology to the client but as a clarification and reminder that the power of spirits operates above human etiquette and that the objective of spirits justifies their means. After delivering extremely harsh, blunt words to a client, Haydée immediately explains, "I'm direct, but it's not me who's speaking. Because They speak clear [*hablan claro*] in order to untie the most entangled paths." In a way, these statements cue the client that what will follow are the inspired messages of the spirits, who are never diverted from essential if embarrassing aspects of people's lives. By means of bringing them to light (in spite of the clients' inability to address them), the spirits' harsh words, in fact, unbewitch clients (untie their entangled paths), thereby allowing the healing process to begin.

In addition to opening paths, obscene language signals the presence of transcendental power, which overrides the power of social norms and etiquette. Paradoxically, however, the content of such messages is usually quite conservative in matters of family, job, and love relationships. Geared toward conformity to—rather than the breaking of—social morals, such messages (even when delivered with obscenity-laced speech) direct clients to act in tune with the Spiritist ethos. Though readers by now realize from previous quotes that spirits often "talk bad," a couple more examples may nonetheless be in order.

A woman who complained about her husband's neglect and her fears that he will finally leave her hears the spirits tell her: "*El te chinga* [He's fucking you over]. Men don't like to eat only rice and beans" (Caribbean dietary staple, referring here to conventional sex). Haydée then asks the client rhetorically, "So . . . what do you give him to eat [provide him sexually]?" In another instance, a woman hears the spirits refer to her mother-in-law, who never liked her and now has allegedly bewitched her: "Why is that motherfucking bitch so bad?"

Perhaps the eventual healing power of spirits derives from their ability to speak the socially unspeakable; in the idiom of brujería, the clarity of their words opens up even the most entangled paths. Reflexively and justifying a false sense of decorum, Haydée used to comment, "You see, Raquel, we espiritistas have to speak like this."

A way of speaking that is direct but only occasionally obscene is also considered in many other healing and magic traditions a sign of mediumship and of the presence of the spirits during ritual. Failure to embody these signs might prove that the medium is not yet ready, or mature enough, to allow his or her body to articulate publicly the voice of the spirits. This is what happened to Chini, a Korean shaman novice, whose case as recounted by Laurel Kendall (1996a) suggests that in addition to having the inspiration of the spirits and receiving their messages, mediums need to be able to appropriately "perform" their voices in public to be considered true shamans. "It was the ability to perform that Chini lacked. She failed, the shamans acknowledged, because she was too self-conscious and inhibited. By their logic, she was unable to perform because she could not give herself over to the flow of inspiration conjured by drum beats, dancing, costumes, and by their own suggestive comments—'The spirits are coming!'" (50).

In other words, even though mediums are not the ones who speak, they need to let their bodies exit and voices articulate the spirits' messages directly—without any internal censorship. In fact, as I have seen on several occasions among brujos and espiritistas, this is the very goal of mediumship initiations by other, more experienced mediums, who constantly cajole novices upon their showing signs of entering trance during such initiatory rituals: "Speak clear! The santos speak clear!"

Following Dell Hymes (1975), it appears that what expert mediums expect novices to do is to "break through" into ritual performance: that is, to leave quotidian speech and its criteria and enter the performative realm of spiritual time (and all that it implies). Without questioning the veracity of novices' mediumship, the charisma embedded in their performance (see Kendall 1996a, Schieffelin 1996) reflects this breakthrough into spiritual discourse. Signaling that it is not the medium who speaks but the spirits, this shift calls attention to the implied authority, intentionality, and consequences of spiritual discourse—the rules of which are governed by a unique regime of value and interpretive frame recognized by shamans and healers (and perhaps also by spirits).

Although it is a widespread notion that the purpose of divination is to discover the cause of individuals' problems, this is just one apparent—and indeed, the least important—layer of its significance for practitioners. When clients say, *Vengo a resolver*, they are implicitly suggesting that the divination event itself will effect a healing process for them. Within the unique space of discourse and action created during divination, where magical chains link perceptible and spiritual realms, their misfortunes acquire a transcendental significance. Ulterior cosmic motives replace quotidian time and space as well as human volition and man-made morals. Embodied, for instance, in the impromptu shifts of voices between spirits and brujos and shifts of alternate styles of speech, these mysterious cosmic motives emerge, promoting the healing efficacy of divination. Clients not only end up "knowing" the source of their afflictions but also "sensing" it: they are made aware of it in an experiential manner. Participation in such an alternative reality—which I have characterized as "spiritual time"—albeit only for the duration of the divination session, reframes a client's problem and its eventual resolution on multivalent layers of experience, where the present, the past, and the future coalesce.

Words and Thoughts That "Do"

When brujos become possessed during divination by the evil spirits that have allegedly caused misfortune to their clients, exorcism is usually recommended (or at times performed as part of the divination ritual itself) to cleanse and liberate their clients from the harmful effects of such spirits. Although in some societies these exorcisms are held publicly and performed in elaborate, multichanneled ways (which may include drumming, trance, chanting, and the ingestion of potions), within brujería these duels between humans and evil spirits are more intimate and personal. A forceful yet impossible—by standard discursive rules—interaction between evil spirits and mediums develops discursively by means of which the mediums order the evil spirits to leave their clients' bodies and this world and to become enlightened in the spiritual world. When Reina became possessed by the underdeveloped spirit (*cogió un muerto*) that was pestering one of Haydée's clients, Haydée intervened, vehemently ordering the evil spirit, "Go away to the celestial mansions! Your place is not here! You shouldn't bother this poor woman." Turning to the client she said, "Forgive him." And as the spirit resisted leaving, she ordered it again and again, "Withdraw now, demon!"

As they manage the forces of good and evil, brujos utter words (not always authored by them) that have the power to "do." When a vision is expressed during divination—for example, "I see you without a leg"—it is a serious warning not to be taken just as a mere descriptive statement about the future. Rather, it is a reminder that it is up to the client (who is now aware of the warning) to amend his or her behavior through free will and thus to change what has been foretold.

But it is not only brujos who can endow their words with magic forces. Anybody can have the potential power to (unknowingly) cause harm or promote well-being just by means of his or her words or thoughts. Uttered or not, thoughts can "do"—as when Haydée asks her clients to "think strongly" while they buy the ingredients for a trabajo—and thus can become as powerful as brujos in producing, managing, and controlling good and evil energies.

Reclamar (to demand), as I mentioned earlier, suggests a verbal invocation (performed either mentally or aloud) for certain outcomes to materialize. Brujos sometimes tell their clients, "You have to 'reclamar' in a loud voice for things to happen as you wish." When they dictate the ingredients of a trabajo, they might direct clients about the mental state they need to be in when purchasing the specific ingredients. "When you buy this goblet [that I have asked for], make sure you invoke the first and last name of that man [the one the client wants to be spiritually united with], you know?" Clients may be asked to invoke the names of the individuals they want to affect when they perform, say, a cleansing or retaliation ritual in their homes. When a woman was instructed to light various candles in her home, one for each of the enemies that had just been revealed to her, Haydée instructed her,

> You should light the candles today because tomorrow is Friday, and you want them to be well lit [fully working] by then.. And remember that you need to concentrate on the names of your enemies and whatever you wish to accomplish as you light each candle. I will put these names in your mind this afternoon from here while you light the candles and will also help you make your pleas at home. It's best if you page me just before you're about to light the candles, OK?

Brujos, unlike most people, have the mental force to empower the pleas their clients make by themselves. Since words may have magical power, special care has to be taken for their management. Invocations need to be clearly spelled out, even if mentally, because it is not enough to wish for a certain result; it has to be spelled out straightforwardly to be effective.

But what happens when someone *reclama* (invokes) a person's name, that is, his or her personal energies? If the person's ears itch and he or she suffers from sudden headaches and insomnia for no apparent reason, somebody might be invoking his or her name. Clients who are desperate often do that unwittingly to the brujos whose help they are seeking. But brujos, again unlike most people, have the spiritual power to be aware of and counteract this effect. For other people, it can be the cause not only of headaches but also of unusual havoc and distraction, sometimes leading to harmful forgetfulness and accidents.[19]

Sounds, Onomatopoeias, and Nonsense Vocables

Some semantically meaningless vocables, onomatopoeic expressions, and the sounds produced by banging on a table, clapping hands, and tapping

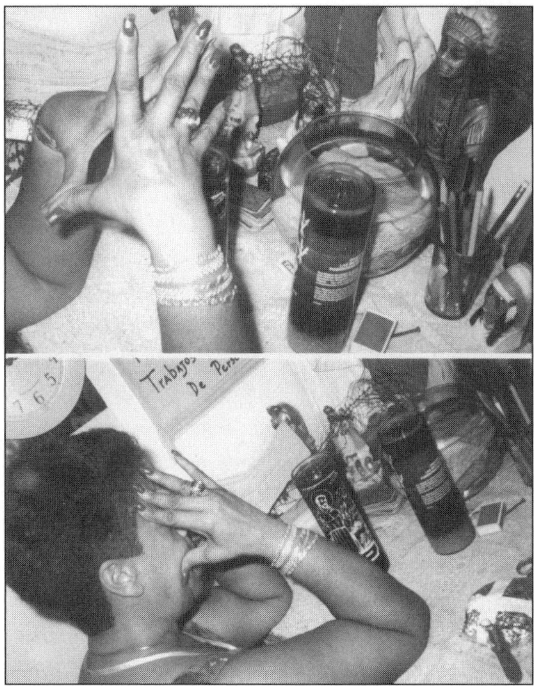

Haydée invoking her protecciones while making a trabajo.

on a bell may suddenly be heard in the midst of a consultation, adding to the opacity, excitement, and sometimes anxiety of what is going on during divination.

Paul Stoller draws our attention to the importance of the senses, particularly of sound, in Songhay possession ceremonies (1996:178), showing that the sound of "praise-naming," accompanied by the sound of musical instruments, has a ritually transformative effect. The *sorko* (praise-singer) "shouts out the names of the spirits, recounting their genealogies and their supernatural exploits." When a praise-singer approaches a spirit medium who is not yet possessed and shouts spirit names into his or her ear, he ensures that "the sounds of the praise-names penetrate the medium's body." The social and spirit worlds fuse through words, the "cries" of the violin, and the "clacks" of the gourd drum. "Through the medium's body, the spirit is ready to speak to the community." Charles Briggs in his microlinguistic analysis (1996) of curing rituals among the Warao of Venezuela, attributes metadiscursive power to cries, interjections, vocables, rattle rhythms, and onomatopoeias. Drawing on Julia Kristeva, he defines these nonsemantic signs as "genotexts," showing that even though they lack a referential content and have no denotative value, they have an indexical value (refer to the speech situation) and thus acquire a metapragmatic role during these curing events (213). These semantically nonsensical elements (unintelligible to patients) help establish the connection between spirits and healers as well as establish the ritual power of healers.

I have noticed that even if these genotexts are initially unintelligible to clients during divination and magic rituals, they are meaningful in their overall role in constructing such events. Perhaps if I asked clients to spell out the significance of each and every sound and vocable they hear during divination, they would find my question irrelevant and nonsensical, for separating the component elements of the whole session is outside the scope of their experience of divination. Rather than decipher these signs individually, clients need to be able to react to them in appropriate ways—an ability they acquire as they become habitués of these rituals.

In the process of participating systematically in divination rituals from morning to night, I was able to react emotionally to these recurrent nonsense vocables and sounds, as they cued the purpose and desired effects of spiritual events. Onomatopoeic words such as *pam, pam* and *pángana,* expressions of speed such as *uan-tu-tri* (one-two-three, pronounced in Spanglish), and the sounds of loud bangs on a table, the clapping of hands, or the snapping of fingers were meant to index both the rapidity and the effectiveness of trabajos and, by extension, of brujos and their power.

Speaking of her own spiritual power, Haydée told Armando when he came to visit her for the first time:

> I'm the bruja of Loíza. What God gives cannot be learned from books. It comes from the sky. It is given to us. When the client parts the cards, I say to myself, "And what am I going to say?" and then—pangana, pangana, pangana [snapping her fingers after each word]—she is witness [pointing to me and raising her voice] that there're comprobaciones here. Right, Raquel? Isn't it right, Raquel, that today I had three comprobaciones here, when—after having told the last client [some time ago] that she wasn't going to inherit a cent because she wasn't legally married to that man—[she confirmed today] that this is [exactly] what happened?

The exclamations *¡Uy, carajo!* and *¡O, cará!* are not easily translatable; the closest would be "Holy shit!" or some such expression that indexes raw awe and surprise.[20] Such exclamations signal not only the imminent arrival of the spirits and the trance of the medium but also that what follows is inspired directly by their words and motives or is a confirmation of what brujos have revealed to clients. Sometimes the latter are also marked by a loud, ritualistic laugh. All such markers indicate a shift of register from ordinary to spiritual, performative discourse. This is what happened right at the beginning of Elena's consultation with Haydée.

> —Aren't you the one who works at The Conquistador [resort]?
>
> —No, at Country Chicken.
>
> —I gave you a recipe for a trabajo, didn't I?
>
> —Yes, but I couldn't bring it [the ingredients]. I was about to do it twice but . . .
>
> —You always come when the problem is in your face. ¡Pángana! That's when you remember. But the cards don't solve problems. The cards tell you what will happen. You have a problem with your work, and that's why you came. Somebody wants to remove you. . . . Ha, ha, ha! You're involved with a man at work, and you quarrel with everybody . . .
>
> —Yes . . .
>
> —¡Pángana! What I saw then, I see now!

That this woman came back with this problem confirmed to Haydée that the diagnosis and recommendations she had made months earlier, when the client first came to her and when the current developments could have been prevented, were right. Signaled by "Ha, ha, ha," the consequences of failing to follow through on the advice given to her are now visible and painful for this client, evidence that one should not toy with divination, that is, take lightly the messages of the spirits delivered by brujos.

Another kind of shift of register is announced when at climactic moments during divination brujos suddenly ring a bell, sometimes even in the middle of trance. It is an indication that the spirits are present and are assuring that what has been said is true or will happen exactly as uttered. Upon hearing the bell rung, accompanied by bangs on the table during her consultation with Haydée, a woman heard the key to all her latest problems: "You were put 'face down,' you know? With a black candle, so everything [in your life] will be upside down!"

Accentuating a statement by banging on a table, clapping, or snapping fingers indicates its gravity and truthfulness. In consultation with another client, the spirits revealed that the woman's main problem was believing that consultations solve problems. She kept consulting with different healers but failed to follow through on the advice that was given to her. Haydée told her, "Because you go to places [for consultation] and don't see results immediately, you become very defiant and negative. Remember that for spiritual matters you need to wait in order to see." Banging hard on the table to establish a series of (cosmic) facts, she added, "Look, I guarantee my work—[bangs] nine days; [bangs again] twenty days; [bangs again] or forty-five days, depending on the kind of trabajo!"

Especially during public veladas where some participants are not previously known to the mediums in attendance, every time a medium rings the bell just before or during the deliverance of a vision for one of the participants, it is an indication that a critical revelation is about to be heard. As the object of such revelation is asked to stand up, he or she must understand that such messages are magically powerful, for they are dictates emanating, word by word, from the spirits. When messages are accompanied by the sound of a bell, addressees should pay special attention to them since the bell signals that they embody a cosmic verdict that may disclose a hidden aspect of their lives or a spiritual debt they may have contracted with someone living or dead and which needs to be settled with the utmost urgency to prevent future misfortunes. Since the personal motivation for attending the velada is not known by everyone, these messages are usually received by individuals with mixed feelings of awe, surprise, gratitude, and, sometimes, embarrassment.

At one velada, a short, chubby man was asked by one of the mediums to stand up, and in the middle of the message he was receiving he heard the bell ring at the very moment when Haydée, who was presiding over and hosting the velada, became possessed. In the words of bozales, the man heard, "You is depressed, you quarrels with somebody at work. . . . At home . . . ? You wants to cry!" And as Haydée rang the bell a few more times, she said, following her vision, "Cry! I know you want to cry! You need to cry to purify your spirit. If you have bitterness in you heart you cannot be happy. Gather your tears. These are *espíritus llorones* [crying spirits]." The man was stunned at this dramatically public diagnosis, which, as seen by his reaction, was right on the mark. He then heard the words of the Madama, who warned him in her typical bozal language: "Your car to crash. You can't to raise . . . you blocked . . . that spirit to have you crying . . . crying. That crying not belong to that body." Haydée then asked, "Do you want to say publicly what's bothering you? Why you always have a dog face? Have you ever thought of poisoning yourself? Or of using a gun [to kill yourself]?" This was evidence that he had a causa with espíritus llorones, who caused him to be depressed all the time and even to contemplate suicide. This revelation was apparently too much for him, for he opted to schedule, instead, a private consultation to deal with his problems.

On one occasion during divination at her altar, Haydée warns Denia, a woman of about forty-five, not to inform her son about her own suspicions that his girlfriend is not being faithful to him; certainly, Denia is not to tell her son that she saw his girlfriend being dropped off many times at night at the house they are sharing by a man the girlfriend said was a colleague from work. After Denia confirms Haydée's revelation (that she believed her son's girlfriend was not good for him), Haydée asks,

> —What do you want? To open the door so his girlfriend leaves?
>
> —I think one thing, and then the other. It's delicate. I don't want my son to be soiled with anything; his whole life is to work and that woman. . . . He will not believe anything I tell him about her anyway.

Without any further questions, Haydée begins to dictate a recipe for a double trabajo. One will make her son's girlfriend have the sudden urge to leave the house (and him), thus freeing him from his (presumably magically induced) obsessive attachment to her: "nails . . . a lock with three big keys . . . a cloth doll . . . a piece of black fabric . . . a twig of *pazote* [wormseed, *Chenopodium ambrosioides*] . . ." Suddenly Haydée rings the bell to assert a confirmación of the cosmic Law of Cause and Effect (which appears to non-espiritistas to be mere coincidence): "Tonio told me he has some in his yard! I told him we would come by to pick some [pazote] in a few days," not knowing then when she would need it. Haydée then begins to dictate the ingredients for the second trabajo, aimed at lifting the bewitchment hanging over Denia's son, the alleged cuckold:

> For your adored son I want a white and red wax doll, yellow ribbon, six wooden nails, and 'The Seven Swords of Michael the Archangel' candle [vigorously ringing the bell again] because they [the Seven Swords] are going to cut the bewitchment that ties her to him.

If the first ring signaled a spiritual confirmation of her wish to gather pazote some days ago (even before knowing for whom she would need it), the second ring indexes the effectiveness assured for the trabajo when performed in the near future, especially of the power of the Seven Swords of Michael the Archangel to cut the bewitchment (caused by the girlfriend's mother, according to what was revealed earlier in divination) that has made Denia's son blind to his girlfriend's betrayals.

The sounds of the bell also mark the confirmation of the spirits' manifestation. At one point during this consultation, after going through other aspects of Denia's life, Haydée asks,

> —And your son, is he OK?
>
> —Yes.
>
> —That you know of . . . I see him separating. Your son doesn't want to, but his girlfriend doesn't want to be with him. His girlfriend will destroy that relationship. You came for that problem!
>
> —Yes.
>
> —[Haydée rings the bell forcefully several times.] *¡Aché pa tí!*

The sounds of the bell vividly confirm that the spirits have manifested themselves and spoken in a clear manner, assuring success in the eventual resolution of Denia's main concern—undoing the bewitchment of her son and his eventual separation.

Opacity and Revelation

Initially, as an outsider I had reacted very differently to what I experienced as discursive opacity and ritual unpredictability. While the fantastic and esoteric narratives I heard made me feel somewhat incredulous and uneasy, the volatile shifts and breaks I experienced during rituals elicited in me very emotional, sensuous reactions. My earlier responses perhaps correspond to typical interpretive assumptions about the differential logics of language and ritual and how we experience each. Making sense of discourse and ritual, finding their sense and sensing them, do entail qualitatively distinct cognitive and sensorial engagements. Initial opacity and disorientation might define rituals in general and be part of the overall experience of spiritual time, operating at the metacommunicative and metapragmatic levels.

I am aware that by making the obscure transparent and the metapragmatic evident I unwillingly undermined in this ethnography the accuracy of the experiential significance of opacity in a ritual context (unavailable to readers except as a written account), that is, its force in creating a total divination experience.[21] During my fieldwork I experienced and sensed (felt the effects of) both the allure and skepticism of this ritual opacity—the various kinds of shifts and discontinuities as well as the startling sounds and puzzling nonsense vocables—even before I was able to have a sense (knowledge) of how such shifts create this overall experience of spiritual time. Brujos define this experience succinctly for clients, saying, "I will tell you not just about your future; I will tell you about your past, present, and future."

Most of the premises that guide standard speech—the lineal conceptions of time it assumes, the coherence of the speaking subject (the agreement about whom personal pronouns refer to), and the pragmatics of various speech styles—are broken during divination. Apparently, the rationalist premises that guide standard language and its linear-temporal foundation are inadequate for capturing the holistic world of divination experiences. Resembling a Spinozean world in which everything—every action and different spaces and times—intersect, spiritual time encapsulates the interrelatedness of past, present, and future as well as the interlacing of transtemporal motives and goals.

It is no coincidence that Vincent Crapanzano chose the montage for its "rhetorical effect" in his *Imaginative Horizons* (2004), where literary, ethnographic, and philosophical texts are placed side by side in order to capture the interstitial character of anthropology, its "inter-space-time." In choosing this writing strategy, he aimed at conveying the inter-space-time that emerges from the interaction of various cultural practices not as a space of confrontation but as a "constitutive space-time" (3, 5–6).

In characterizing the experiential frame of divination as spiritual time, I have suggested that breaks in standard speech are constitutive of a different kind of holistic epistemology (and nosology). It is not just the result of the addition of all its parts. Rather, its fragments contain (as in ellipsis) the whole; each time they are delivered, they constitute a whole in slightly different ways. Though intimations of such cohesion can hardly be expressed in standard language, they surely can be experienced or expressed in poetic language and in myriad other forms of artistic creation (see Gibbal 1994 [1988]).

Healing and poetry are thus not so different. As Czech literary theoretician and aesthetician Jan Mukařovský suggests (1964:18), "The violation of the norm of the standard, its systematic violation, is what makes possible the poetic utilization of language; without this possibility there would be no poetry." When the voices of the spirits and the dead become manifest during divination and trance, they violate various rules of standard discourse. Accompanied and introduced by sounds, cries, and semantically nonsensical exclamations, these voices evoke the spirits' presence. Their sacredness can be sensed in spite or because of the opacity of their discourse. This is when the spirits reveal the true source of afflictions (and their solutions) to the living in a totalizing, timeless, and spaceless discourse. Obscure in linguistic terms, the evocation of the divination event nonetheless clears the spiritual paths of the afflicted, making them experientially (somatosensorily) apparent, transparent, and most of all manageable. Like the evocation of poetry, when the initial opacity of divination creates spiritual and emotional transparency, it is when the timeless and spaceless cosmic order is experienced; in sum, it is when the spiritual time thus experienced can clear, as brujos say, the most entangled paths.

Chapter Five
THE SENTIENT BODY

As planned, I arrive at Mauro's at one in the afternoon. We are going to a *toque de tambor* (also *toque de santo*), a Santería drumming celebration in honor of the orishas. But we leave at two-thirty in the afternoon because we need to wait until Ronny (the other Cuban babalawo) arrives as well. While we wait Mauro tells me about his plans to start a spiritual spa in Miami with the help of some of his influential godchildren. He talks about his relationship and spiritual work with his wife, Lorena—her demands, the fact that she is in charge of everything practical (such as the house budget) and her intention to work in Miami as an accountant. Castro's politics, the revolutionary Camilo Cienfuegos, and the rivalry of Castro with El Ché acquire intimate significance once Mauro weaves them into his own life story:

> While in Cuba I had a house, a chauffeur, and a Cadillac. I used to work for only four hours. Castro used to send me new tires made in China for the car. His mother read cards, and his brother was a homosexual. I left in December 1971. Those that left with the Mariel [in 1980] were very mistreated by Castro—I wasn't, I used to live like a king. I was mistreated when I arrived to Puerto Rico; here I was never accepted [by Puerto Rican babalawos].

When Ronny arrives, they go to change clothes, then come back all dressed in white, covered (to my surprise) with very flashy jewelry—gold and diamond rings, necklaces, and bracelets. Only later did I learn the spiritual, symbolic meaning of this flamboyant display.

We all get into my rented car and head to the toque de santo. The weather starts to get quite hot, and the sky remains clear blue. As we approach we sense the festive atmosphere on the block, we know we have arrived at the right place. The single-story house, similar to all the others in the development, stands out only because dozens of people are standing outside it, and loud drumbeats reverberate in the otherwise deserted street. Mauro and Ronny greet a few people and push me softly inside the house to the room where the actual toque is taking place. The room is decorated with green leaves hanging everywhere from the ceiling; in one corner is a bunch of branches arranged in the shape of a tree, under which stands a young man dressed as Eleggua in red and black sequined pants and shirt with a sash across his chest. He has feathers in his cap and holds a baton festooned with matching small red and black balls. Next to this man stands a woman dressed in green and black, her cap decorated as well with feathers. Ronny tells me that the novice woman "receiving" Ogún and Ochosi (in her head) is the one giving the toque; the other novice, the one receiving Eleggua, is co-hosting this celebration. The woman receiving Ogún and Ochosi stands like a statue, her eyes fixed in a distant gaze, repeatedly puffing big clouds of smoke from a cigar wedged between her lips. She holds a machete in one hand, resting the other on her hips and occasionally raising it to adjust the cigar. I notice a few red stripes painted on her face and legs that bestow on her an animal-like camouflage. Against my first impression, I see that even though both initiates stand quite motionless, locked in an iconic stance, they do move slightly back and forth to the rhythm of the entrancing drumbeats that pervade the whole space.

In the center of the room five musicians play and sing sacred music: one beats a tall drum forcefully yet seemingly effortlessly; another shakes two large beaded gourds (*chequeres*) in alternating vertical and circular motions; another beats a cowbell with a stick at measured intervals; and a ten-year-old boy keeps the beat with a small, hand-sized *maraca* (gourd filled with rice). A *cantador* standing in the front, next to the boy, leads the praise-singing in the prescribed order of *orus* (invocations for the orishas). A series of call-and-response sections develop between all the musicians, who accompany the lead singer and the participants at the toque. The participants, in addition to singing, dance in a spontaneous circle created at the center of the room in honor of the orishas that are summoned by each specific drumbeat and praise song. I feel privileged that Ronny stands by my side explaining to me who is who and what is going on and why.

Ronny tells me that the spatial arrangement of branches and green leaves corresponds to initiation rituals with *guerreros* (warrior orishas). The warrior Ogún, according to one myth, used to carry Ochosi (the hunter) on his shoulder when they went hunting together; Ogún would open the jungle with his machete, and Ochosi would shoot the arrows. When initiation is performed with orishas who are not warriors, the decoration of the ritual space is made with fabrics of different colors, matching the colors associated with each orisha. In an adjacent room I see the host's *soperas* (soup tureens that contain the instruments and sacred stones of the orishas), which embody the spirit of their owner. Big sheets cover them, Ronny tells me, to prevent both deliberate and unintentional bewitchments.

In the main room, the music and dancing go on while the musicians are offered rum. On the ground in front of the musicians lies a dead rooster on a plate covered with grains. This is an offering for Changó (the owner of drums), who has been summoned to promote the success of this drumming session for the orishas. Reacting to my look of surprise at seeing everybody leaving, Ronny tells me that after all the orishas have been called by the drums in the prescribed order, the toque de santo for guerreros typically proceeds onto the street. As everybody starts moving slowly outside, Ogún possesses ("rides") the novice woman (his "horse"), who gradually changes her demeanor. Her eyes begin flickering, and she starts walking toward the main door with a heavy step—a few seconds elapse before she lifts each foot. A tremendous force seems to be involved in each movement—both while lifting and lowering each foot. The transfiguration takes place with each movement. As if stuck to the floor, one foot rises only with great effort, then with trembling force goes heavily down. Sighing loudly and heavily through the nose like a bison, Ogún now swings the machete up and down, and side to side, with each step as he passes between the guests, some of whom try to restrain him from behind to prevent him from hitting someone or hurting his "horse" (the novice) by the machete. Carefully, the cantador tries to release the machete from Ogún's hands, but Ogún continues pacing forward as if blind to the commotion he produces on his way. As he approaches where I am standing, I become alarmed. Fortunately, he passes me by, heading straight toward the street, mumbling some indecipherable words. Ronny explains to me that Ogún always likes to wander the street.

A young, extremely thin woman dressed in white who had earlier been singing begins to have convulsions that show signs of her entering trance. A santera, the *madrina* (spiritual godmother) of the novice, comes to her aid together with several other women. While the madrina blows air in the woman's ear and face, the other helpers bring half a coconut shell filled with water. Each sips some of the water, then sprinkles the young woman's face and body with it until she gradually relaxes and comes back to herself. As the helpers calm her down, the madrina runs out to assist Ogún's horse bearing another coconut cup with water to be sprinkled upon his novice.

On the way out I notice a black, two-foot-tall doll, dressed all in white, propped in a chair right at the entrance to the parlor, surrounded with flowers, small plates of food, and lit *velones* (candles in tall glass containers) arranged in an altar-like manner. As I go out to the sidewalk, where most of the participants are now assembled, I notice a plate at the street curb drain with some scraps of food leftover from the previous day's feasting, next to which is a cluster of lit candles. I am told it is an offering for a santo (orisha) that lives and feeds at waste sites. Ogún is parading the street swinging his machete, while the madrina and the other women make sure that nobody—especially his horse—gets hurt while Ogún possesses her body.

Gently guided back into the house, Ogún gradually leaves the novice's body, and the novice, together with all the guests, moves back to the big area of the house, where the music and dancing resume. Mauro, Ronny, and I find a good spot on the side and observe the dancing. One of the santeras, a woman of about sixty, ritually greets those members of the religious community who—regardless of their actual age—are higher in the spiritual hierarchy, prostrating herself on the ground (as I saw Chris do at Mauro's) while the recipient of the greeting marks a cross on her back, patting her twice before helping her stand up. Then they embrace ritually, bringing each side of their bodies together several times, shoulder to shoulder. When she approaches Mauro and Ronny, who occupy the highest level of the religious hierarchy, she touches the floor with her fingers while they bless her with some prayers. When she greets those who are lower in the hierarchy, she taps them after they prostrate themselves at her feet.

At this point Ochún, another orisha, possesses the madrina, who is moving graciously and sensually among the participants. As she approaches some participants standing around the dancing space, she delivers messages for them. A few of the chosen ones break into an emotional sob upon receiving Ochún's messages. She then approaches Ronny (who is standing by my side) and prostates herself in front of him. Ronny crosses her back. As she stands up, Ochún caresses him sensually from head to toe, whispering a message to him in the words of bozales (words I unsuccessfully try to hear). I see Ronny nodding his head, registering her message. Ochún then grabs him and takes him to dance with her.

Mauro in the meantime gossips with me about the guests. "Some here are homosexuals," he tells me, following up on comments he had made days earlier about the recent increase of practitioners who are homosexuals—a trend he dislikes and which he attributes to the development of Santería in the United States. Pointing to a chubby man, he says, "Look, that old one even has breast implants; and the younger one over there, with a handkerchief, is also a homosexual. So is that one wearing green and white, holding a fan."

Seeing Mauro's and Ronny's casual behavior, I realize at this point that neither of them came to officiate in any manner. They have come just to lend their support to the madrina and to honor the initiation festivity. Around seven in the evening the babalawo in charge, who is the godfather of the two novices, arrives and greets Mauro and Ronny as we are leaving. He is dressed very informally, not in white as most of the participants; I recognize him, for he was there earlier wearing shorts. The three babalawos gossip about other babalawos—especially about the one whose son was murdered a few days earlier. Two other babalawos arrive, pay their respect to the officiating babalawo, and join in the conversation about the latest news in the community of practitioners. Unable to understand whom or what they are gossiping about, I reluctantly move to a side of the room away from the group of babalawos and turn my attention elsewhere.

All this time, the madrina—still possessed by Ochún—is dancing among the guests and only stops now and then to give messages to this or that person. Out of nowhere, the madrina/Ochún is now standing in front of me. This is unexpected—my heart starts beating very fast—for I had assumed that my role as observer excluded me from any further participation in the ritual. Ochún gets incredibly close to me and begins whispering unintelligible words that only remotely resemble Spanish. Frozen in place, I feel her heavy huffing and puffing on my face and in my ear. Chills go up and down my spine as her breath touches my skin. My whole being is engulfed by her ascending and descending undulating movements; barely touching me, she strokes my body from shoulders to fingertips, then torso to legs. I find myself responding to her hip movements and heavy sighs and exhalation with my own in-synch movements. But I cannot respond to the words she whispers, for they remain obscure to me. Behind her I faintly see the other women, who in the meantime have begun translating Ochún's message to me. But their words, too, remain mostly opaque to me. Overtaken by the warmth, tenderness, and sensuality of Ochún, I gradually lose a sense of my surroundings. I tease out one sentence of the women's translation as, "Ochún says you have a man mounted on your shoulders." Then, as Ochún caresses my belly, I vaguely hear, "You have problems in your stomach," even more faintly followed by, "and your feet." Ochún then leaves. After only a few seconds, she returns with a calabash painted green and purple and hands it to me. As Ochún again speaks to me in the language of bozales, the translators say, "You have to toss it in the river and let it go with the current." At this point I am standing in the middle of the dancing area, trying to absorb what I have just heard, when Ochún, mumbling some more words, unexpectedly opens the chignon I am wearing and spreads my hair over my shoulders. From a bowl I had not noticed before, she begins to pour honey over my hair, face, arms, and body—of course, the honey goes also on my sleeveless, cotton dress!—slowly, sensuously licking some of it that falls on her hands, delighting herself with each drop. Honey is Ochún's favorite food.

My whole body is sticky, and the heat of the afternoon melts the honey in my hair, dripping it onto my face and neck. Circling my body, Ochún first stops at my back, rubbing her back against mine in a rolling movement in synch with the rhythm of the music—an action that I instinctively reciprocate. Returning in front of me again, she rubs my chest over my dress and neck with the rest of the honey from the bowl. I have no sense of how much time this has taken, but at one point, as abruptly unannounced as she had approached me in the first place, Ochún moves away to give messages to others.

As the object of such attention, I felt transfigured, experiencing a kind of sensorial shock—Ochún's energy and force from without and my own changes of perception from within. The female helpers/translators accompany me to a nearby laundry sink to wash the honey off from my body and dress, preparing me for my safe return from that experience, and make additional comments about the message given to me by Ochún, repeating parts I had not managed to retain. Most of all, they reveal to me that Ochún had claimed me as her daughter.

As I drive home soaked with water (there were no towels at the sink), behind the wheel I still savor the intimate encounter and taste I had of Ochún under the burning sun of the afternoon. I tell Mauro, my protector, what Ochún said to me, and show him the painted calabash I was given. Unsure of what all this means for me, I ask him what I should do. Here I am at the very beginning of my research wondering whether I am ready to get initiated in the religion. He says not to worry. Until I make up my mind one way or another he will offer the calabash to Ochún the next time he performs a ritual at a river. With this small ritual, he assures me, I will bear no debts to Ochún's demands for the time being.

Risking exaggeration or mystification, I retrospectively regard this ritual experience as an unforgettable imprinting experience. Feeling the need to share it with friends and students over the years, I have described it as a unique bond established between Ochún (and, perhaps by extension, with this religion as a whole) and myself via very basic somatic sensations. Although a personal experience, it was hardly outside the cultural significance of the sensory realm of Santería. Not unlike the apparent incursion of this world into my own personal dreaming, it seems that my most personal sensorial experiences during fieldwork were part of a collective world of meanings pertaining to the orishas.

Somatic Modes of Attention

Relevant here are the questions Csordas poses (1993) about somatic modes of attention in ritual healing processes. He proposes embodiment as a paradigm or methodological orientation that requires that the body be understood as the existential ground of culture—not as an object that is "good to think" but as a subject that is "necessary to be" (135). Somatic modes of attention are culturally elaborated ways of "attending to and with one's body and surroundings that include the embodied presence of others" (138). Because attention implies both sensory engagement and an object (as well as attention to the position and movements of others), Csordas means both attending "with" and attending "to" the body, which in fact "must be both" (ibid.). But even if attention to our bodies is acknowledged, he continues, how do bodily sensations acquire their significance? Is the heat felt by healers the same others feel when they blush or the tingling healers experience the same as the tingling others feel in other meaningful situations? Specifically, Csordas ponders "whether the 'pain backup' in the healer's arms as she lays her hands on a person's shoulder is really the same feeling we have when our arm 'falls asleep' after remaining too long in an uncomfortable position" (148).

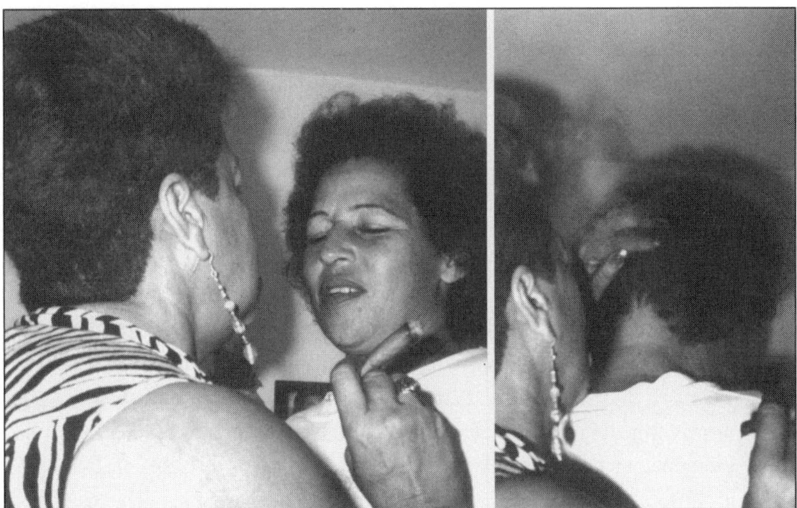

"Somatic modes of attention."

Indeed, particular events have the power to establish the connection between certain bodily responses and their emotional significance. I am thinking about the somatic reactions during the seclusion stage of her initiation ritual in Vodou that American dancer Katherine Dunham reported having while doing research in Haiti during the 1940s. While attending rites at an *ounfo* (Vodou temple) in the Cul de Sac region, Dunham was convinced by the *manbo* (godmother), Téoline, to undergo a *lave tèt* (initiation) ceremony called *kouche* in preparation for her spiritual marriage with the spirit Danbala (Murphy 1994:19). In *Island Possessed* (1969) Dunham describes the days she spent amassing the ingredients and gathering the special clothes, food, liquors, and lotions necessary for the ceremony, setting the mood of a special sacred space and time: "I began to feel in the personal care and effort in the choosing of each object, its 'mana,' its mystic power, as different from the object next to it—similar in appearance, but utterly profane and unmystic" (quoted in Murphy 1994:21). After the ingredients were collected, Joseph Murphy notes, Dunham was led off to isolation in the *djèvo* (a sanctuary room within the temple), together with eight other female novices, where they were

> confined to the floor on their sides, spoon fashion, for most of the three days and allowed only the most minimal movements. Every few hours the officiating manbo Téoline would appear in the doorway to shake her *ason* [rattle] and call "*ounsi lave tèt*, rise up and turn." Then the nine novitiates would merely roll over and fit themselves together on their opposite sides. They ate only unsalted sacrificial foods of their *mèt tèts* [spirits who own their heads], and could wash and relieve themselves only at morning and at night. (Murphy 1994:21, my brackets)

Dunham describes the physicality—not the religiosity—of that experience. For her, initiation appears to have been a social-physical-spiritual imprinting process rather than a cognitive learning process.

> Perhaps it was the physical need for some change, if only to turn over on the dirt floor and bring momentary relief from the cramp of our awkward positions. Perhaps the fasting, the incessant subdued drumming, the intermittent ring of the bell and the rattle of the ason, the smell of burning charcoal, fresh and dried blood and incense, the intoned instructions at our departing "selves" and entering "*loa*" [spirit] were gradually effecting hounci [priestesses] out of bosalle [bozales]. (Quoted in Murphy 1994:21, my brackets)

About her sensory deprivation, Dunham writes:

> Lying on the damp floor of the *houngfor* [temple] in a cold chill, probably because I had forgotten a supply of quinine, aching from heat to foot, I condemned all mysticism, all research, all curiosity in the ways or whys of other peoples, all "calls," all causes. . . . With aching knees tucked under the buttocks of the woman in front of me I even wished I was back in Chicago or in Jolie, which indicated a state of total eclipse. (Quoted in Murphy 1994:22)

But then, realizing the connection between altered awareness caused by physical deprivation and somatic learning, Dunham describes how, during breaks in the "flooring" stages of those three days, sacred knowledge was imparted to her that included esoteric salutations, the proper service to Danbala, its ceremonial clothing, foods, dances, and emblems, and the import of this spirit to her own personality (Murphy 1994:22–23). This learning was enhanced by actual contact with a novice in trance during the "flooring" periods, which Dunham suggestively describes as follows:

> The woman fitted into the curve of my lap began to tremble. Softly at first, so that it might have been a chill from the damp earth, then violently, so that all of us were jarred by her cataclysmic tremors and knew that her god had entered. To me it was a great relief because it meant that I could move, even stretch without attracting attention, without breaking that somber expectancy that we had lived in for twenty-four hours. (Quoted in Murphy 1994:23–24)

I would hardly have remembered what was said at the toque de santo had I not recorded it (however fragmented) in my field notes, but I cannot forget the worlds of meaning that were enacted throughout that afternoon. The sound of drums, the heat, the stickiness, and the sweetness of my encounter with Ochún: these were all part of an imagined intersubjective reality of Santería practitioners that I was able to taste with all of my senses (Stoller 1989b, 1997).[1]

Our bodies indeed remember. But as Marcel Mauss (1979 [1950]), Paul Connerton (1989), and others argue, their modes of remembering resemble more a branding, an imprinting, than a narrativized memory. Certain movements—such as those involved in riding a bike, dancing, crossing oneself, and spiritual cleansing—involve what Connerton identifies (1989) as "habit memory" and what athletes and scientists term "muscle memory," which, once acquired, is forever imprinted in one's body. Likewise, ritualized behaviors, possession, bodily trauma caused by illness, and (in a lesser degree) dreaming are all anchored in sensorial memory or the physicality of experience. Like the "primary processes" which Freud recognized (1994 [1911]) in dreaming, they belong primarily to a preverbal realm.

Relevant here is Bourdieu's observation (1990 [1980]:66–69) about *doxa*, which refers to "practical faith" or "practical belief" and is premised on individuals' "undisputed, pre-reflexive, naïve, native compliance" with the fundamental presuppositions of a field of social action. Doxa encompasses the quotidian "pre-verbal taken-for-granted reality of the world that flows from practical sense." Indeed, "Practical belief is not a 'state of mind,' still less a kind of arbitrary adherence to a set of instituted dogmas and doctrines ('beliefs'), but rather a state of the body" referred to also as "bodily hexis" and "permanent dispositions" (69, 70). Connerton puts it in simpler terms in his study about social memory (1989:4–5), when he suggests that social memory, easily accessed in commemorative events (since these are basically performative), depend on habit, which "cannot be thought without a notion of bodily automatisms." With this analytical model Connerton aims at contributing to what he identifies as a much-needed study of the "inertia" between the individual and social structure.

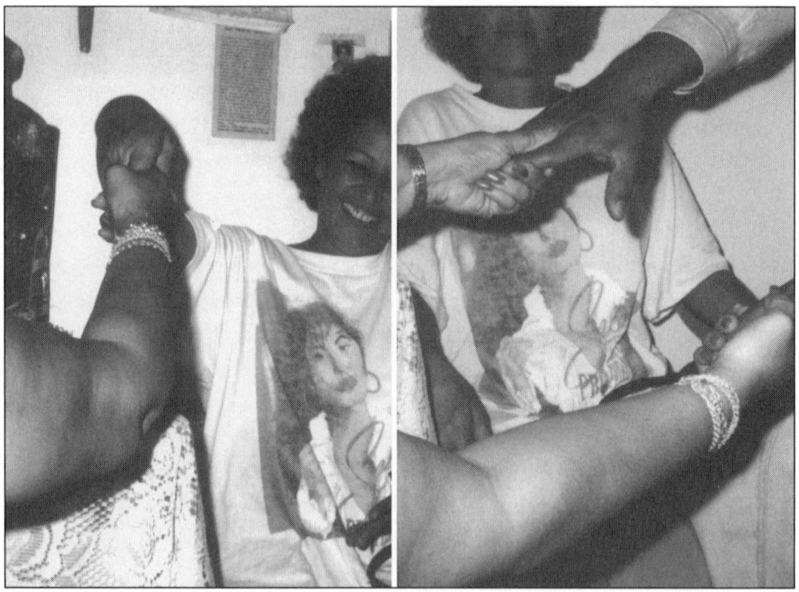

"Enacted beliefs."

Premised on the ideas that the body operates as a "living memory pad, an automaton that 'leads the mind unconsciously along with it,' and as a repository for the most precious values," Bourdieu proposes the notion of "enacted belief" as the par excellence form of what Leibniz identified in his *Opuscula philosophica selecta* as "blind or symbolic thought " (Leibniz quoted in Bourdieu 1990 [1980]:68). This form of unreflective thinking, Bourdieu continues, "is the product of quasi-bodily dispositions ... analogous to the rhythm of a line of verse whose words have been forgotten ... [or] the rules of thumb, which generate through transference countless practical metaphors" (68–69).

What Bourdieu suggests is that these linguistic and bodily dispositions (Connerton's "bodily automatisms") "function as depositories of deferred thoughts that can be triggered off at a distance in space and time by the simple effect of re-placing the body in an overall posture which *recalls* the associated thoughts and feelings, in one of the inductive states of the body which, as actors know, give rise to states of mind" (69; also see Halbwachs 1980, Stoller 1995). Often staged in great collective ceremonies, singing and dancing serve not only the purpose of giving a solemn representation of a group but also "the invisible intention of ordering thoughts and suggesting feelings through the rigorous marshalling of practices and the orderly disposition of bodies, in particular the bodily expression of emotion, in laughter or tears" (69). Bourdieu, of course, stresses the symbolic (and reproductive) power that arises from such social imprinting—of bodily dispositions and emotions—suggesting that the range of emotions triggered by these bodily dispositions may thereafter be controlled "either by neutralizing them or by reactivating them to function mimetically" (ibid.).

Transposed to ritual contexts, practical belief or bodily hexis would encompass those preverbal experiences inscribed during heightened events (such as initiation rituals or religious festivities) that have the power of eliciting emotions in an uncritical manner simply by means of a reactivation of certain bodily gestures and somatic predispositions (see Deren 1985; Rouch 1960, 1971; Stoller 1989b). Even though somatic predispositions usually stem from sets of transcendent beliefs (such as in particular cosmologies, eschatological myths, and ancestral beings), they are nonetheless experienced as second nature to practitioners. "The enemy of ritual is one who is incapable of or unwilling to voluntarily suspend disbelief—the spoilsport," according to Barbara Myerhoff (1977:199).

Religious gestures elicit religious beliefs. This is what Blaise Pascal (1623–1662) suggested in his well-known, controversial, pragmatic

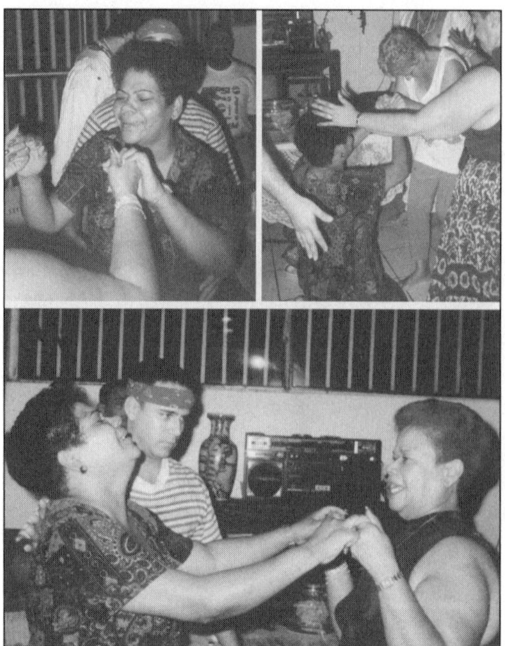

Bodily dispositions and enacted beliefs during a velada.

argument for believing in God.[2] By acting as though we believe, we end up believing, a phenomenon encapsulated in Pascal's famous dictum "Kneel down and you will believe!" In the section "Of the Means of Belief" (1901 [1670]), Pascal argues that the belief of the mind (reason) and of the heart (sentiment) will eventually follow the practical belief of the automaton (ritual, external).[3] "The external must be joined to the internal to obtain anything from God, that is to say, we must kneel, pray with the lips, etc., in order that proud man, who would not submit himself to God, may be now subject to the creature: To expect help from the externals is superstition; to refuse to join them is pride" (91). Pascal, explaining how custom together with reason shapes our beliefs, states:

> We must acquire an easier belief, which is that of habit. With no violence, art or argument it makes us believe things, and so inclines all our faculties to this belief that our soul falls naturally into it. When we believe only by the strength of our conviction and the automaton is inclined to believe the opposite, that is not enough. We must therefore make both parts of us believe: the mind by reasons, which need to be seen only once in a lifetime, and the automaton by habit, and not

> allowing it any inclination to the contrary: *Incline my heart*. (Pascal 1966 [1670]:274)

Secular Rituals (1977), a collection of essays edited by Sally Falk Moore and Barbara Myerhoff, proposes various ways in which previous anthropological understandings of religious rituals can be applied also to nonreligious situations, revolutionizing the way anthropologists approach everyday life interactions, political meetings, games, sports, parades, and festivals. What, they ask, are the social advantages and effects of ritualized—repetitive, formally structured—behaviors? To get at the issues of embodiment in ritual, I propose to reverse the analytical trajectory that informed *Secular Rituals*. Instead of drawing from religious rituals and making inferences about secular behaviors, I propose drawing upon those taken-for-granted, quotidian "bodily automatisms" (such as brushing one's teeth, opening a can, and so on) in order to shed light on religious gestures (such as those involved in spiritual cleansing). When acquired as permanent dispositions, spiritual gestures become forms of incorporated knowledge or bodily hexis; that is, they are experienced as second nature, "sensible," and judicious by practitioners. Even though these "bodily automatisms" are informed by complex religious beliefs, they actually escape any conscious reflection. And this is where I see their power. The question still pending, and which I cannot address here, is whether the efficacy of these gestures in not only symbolic but physical, perhaps also affecting the autonomic nervous system.[4]

For Pascal (1966 [1670]:154), the acquisition and reproduction of these somatic dispositions would explain why "the heart has its reasons of which reason knows nothing." In making a case for the belief in God for skeptics, Pascal insists on the nonrational nature of faith and compares it to self-love, asking, "Is it reason that makes you love yourself? It is the heart which perceives God and not the reason. That is what faith is: God perceived by the heart, not by the reason."

In line with this theological approach to belief—but from a sociological and historical (nontheological) perspective—Marcel Mauss, Michel Foucault, and Pierre Bourdieu (among others) have suggested that it is through elaborate sociocultural "techniques of the body" that human bodies become sentient social bodies. Bourdieu's life work has been invested in showing how the body and the processes of embodiment in complex societies are engaged in particular sociocultural fields such as the arts, education, and (most obviously) gender relations. In assessing how

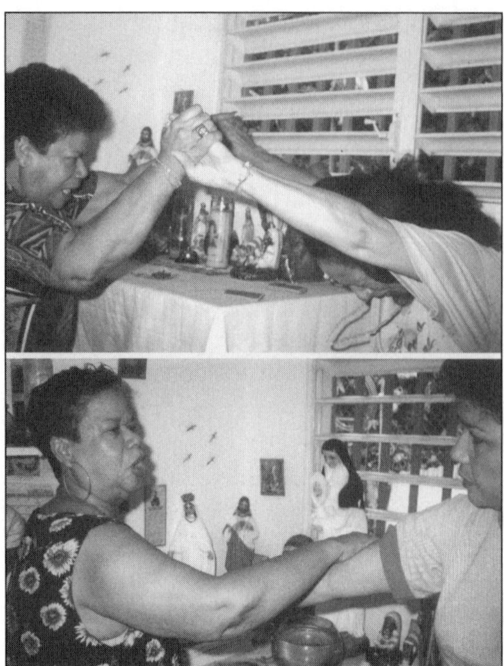

"Incorporated knowledge."

the body is engaged in the process of acquisition and reproduction of the habitus, Bourdieu distinguishes between practical mimesis and mere imitation:

> [T]he process of acquisition—a practical *mimesis* or mimeticism which implies an overall relation of identification and has nothing in common with an *imitation* that would presuppose a conscious effort to reproduce a gesture, an utterance or an object explicitly constituted as a model—and the process of reproduction—a practical reactivation which is opposed to both memory and knowledge—tend to take place below the level of consciousness, expression, and the reflexive distance which these presuppose. The body believes in what it plays at: it weeps if it mimes grief. (Bourdieu 1990 [1980]:73).

In the case of religion, Csordas suggests (1990), this kind of embodied knowledge is acquired through a host of somatic images that are inculcated as techniques of the body and dispositions. These somatic images "embody dispositions characteristic of the religious milieu" (20), which if changed will also effect a change in the techniques of the body. Csordas shows

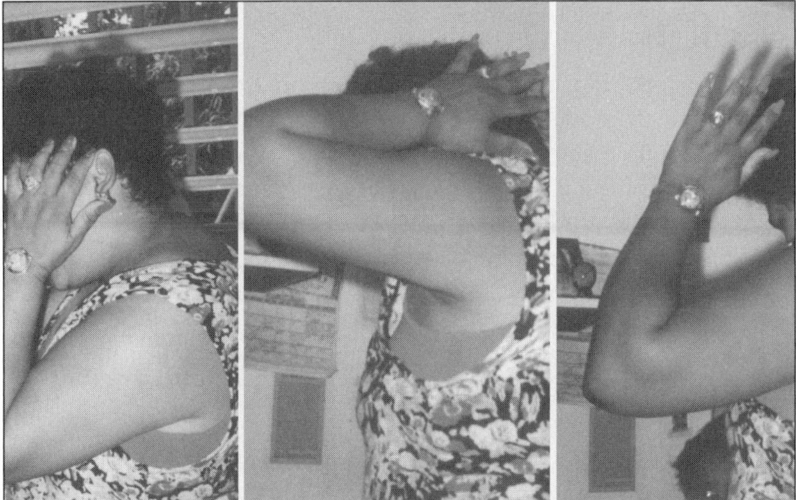

Habitus of possession.

that different techniques prevalent throughout the history of the Christian Charismatic movement, such as speaking in tongues (in the 1960s) and resting in the spirits (in the 1980s), reflect demographic changes; each technique "represents the embodiment in ritual practice of differences in generational and class habitus" (29).

At the toque de santo that afternoon in the summer of 1995, I did not need to *believe in* Ochún to experience her presence. The physicality of my encounter with her was primarily emotional and sensual (not cognitive), and (at least) for that moment, my body reacted to her *as if* I had believed in her. Perhaps this is what defines "embodiment" as an interpretive framework that paradigmatically distinguishes cognition from emotion (Csordas 1990:37, Crossley 2001). In Bourdieu's terms (1990 [1980]:73), the body "does not represent what it performs, it does not memorize the past, it *enacts* the past, bringing it back to life."

Somatic Imagination

Certain traditional theater genres, such as Chinese opera, are based on the development of specific plots that depend on archetypal (social and mythical) characters that enact, rather than represent, their physical and moral attributes on stage. The Beijing Opera, dating from approximately the twelfth century, synthesizes music, drama, dance, and acrobatics performed in very elaborate costumes and with a minimum of props. Similarly to religious practices such as Santería, Vodou, and Candomblé in which deities possess devotees, each character in a Chinese opera is identified by a specific dress, color, gesture, mood, demeanor, personality, tone of voice, and moral attitude. And there are as numerous regional variations as there are dialects (*Travel in Taiwan* 1995).[5]

In the documentary film *Beijing Opera* (Quiquemelle 2003), one can see how actors are chosen at very early ages—regardless of their gender—according to their innate physical and spiritual dispositions to specialize in one of the four principal types of roles: *sheng* (male), *tan* (or *dan*, female), *ching* (or *jing*, painted-face singers, warriors, and demons), and *chou* (clowns), all of which are subdivided into a variety of characters.[6] As a result of years of training, their bodies acquire the dispositions of the characters they enact on stage; that is, the gestures, pitch of voice, and attitude of the character become second nature to an actor, who will typically enact the same character in different plots.[7] One could say, especially due to the training of these actors, that they *become* the characters themselves.

The apparent affinity of this theatrical genre with possession religions suggests its connection (actual or coincidental) to religion as much as to the arts.[8] Similarly, one can say that the spirits and deities in the Spiritist pantheon (as well as in Santería, Candomblé, and Vodou) have personalities and are in charge of cosmic powers that correspond to ways of being and dispositions, which are adopted and enacted by possessed mediums or their initiated children. Members in a community of practitioners not only might be able to identify these typical gestures with a deity that is possessing a medium but also might show signs of being intrinsically affected and moved by them. Like the typified movements and speech of the Chinese opera characters, the particular dispositions of each orisha or spirit become imprinted in the bodies of initiates and in the somatic imagination of practitioners, eliciting prereflexive spiritual effects among them.

Is it possible that the enactment of the various characters of the Beijing opera on the stage elicit—as in Santería, for example—their spiritual presence? If so, is it with the essence of these traditional characters, not with their mere representation on stage, that local audiences engage during the performance? Are actors actually *possessed* by these characters, or are they simply bringing them to life, impersonating them, at each performance?

Ethnomusicologist Katherine Hagedorn raises similar issues in her book *Divine Utterances* (2001:116–117) when she refers to the blurring of folkloric performances representing Santería toques de santo (like the one in which I participated) on stage. She argues that the corporeal memory of sacred utterances such as singing, drumming, dancing, and praising

> might imbue a secular folkloric performance with possible sacredness. . . . In fact, the primary goal of a mimetic folkloric performance seems to be the resurrection of potential (if not actual) sacredness during the circumscribed length of the sacred performance. The dancers, singers, and drummers labor to recreate a bit of the magic that exists in a "real" toque de santo. . . . But the performers cannot control the effects of their divinely inspired utterances on the audience. This re-created magic often evokes spirit possession among the faithful, even when the context and the intent of the performance are apparently secular.

Similar blurring of boundaries between performance and possession has been widely recognized by practitioners in various possession religions. In Songhay, "fake" possession is highly problematic. Within Santería, on the other hand, the characterization made by several santeros interviewed by Lydia Cabrera (1975) in the 1930s seems less harsh; they referred to "exaggerated" possession as "santicos." I myself have overheard mediums being judged (and slightly dismissed) based upon the degree of "appropriateness" (rather than truthfulness) of their particular mode of possession, a recurring topic of conversation and gossip among practitioners today. Yet, no resolution or final verdict seems to ever be expected. Instead, the indulgence in such speech among practitioners seems to be aimed just at reflecting and maintaining an apparently intrinsic wariness about the boundary between belief and skepticism at large and truthful or appropriate and fake or exaggerated possession in particular (reflected also in Eco's incisive depiction of Amparo's reticence and the German woman's inability to become possessed during the Umbanda ceremony in Rio de Janeiro).

Spiritual Gestures

One of the most visible and typical techniques of the body found in espiritismo and other Afro-Latin religions such as Santería and Vodou that is repeatedly enacted during veladas, rituals, and public and private consultations pertains to the cleansing of the spirit; cross-cultural similarities of these gestures are too extensive to mention here. Cleansing of the spirit consists mainly of a wrapping movement that one can perform for oneself or others in which arms encircle the body from head to toe in a manner that signifies the gathering of negative energies assumed to be lodging in it. This wrapping movement or gathering then turns into shaking-off and throwing-out gestures that signify the shedding of the negativity that is assumed to have lodged in a person's body. Usually it involves shaking this negativity out through the hands and fingers over a fuente, as if depositing it there, or simply in the air, away from the body. But not all spiritual cleansings take this form.

Ken, a Nuyorican healer now residing in Puerto Rico, was raised within espiritismo; but while living on the mainland he had been initiated also in various Native American and Asian healing traditions. At various veladas of espiritistas-brujos we attended together, I saw him participate in collective cleansings. His cleansing gestures, however, were slightly different from those of other espiritistas-brujos. "I use small brooms to cleanse the aura of people, to gather the negativity of their spirit, and then dispose of it similarly to what espiritistas-brujos do," he explained. "But it does not make any difference whether you use brooms or your hands—the intention and effect are the same."

As far as I can venture based on my knowledge, almost every Puerto Rican is familiar with espiritista ways of cleansing oneself. As a learned disposition acquired actively or vicariously during rituals, the gestures involved in cleansings are part of a collectively shared, embodied knowledge that allows for their enactment in ritual events or at least informs their recognition when performed by others. When Fanny, a longtime client

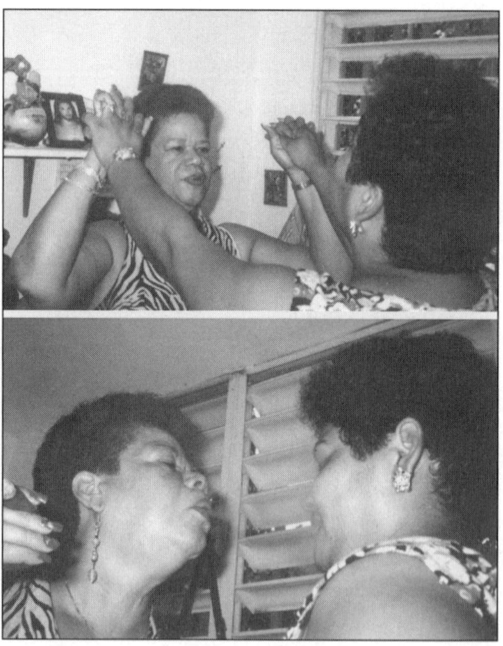

Reina being empowered and cleansed by the Indio.

of about forty, heard Haydée banging on the table in the course of her divination session, she must have understood not only that what would follow was a dictate from the spirits for her but also that she would know what to do when she heard "*¡Sacúdete, despójate y pásalo!* [Shake yourself, cleanse yourself, and pass your cuadro on!].[9] You have to cleanse yourself here, Mama [endearing term]. This water [in the fuente] is clean. Cleanse yourself here. Cleanse yourself and pass it!" Indeed, without a word, Fanny stood up and began waving her arms over her head and encircling her body from head to toe. After performing a few cleansing gestures ending with her hands in the fuente, Fanny unsuccessfully attempted to pass her cuadro.

The divination session went on. And as Haydée kept revealing painful and worrisome aspects of her client's life, Fanny started crying. Haydée stopped her divination. *Y no me llores que me cortas* (And don't cry because you cut me off, she reprimanded, meaning that Fanny's crying would bring to a halt the ongoing deliverance of the spirit-inspired divination

¡Sacúdete, despójate y pásalo!

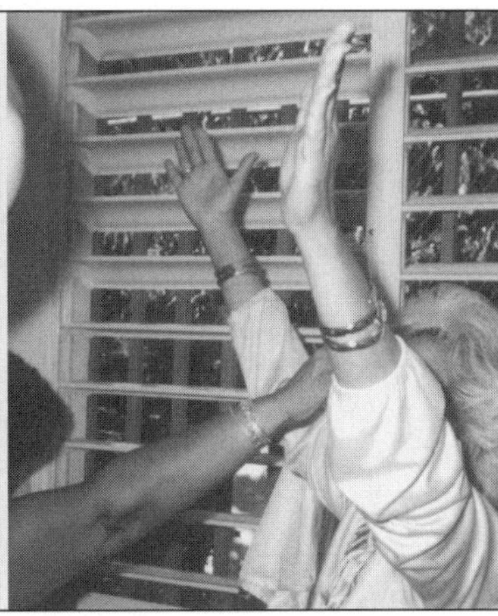

messages for her. As on many other occasions during divination, Haydée ordered Fanny not to cross her hands (*No me cruces las manos*) because she would thereby cut her off (*que me cortas*). Apparently, certain gestures such as crossing one's legs or arms suggest (semantically and iconically) the cross, which—by recourse to its historic-folkloric uses—has been invoked for centuries as an overall shield meant to protect oneself from dangers of all sorts, particularly those arising from contact with the dead and from possession.

Poses That "Do"

One of the most memorable self-revealing times I shared with Haydée was our looking together at the album of photos I took of her, a reflexive experience comparable only to our listening to the tapes I had recorded of her work. Certain photos attracted her attention more than others and were the objects of extensive comments, which she often shared not just with me but also with her friends, kin, and select clients. When Armando came for the first time to Haydée's home after they decided to work together, one of the first things she did after greeting him was to show him the photo albums of her at work that I had helped her put together. Observing him closely as he was looking at these photos again and again, studying them in detail, she wondered aloud with a sense of false modesty, "You're looking [at the photos] 'up and down, down and up.' . . . Why?" In this context, it was a remark about what appeared to be his fascination with the photos and, by extension, her work and implicit fame—not every bruja has an anthropologist documenting her work in such detail.

Further, within brujería practices, there is a magic significance to the visual trajectory drawn by the eyes (especially those of powerful brujos) as they gaze at something or somebody. This is the power mentioned by Tonio of "tying" the object of their gaze to their own will. The power of the gaze to assert, to make happen—not unlike the performative utterances Austin discusses—is recognized by brujos and finds ample expression in Puerto Rican popular culture. Songs, jokes, and proverbs recognize this magic power of the gaze effected by means of fixing one's eyes on a desired person, which ties this person emotionally (even against his or her own will) to the owner of the gaze.

As Armando was flipping through Haydée's photo album, he stopped for a few minutes at a photo in which Haydée is posing on the porch holding La Caridad. Noticing this, Haydée asked him, "What do you say?" Without waiting for an answer, she continued, "Look at the firmness with which I am securing that Santa there on the porch; I am holding her

"Look . . . I am holding her by the crown!"

by the crown!" I remember that when Haydée posed for that photo, she clearly was intending to fix—by means of the magic of gesture and the technology of reproduction—a sacred moment of commemoration: the spiritual bond between her patron saint, La Caridad, and herself. The way she held the figurine of her patron saint in more than a dozen photos I shot of her in subsequent months varied only slightly. These photos, taken over the course of a year, parallel iconically her discursive devotion to La Caridad, best illustrated in the opening and closing prayers she performed every day before and after her daily consultations.

Along with the care Haydée took in posing for photos, she also paid unusually careful attention to arranging the way another healer embraced her or held her hands. Standing physically above the level of another brujo conjures an overpowering standing in the spiritual realm and submission for the one positioned beneath the other. Even when performed unintentionally, brujos are aware of the magic effect of what for anyone other than a brujo may seem innocuous gestures. Whenever another healer happened to be standing next to her while she was seated and tried—in this position—to stroke her head or shoulders in a friendly embrace, she would make an effort to stand up and only then allow the other healer to lay a hand on her. It became evident after such occurrences that the physical location of one brujo vis-à-vis another carries an utmost mimetic meaning within the field of magic.

Consider the dream Haydée had about me. When she narrated it, she insisted on being precise in describing how I held her hands, cupping them in mine, a symbol of protection and nurturing. While working with Armando, Haydée made sure on numerous occasions that he did not cover her hands, not even when handing objects to her, in order to avoid positioning herself in a spiritually submissive level. To avoid this at all cost, she sometimes would reverse a spontaneous, natural movement, performing one that instead appeared quite contrived and unnatural. On one occasion, Haydée changed the direction of what appeared to me to be an innocuous movement: when Armando was about *to hand her* a velón, she ordered him to hold it instead in order for her *to take it* from his hands.

Other ordinary gestures that would go unnoticed by outsiders might well carry significant magical meaning among brujos. While dancing with Armando one morning to the sounds of música santera to get spiritually ready before consultations, Haydée intentionally wagged her skirt over him—while winking to me—to assert that her mediumship was more powerful than his, as well as to magically control his will—a gesture that I am sure did not escape him. To waggle (*sacudir*), to bind (*ligar*), and to blow (*soplar*) are actions that have magical significance derived from their use in the making of trabajos. Thus sacudir means to cause harm (when something is jiggled); ligar, to hold and control the will of another person (when staring at a person); and soplar, to bewitch (when magic powders are blown). Note Tonio's comment about the bruja who billowed her red-and-white dress over a man to bewitch him and the expression *te menean el cacharro* (someone is wobbling your pot) to signify that magic has been performed by mixing potions in a cauldron. If one is anxious and distressed but cannot identify the cause, people might say, *Te están meneando el cacharro*, to suggest that somebody could be stirring potions in a cauldron to bewitch the person, causing his or her emotional imbalance. To cover, to shield, and to wrap (arropar), however, are movements that signify the healing protection of saints and other enlightened ancestor spirits unless they are performed with the intention of dominating others without causing them harm.

Evidence of their intertextual spiritual significance as well as historical precedence since the colonization of Puerto Rico, these various symbolic movements are widely referenced in folk narratives, folk songs, and proverbs, typically conveying (in serious and comedic tones alike) the centrality of love-producing and other magic works in the popular imagination. A common onomatopoeic word for the act of blowing magic powders, *fufú*, stands for bewitchment. The first time I heard this word I was at the

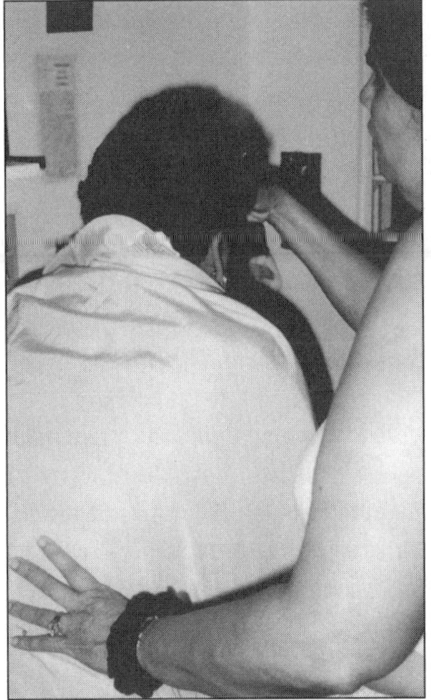
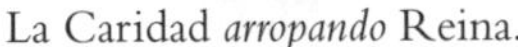

La Caridad *arropando* Reina.

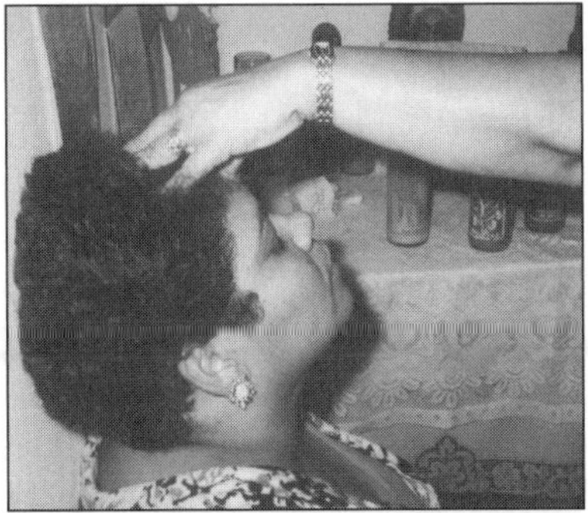

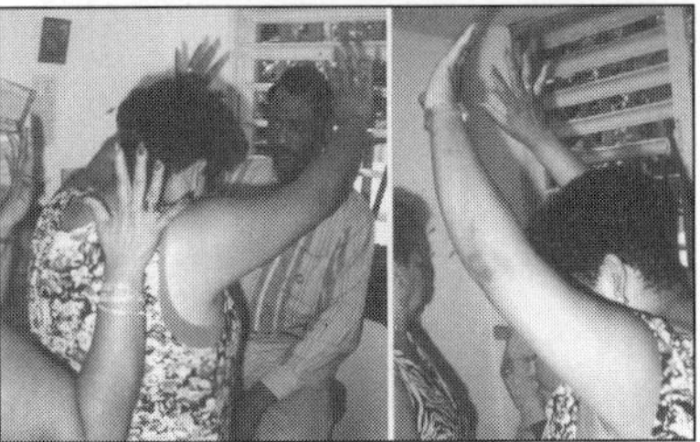

Haydée transferring positive energies and protecting Reina's materia.

National Archive, where a very friendly researcher said—upon learning I was searching for documents about witchcraft accusations and trials—"Beware of a fufú popping up for you" (*A ver si le sale un fufú*). To a client wanting someone to fall in love with him or her, a brujo may suggest: "Do you want to have so-and-so fastened to you?" In such a trabajo the brujo literally straps together two figures to represent joining the client to the object of the client's desire. Similarly, *ligar* (to bind by means of fixing one's eyes on a person) means to control or to be tied to another person in such a way that the desired person feels an inexplicable attraction for the one who is gazing at him or her. On the radio, I heard once an anchor jokingly use this word for commenting critically on the recently imported bourgeois bodybuilding craze, particularly pervasive among yuppies in Puerto Rico. Implying that the apparent Americanization of Puerto Rico cannot erase ingrained Puerto Rican folk beliefs, he told of a man who, rather than paying for his apparently very attractive wife's membership at a local gym, purchased some widely advertised, very expensive home-gym equipment, maxing out his credit card so that "she wouldn't have to join the local gym and risk having somebody fix their eyes on her (*ligarla*) as she exercised."

There is a spiritual rhetoric to gestures. Certain gestures plead, others invoke and summon, and still others assert and establish. As performatives, spiritual gestures not only invite, persuade, or mark and certify but also become offerings and signs of recognition. Holding arms up high might both index and summon a spiritual bond. Of course, the boundaries are very subtle; particular situations define whether gestures are meant to commemorate or invite deeds. As with icons, they often encapsulate complex messages. For example, when brujos cross their hearts they signify both their humility as healers and their submission to the spirits. Gestures actually "do." They afford complex ways of communicating with the living and the spirits.

Indeed, something I learned to recognize very early on was a language (a *parole*) of gestures through which healers speak and communicate with the living and the spirits. When I accompanied Haydée, her son, and several friends on a private pilgrimage to a Marian chapel at a mountaintop in Juana Díaz, Haydée insisted on being photographed with some babies. It was as if she were recreating an image she had of the Virgin with the Child that she wished to emulate as a symbol of the sacredness of her pilgrimage.

One could obviously speculate about the centrality of gestures among brujos in relation to the long-held iconographic centrality of the colonial proselytizing project, discussed earlier (Augé 1999, Cole 1989, Consentino

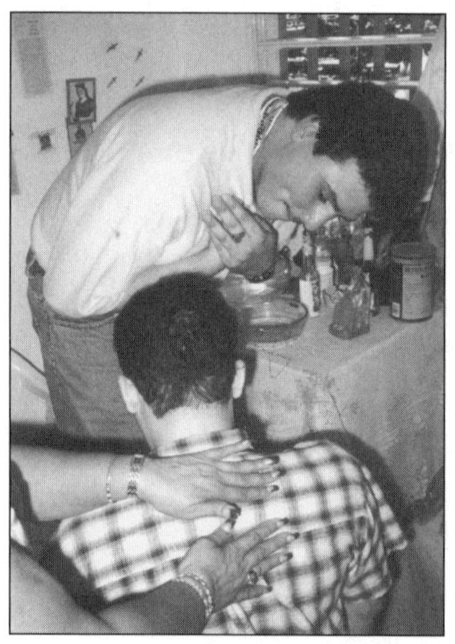

Armando manifesting his humility and submission to the spirits.

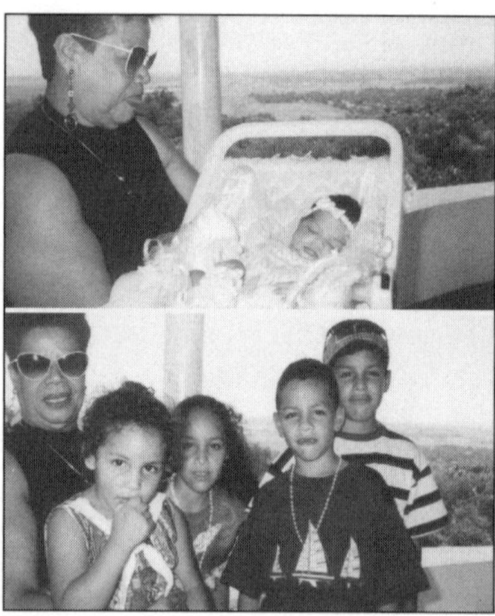

Haydée manifesting the sacredness of her pilgrimage.

1995, Gruzinski 1990, Taussig 1987, Rouch 1960). Religious iconography both represented and interpreted sacred passages in the gospel, adding to them images of collective and individual sources. Artists represented these in the local visual imagery: chubby, hovering angels with facial expressions, body postures, and elements of dress, architecture, and landscape characteristic of the folk imaginary.

A parallel could be drawn with the ways in which Catholic iconography and hagiography were incorporated, recreated, and creatively remade by brujos since colonization. Elsewhere (Romberg 2003b) I show the parallel between the way in which colonial Catholic miracles and visions were institutionalized as a mark of the godly civilizational, sacred stature of the founding of new towns and churches in the colonies and the way brujos have since included these visionary experiences in establishing the legitimacy of their healing and magic. Composing one of the layers of their practice, the enduring rapture of that mystical world keeps reappearing in new forms and faces through a process or creolization or "ritual piracy" (Romberg 2005b), giving new spiritual meaning to the current realities and aspirations of capitalist modernity.

Colors and Styles That "Do"

The way people dress, the colors they choose, and the activities they enjoy reflect their personalities while also revealing the kinds of protecciones or guardian spirits they have. When a young woman, Marta, came to consult with Haydée, one of the first comments she heard was about her sloppy way of dressing. Implying that this was an indication that Marta was sad and depressed, Haydée told her,

> Your mother is not here anymore, and your father might not be present at your wedding. In spirit, however, they'll accompany you. You love your father so much. . . . You're afraid he'll not be at your wedding. All of us have to die, but others *have to live*. I'll give you a son who will reincarnate your father. You ask yourself, "How could I stand the death of my mother and [eventually] my father?" She's dead for six years now. Remember that when God claims (*reclama*), demands, you go, you go. . . . Your mother used to love this [spiritual work]. I see her with long skirts, dancing, dancing. The day you feel like this, do it; you will be liberated.

Even though Haydée never knew Marta's mother, she apparently felt her cheerful spiritual presence and contrasted it with Marta's gloomy personality.

Following the logic of protecciones and possession, if Marta would allow her own dead mother's benevolent and cheerful spiritual force to lodge and manifest itself in her own body, it would free her. Paradoxically, freeing this force—that is, allowing it to manifest through its typical behaviors (dancing)—Marta would be letting the healing force of her mother's spirit effect its restoring influence—and hence liberate her.

Carina, a teacher in her mid-forties, received similar advice when she came to consult with Haydée. Although she had come to solve work-related problems, these were soon identified as less important than problems she had with her second husband, the mother of her first husband, and her son from the first husband. Haydée began the divining process by stating: "You have a beautiful cuadro. Why haven't you developed it? In the next velada I'll have some people develop theirs [and you can develop yours]." Continuing the process, Haydée asked, out of the blue, "Why is your hairdo like this? I don't like you with this hairdo." And while Haydée opened up Carina's ponytail and rearranged her hair on the sides, she added (relinquishing the intention of this action to the spirits—as on many other occasions), "It's not me. I'm being led to do this." (When I saw Haydée do this, I remembered how my own hair had been released at the toque and the sensation I felt when Ochún opened the tight bun I had my hair in and what that act meant to me in that ritual context.)

"You are new to this area, right?" Haydée said while welcoming a beautiful young woman to her altar for the first time. "Who's Evelyn? You

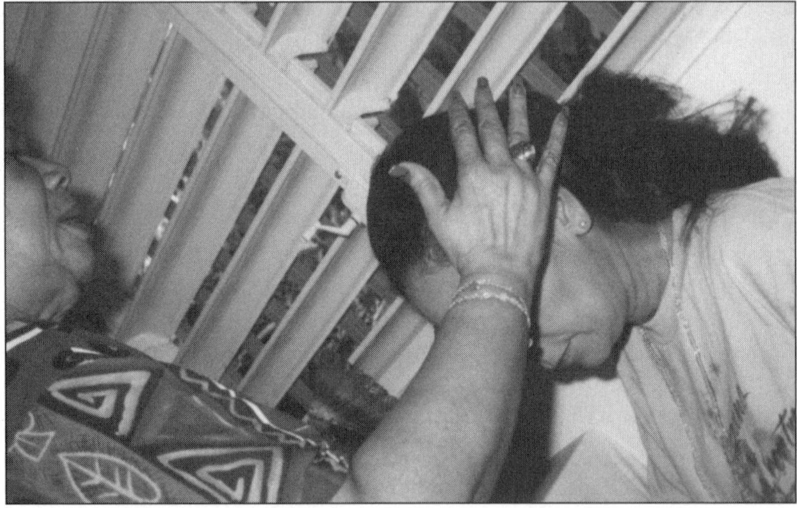

"It's not me. I'm being led to do this."

are not married, but you're not a señorita. All those who get close to you leave. I speak everything I see here. You are nineteen, and you're afraid of remaining single. Why is it that the bewitchment that had been sent to your mother got picked up by you? You are not to blame." Shifting slightly the tone of the divination, Haydée asked her inquisitively, "Why do you so much like wearing red clothes? Don't wear them! Santa Bárbara doesn't let men get close to you. Make sure you don't wear red clothes."

A few months earlier I had heard Haydée comment on my own style of dressing. She asked me why I was always dressed in black, brown, and other dark colors. Coming from an East Coast academic milieu, I thought I was following a fashionable dress code. But Haydée was thinking about other sources of my choice. She told me I should wear bright colors and wear big hoop earrings because I had a *gitana* (Gypsy) within me. On the first opportunity I had, I bought myself a pair of bright-green, high-heeled sandals (under her influence, of course) and a few sets of brilliantly colored clothing. If indeed the colors we wear reflect our energies—revealing the protecciones who "own our heads"—my initial university-style dress was read as reflecting not simply an urban style of dress but rather a somber, troubled spirit that hindered a cheerful, lively gitana spirit from manifesting itself in me.

Ken, the Nuyorican healer I mentioned above, also commented on the colors I wore. The colors we choose to wear (in general and on particular days) both reflect and affect our aura, he explained. He advised me to begin wearing bright-colored underwear as well, for the closer to one's body the colors are, the more effective their influence is. Doing so would balance what he considered were the overly intensified vibrations of my head *chakras*. He explained that chakras, or energy points, in our bodies emanate certain waves of varying vibration that correspond to each color of the rainbow. When the vibrations of our chakras (the intensity of their colors) fall out of balance, particular colors—if worn close to those out-of-balance chakras—may raise their vibrations and help adjust the balance among them, thereby restoring harmony to our energies. Santería healers have a different explanation while also being very much attuned to the energetic value of colors in summoning their guardian spirits or orishas. When I saw Mauro wearing a red cap during one of my visits, I asked him why he was not wearing his usual white cap—the one I had seen him wearing several times during rituals. Nonchalantly, he explained to me that he wore it for protection while stripping an electric cable: "This red cap belongs to my santo. I also sleep with it."

Gradually over the months of my fieldwork I became increasingly sensitive to the spiritual meaning of colors and their correspondences with bodily functions, cosmic energies, moods, and of course the orishas and santos (prevalent in West African religions and their creole reworkings in the Afro-Americas). These correspondences pertained to ancient cosmologies that had been completely foreign to my upbringing, so much so that on my short visits home I carried back with me this new, second-nature attentive sensitivity to colors and their spiritual influence, which amazed my family.

Choosing an adequate gift for Haydée on my trips back to Puerto Rico, there was no doubt in my mind that it had to be golden or yellow and surely luxurious and fancy. (I felt by that time that colors, plants, and any number of other elements correspond to our protecciones and our personalities.) One such time, I wanted to buy her a piece of jewelry. A particular bulky, elaborately inlaid, amber-studded silver ring stood out among other less attractive ones at a local jewelry store—it was perfect. Not only was amber Ochún's favorite color, but also the ring's extravagant design felt just right for her. Though very tempted to buy it, I had already spent quite a big sum for an impressive golden-sequined nightgown for her. Realizing I could not afford the ring, I looked around for another, less expensive one. At the point when I almost desisted—some rings had just a tiny amber, others none, and so on—I saw a silver ring with a turquoise stone delicately placed in the center of a unique inlay of Native American motifs. The Indio, one of the entities of Haydée's cuadro, came instantly to mind. I interpreted that as a sign that the ring was "meant" for her—that she needed the Indio in her life.

Upon my return to the Island I gave her the dress and the ring, accompanied by the anecdote about its purchase and my vision. She loved both gifts and wore the ring immediately on the pinkie finger of her left hand as an amulet, "not taking it off, not even to bathe." After a few weeks, however, while Haydée was in the middle of performing a trabajo in her altar, I noticed she was not wearing the ring. When I later asked why, Haydée responded: "Ochún took it yesterday when I went to the shore to cleanse myself." She then mimicked the gesture she had made at the shore. Encircling her body and head with her arms, she enacted the moment when her hands tossed away the negativity that was lingering in her body. With that very movement the day before, she had "accidentally" hurled the ring off her finger and into the sea—the abode of Ochún. Since, as the espiritista adage imparts, "There's no coincidence, only causality," the ring was meant to be given to Ochún as an offering: "Ochún claimed that ring. It was my gift for her for helping me get rid of my pain. I was very sad yesterday, but she cleansed my tears."

The Magic of Representation

I realize that even now, years after I first saw Haydée manipulate photos for making trabajos, I cannot tear poor-quality photos of people I love before disposing of them. It is as if I do not want to trigger, even unwittingly, any tragic sequence of events that might hurt, via the laws of invisible magic correspondences, someone I love. Although I rationally "know" that it cannot happen, I still cannot do it, reminding me of what Stoller identifies as "embodied rationality" (1998). At the risk of appearing to be a "superstitious" anthropologist, even disposing of blurred photos in one piece is hard for me, though easier because I do not rip them apart. Apparently, tearing an image has become—after working with brujos—unbearable to me. The same is true with laying down photos of people I love upside down even for the few seconds it takes me to place them in picture frames or albums: I just will not do it.

Tied by Mimetic Somatic Reactions

A mother and her two young married daughters came to consult together. At one point, interrupting the reading of cards for the mother, Haydée complained, "I have nausea. Which of you here is pregnant?" The mother, whose age was clearly well above the fertility limit, smiled matter-of-factly: "Not me!" The two daughters simply looked at each other, shrugged their shoulders, and waited for Haydée to continue. After a half-hour of divination, Haydée, again referencing her own somatic reactions to these clients, asked, "Which one of you has a headache? I didn't have one, but my face feels fatigued now." One of the daughters revealed she was suffering from a headache; in a subsequent visit, the other daughter confirmed she had found out that she was pregnant. As on this occasion, many other times I have heard healers complain about the often painful somatic reactions they experience as a result of their material as well as spiritual identification with their clients—an identification that indexes their gifts and sacrifices as healers.

What should be clear at this point is that somatic modes of attention depend on a cultural-interpretive framework that assigns definite meanings to sensations that emerge in exchange with objects in the world. Not every time Haydée feels a headache or some pain is it sensed as a client's ache or pain. When, then, is a pain just a pain—and when a symbol of another person's causa? Here it is useful to draw again on Csordas' notion of "somatic modes of attention," whereby he proposes "to understand revelatory phenomena as forms of imagination" (1993:147). Yet, in contrast to current scholarship, which discusses "imagination" almost exclusively in terms of visual imagery (and by extension, as "mental" imagery), Csordas suggests a phenomenological conception of imagination (following Merleau-Ponty) based on a "*bodily synthesis* . . . characteristic of a human consciousness that projects itself into a cultural world" (148, my emphasis). This bodily synthesis depends upon a specific cultural imaginary—in Haydée's case one composed of sets of spiritual beings and etiological explanations of misfortune and healing—without which the tingling reported by healers would equal the tingling of an arm after it has not moved for some time. In making this distinction, Csordas asserts the indeterminacy of our existence and perceptions, in line with Merleau-Ponty, who "objected to conceiving perception as an intellectual act of grasping external stimuli produced by pregiven objects. Instead, he argued that the perceptual synthesis of the object is accomplished by the subject, which is the body as a field of perception and practice" (148–149). By collapsing the subject-object duality, Merleau-Ponty asks more precisely "how attention and other reflective processes of the intellect constitute cultural objects" (in Csordas 1993:149).

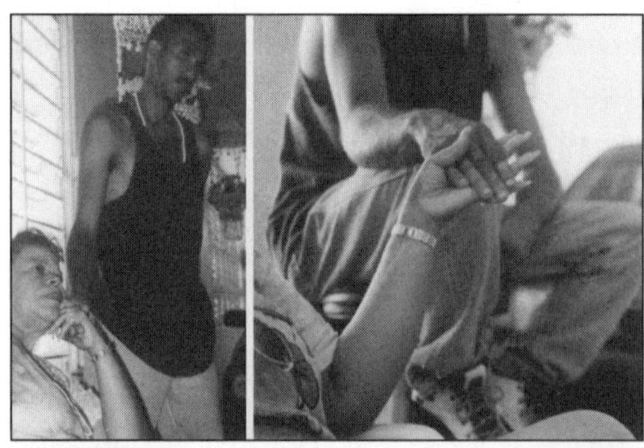

Haydée in spiritual communion with a client while Reina "catches" his causa.

How to understand this mimetic somatization from an experiential perspective? Somatizing or imagining with their bodies what their clients feel is indeed one of the ways brujos are able to reveal the nature of their clients' misfortunes. That is, as a conduit for elucidation, the healer's body mediates between the overall misfortunes attacking their clients and the causas that have caused them, as well as between the causas and their resolution.

Being possessed by evil spirits and muertos that have been sent to harm their clients is an unmistakably extreme form of somatic mimesis and sacrifice by proxy on the part of brujos, by means of which the healer's body intercedes in order to restore the well-being of the victim. A milder form of intervention no less motivated by sacrifice comes about when a healer senses in his or her body the exact pain and location produced by a bewitchment that had been intended for a client. Acting as a sensor or red light, the healer's body indicates that something—in the form of a cleansing or a retaliatory trabajo—must be done to restore the victim's lost harmony.

While reading the cards for Yolanda, a teacher, Haydée held her own throat gently and asked, "Do you have a sore throat? This is a causa, you know. Do you shake [cleanse] yourself?" Later Haydée insinuated that Yolanda's

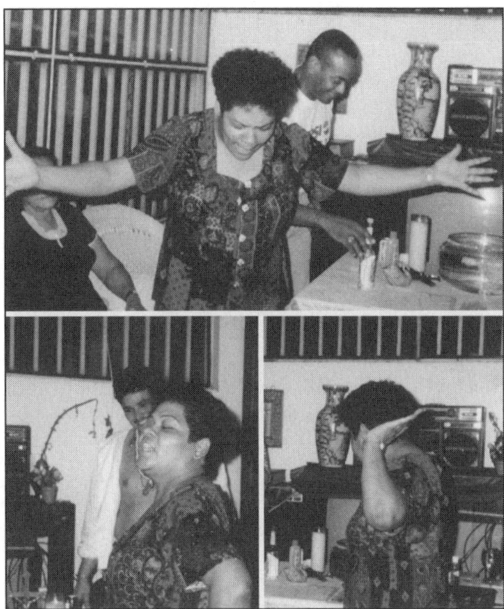

Reina "catching" a causa at a velada for one of its participants.

ex-husband's family was to blame for Yolanda's causa, which Haydée had felt in her own body. To begin solving this causa, Haydée revealed that the source had to be sought in Yolanda's ex-husband's family: "Your son's mind has been poisoned in his grandmother's house; he has tried to disrespect him [his stepfather]. He told him, 'You're not my father.' . . . I see a court problem." First, Haydée's throat ached, mirroring her client's ache, which then opened up the possibility to solve the causa that had triggered it.

This was also the case with Maite, a woman in her mid-twenties who was unable to carry a pregnancy to term for a couple of years, having suffered several miscarriages. Finally she was able to carry a pregnancy to term with the help of Haydée, who spiritually and physically "prepared" Maite's uterus by means of special *ponches* (fruity mixtures) that she prescribed for her to drink during several weeks. These helped Maite conceive and, most importantly, "hold onto" the baby. It was during these first critical weeks after the apparent conception that Maite came to see Haydée. But even before Maite had a chance to speak or tell her why she had come, Haydée vehemently insisted that she "calm down," though Maite manifested no disturbance at all. I soon understood why. The minute she saw Maite, Haydée said, "I feel an anxiety and alarm that is not mine"—an indication that it was caused directly by Maite's state of mind. "Maite, calm yourself, don't get out of control. Whatever you saw or felt will pass as it came. So your blood will not descend; it's been fourteen days now that you have conceived. That baby girl will be [spiritually] mine . . . and she's coming with blessings."

When healers and clients become connected by means of somatic mimesis, the bodies of brujos react as sensors and mirrors of their clients' pain, which—in addition to the cards used in divination—function as instruments of divination, for they materialize (*plasman*) the invisible world of the spirits. For instance, in consultation with Dania, another woman in her mid-twenties, Haydée began the session by stating, "You are not working yet—you haven't gotten a job yet, right? And what about the woman who was driving you crazy?" And then, while her upper body trembled, Haydée cried, "Uy, I have chills! Your leg hurts you, right? This is how I felt it, like an electric shock [*correntazo*]—like an electric flow that kicks you backwards. This is how you feel? How long have you felt this way?" The client asserted she had felt paralyzed for no apparent reason over the previous few days, and this was what had brought her to consult in the first place.

A different kind of bond that brujos often reference is the one they purposely establish with needy clients to help them by means of transmitting their power and bendiciones to them. At the end of a consultation with a young woman who was suffering because, among other problems, her boyfriend had stopped calling her, Haydée said, "Call him. You're afraid that he'll reproach you, aren't you? You're going home with *my* influences [spiritual power]. Call him today. He'll answer with love and tell you something you want to hear." When clients, however, resist the establishment of this somatic bond, brujos may well sense it and disarm them by saying, for instance, "You're fleeing from me. I'm a bruja and see beyond [your aloofness]."

The somatic bond established between healers and clients is paralleled by the one between healers and spirits—the latter also manifested in bodily sensations such as currents running through the torso or by an unusual rise in body temperature. During a consultation with a married woman, Haydée revealed that the client was having not one but several simultaneous love affairs:

> Do you want to kick your husband out? You've been crying a lot because you don't know what to do. You don't want to leave your husband because of the children, but you have to decide. Or are you going to play with fire? You husband hasn't realized it yet, right? Be careful that he doesn't hire a detective to tail you. . . . But there's another man after you. . . . Do you want to go off [with him]? Is there a man among the scandalmongers?

The woman quietly nodded; indeed, she was considering leaving her husband for another man—but she had not yet decided with which one of the two. Just when the details of this woman's complicated extramarital relationships seemed unable to get more entangled than they were, Haydée reacted gravely, suggesting to the woman that imminent dangers were lingering over her due to her irresponsible behavior—letting neighbors see her lovers picking her up, for example—unless she did something about it, both materially and spiritually.

Haydée looked extremely upset and worried for her client. Visibly flustered, Haydée nervously stroked her forehead and cheeks a couple of times in what seemed to me an awkward manner. Seeing my reaction, she explained, "When I pat my face like this, it is a sign that I have the spirits mounted on me." The stroking was a response to the sudden change of body temperature she felt, a somatic reaction to the spirits "mounting" her. This in turn was a sign that the clients' problems were acute and needed immediate, forceful intervention. Immediately after she acknowledged that the spirits mounted her, Haydée began reciting a recipe for a trabajo, which

(I learned later) was meant to guard this woman from an imminent tragedy. For each ingredient she enunciated—such as, "I want you to bring me two bottles of benzene; I need to you to bring pins"—she energetically tapped on the table, as I had seen her do on other occasions when the words she uttered in trance were directly those of the spirits. Indeed, by means of somatic mimesis, healers not only embody the actual pain, suffering, and bewitchments experienced by their clients but also act as alarm sensors, warning of imminent dangers lingering over their clients so that they can immediately take any necessary preventive actions.

About the somatic reactions of healers, Csordas compares his own work on Christian Charismatic healing with what scholars of Spiritism such as Harwood (1987 [1977]), Koss (1964, 1970, 1988, 1992), and Garrison (1977) have documented on Puerto Rican espiritismo healing. From a phenomenological/semiotic perspective, he notes that healers in both systems "learn about the problems and emotional states of their clients through bodily experiences thought to parallel those of the afflicted" (1993:142–143). Corroborated by my own research (conducted a few decades after these authors' studies), Csordas' comparative work attests not only to the commonalities in the two systems but also to the continuity of the basic somatic reactions of espiritistas since at least the 1960s. Drawing on this scholarship, Csordas mentions four basic types of somatic reactions within espiritismo, which Haydée referred to generically as manifestaciones: *videncias (*seeing the spirits), *audiciones* (hearing the spirits), *inspiraciones* (sensing immediately what is on the client's mind), and *plasmaciones* (feeling the pain and distress caused in the client by spirits).[10]

Of all the information Csordas cites from this scholarship (1993:143), the most revealing to me is the range of bodily sensations that healers reported during plasmaciones, corroborating my own conclusions, from "tingling, vibration, or a feeling of elation of being possessed by a guía [guide] spirit" (Harwood 1977) to a "headache, stomachache, or tension picked up from the client" (Garrison 1977) to a "feeling of electrical charge, accelerated heart rate, pain and other symptoms, felt at the corresponding body site, cool air blowing across the skin starting from the head, tingling, energy entering the stomach and leaving the head or moving like a snake in the body, fluídos like sexual energy, buzzing sounds, body lightness, rapid thinking, feelings of contentment and relaxation in the presence of a good spirit, feelings of nervousness, fatigue or fear in the presence of a bad spirit" (Koss 1988, 1992).

Take, for example, what for me is the most visible and extreme form of somatic mimesis: that between physicians and patients as evidenced among practitioners of Siddha medicine in southern Asia. Drawing on Valentine Daniel's research, Csordas notes that physicians coordinate pulses with their patients, "making their own pulses 'confluent and concordant' with those of their patients" (1993:143). Similar modes of somatic attention between therapist and patient have been recognized by some psychotherapeutic schools as intrinsic to the very condition being treated (144). Indeed, countertransference (or the sensing of a patient's psychological conflicts by the therapist) is seen as a "physical, actual, material, sensual expression in the analyst of something in the patient's psyche" (Samuels 1988 quoted in Csordas 1993:144) rather than as a pathological reaction of the therapist, as traditional theories of countertransference suggest (145).

But what might countertransference be like when embodied by brujos? Many times during or after consultations, Haydée would complain of some ache and take some pills because she had "caught the pain and the bad energies" that her clients brought with them to the altar. When Hanny, whose son had been shot, left after a consultation, Haydée asked me to bring her some headache and pain-relief pills, acknowledging that "this ache is not mine—it's Hanny's." On another occasion, after working with Haydée on several difficult cases at the altar, I myself "caught" a horrible headache something like a migraine. Haydée asked Nana, her housekeeper, to bring some ice cubes, which Haydée then applied to my forehead and neck, putting the rest in the fuente. I already knew that ice is in general an excellent remedy for migraines, but in this case her diagnosis made the ice become effective also for "cooling the negativity and the heat of the clients."

Often when brujos feel the pain of their clients, perhaps as a form of countertransference, they might conduct a cleansing ritual right there as part of the consultation. This is what happened as soon as Norma, a tall woman in her late twenties, sat down for her consultation after she heard Haydée say,

> —Your chest is aching; that's a causa. [To Reina and me] I want water with sugar. Open the faucet and let the water flow so that her own tears will end. Her waist is also aching. [To Norma] You deserve pity. . . . You don't eat. . . . [To Reina] Bring a cracker . . .
>
> —[Norma sobs,] As I was on my way, I was choking on my own tears.
>
> —That pain in the chest is a causa.
>
> —I have a lawsuit pending over my house. [All] I want is a nice, white house.

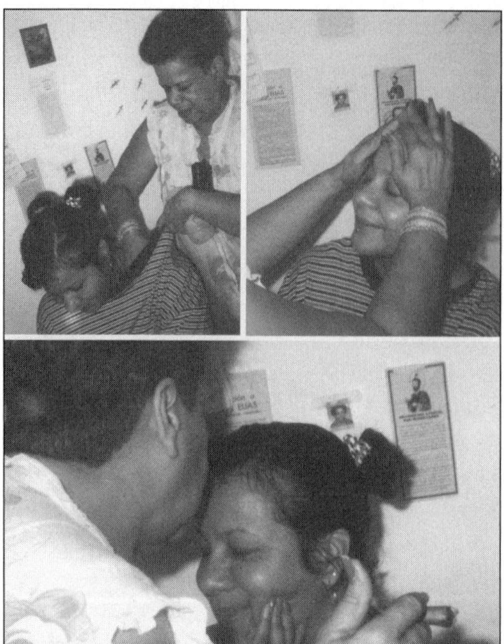

Haydée transmitting her power and bendiciones to a client.

Haydée revealed that Norma never knew her father, who was a merchant marine, nor her real mother and that she was raised instead by a somewhat good woman who, Norma painfully disclosed, disappointed her for not being there for her when Norma had a stroke.

> —I had a brain stroke, but she didn't come to the hospital. Nobody took care of me. I was left lying in the hospital's corridor.
>
> —But with your good cuadro you'll never be left alone. Your cuadro accompanies you all the time; it fights for you . . . [To Reina and me] Those tears that she shed . . . Oh, but I cannot pass that cuadro now. [She shouts and bangs the table three times.] May the peace of God remain here now and forever! My good cuadro, tell me that [her causa] holds only until now . . . [In trance, to Norma's cuadro] Talk! Talk to me! Look at me and talk to me! Now! Enough now [of being silent]! Talk to me! Say what you have to say! Say that you have to pass your cuadro [let it develop so it can speak to you] today! [In the language of bozales she says,] A white piece of cloth for you! [To Reina and me] A white piece of cloth! [Give me] White paper

> [instead]. [To Norma] White cloth over face [clapping]. I'm cleansing the visage as if it were with the wings of Christ. ¡Uy! [I'm] Gathering those serpents and depositing them in the fuente. Cleanse! Gather! Throw! [She directs Reina's hands.] And pat me here, on top [of my forehead] in the name of the Father, the Son, and the Holy Ghost with that cloth. Here, like this, ¡o, cará!

Showing signs of being emotionally charged, Norma moaned, wept a bit, and then sobbed heavily as she heard the following message spoken to her by the Madama:

> [In the language of bozales] Oh . . . Oh . . . Oh . . . you is on the ground but needs to rising, needs to coming back to work, winning lawsuit, having *chavos* [money], buying house. And [I] say, "Caramba that I doesn't see that Señora earlier." But your [enemies] is not letting you to see me earlier—it have to be today! Cry! Cry! You leaving tears here. Caridad del Cobre with you; she gathering and throwing tears to sea. Two times you mine, you mine, you Caridad's. And [I] say today you rise, rise, and rise. Cry! Cry! Cry! And why I being happy today? Knowing that many difficult cases come today for me, but [I] say I being Caridad del Cobre and I doing charity.

Abruptly shifting to her own self, Haydée continued with the consultation, addressing Norma in a medical doctor's tone:

> Your chest is aching very much. This is a causa, you know? I want water with sugar. [She sighs heavily.] I was pulled out of [a sick] bed by *los míos* [my ones, my protecciones] in order to work. That water [with which Norma was cleansed] needs to be dumped. [To Reina] Open the faucet and then dump the water. Throw it into the dumpster so that, as this water goes, her tears will go away too.

Now in the tone of voice and the bozal speech of the Madama she says, "And [I] say to giving her a water cracker." While Reina went to the kitchen to fetch a pack of crackers, Haydée resumed the consultation in her own voice: "How is your stomach? I couldn't eat [lunch] yet. But you don't eat at all." Haydée took a cracker, bit into it and offered it to Norma, ordering her to bite into it. Haydée then took a sip from a glass of sugared water and asked Norma to follow her in alternately biting into the cracker and taking sips of the sugared water. While sharing these sacredly significant bits of food and drink, Haydée recapped the emotional and physical state in which Norma had arrived at the consultation and the legal problems she had been encountering. Haydée told Norma of similar ordeals she herself had experienced in the past and how she had managed to solve them, offering them as models for Norma to follow: how La Caridad has helped her; how she cleansed herself at the sea, cried, and prayed; how she dreamt of a house painted white and yellow (before she could buy a house); and how by having let her cuadro develop, she was now able to materialize that dream.

It was the first time I had seen Haydée share such bits of food like this with a client. Noting my amazement, she added:

> —Raquel, you didn't know that this cracker is cleansing her, right? [To Norma] Drink that water and return it to me; eat your cracker and drink your water; drink and return it to me. With this cracker you'll be cleansed. What did you pledge and didn't fulfill? To which santo did you made a promise—was it Saint Elias, Lord of the Cemetery? To that one you shouldn't make a promise, no way.
>
> —Well, I did make a pledge.
>
> —You don't play with him; you only make an exchange with him when you take trabajos to him.[11]

Haydée began dictating a trabajo to cleanse Norma and to appease any evil spirits that might have been pestering her following an animal sacrifice she had made at the ill-advised (Haydée implied) suggestion of a santero Norma had consulted. In the meantime she and Norma continued to exchange bits of food and drink.

This extremely long and emotional consultation included another form of cleansing right there at the altar: the application and disposal of ice cubes as Norma lamented her dire misfortune of being first abandoned by her husband, of then being fired from a very good job at the airport for no apparent reason, of losing thirty-five pounds, and then of being refused all other jobs for which she applied on account of being overqualified.

Particular manifestaciones (as discussed in Chapter Three) might also index the presence of the spirits and be symptomatic of a comprobación of a previous revelation. Carla, a red-haired client of about forty, told Haydée in the midst of her divination session that the day before, when her son was about to go out with some friends, she said to him, "You won't ride in *that* car." It was a green car, which Haydée, in a revelation to Carla a few days earlier, had said would be dangerous for him to ride in.

> Your son rides in a green car with his friends—tell him not to! They'll take him from you [kill him].

Thus, when Carla reported that indeed some friends came to pick up her son in a green car—exactly as revealed to her some days earlier—and that she had prevented him from riding in it, Haydée's upper body reacted with a quick, snakelike movement, and she said, "I have goose bumps now." These goose bumps were Haydée's somatic shorthand for a confirmación—her own body and words acknowledging the veracity of her previous revelation and warning.

Carmen, a woman who worked in school transportation, came to consult about her husband, but Haydée's first revelation to her was that one of her sons was involved in drugs and was hanging out with dangerous company. Shifting then to Carmen's husband, Haydée stated: "That man will go in his sleep; he's not well. Has he got HIV? Cancer?" Carmen was speechless.

> What are you waiting for?—for him to die? [She touches her own back.] Girl, you have a pain . . . in your spine, a burning pain that goes all the way to here, at the base. This causa that you have, you take it back with you because it's not mine! This is a causa that *you* have of what they [your enemies] toss on to *you* (*te tiran*), and *you'll* take it because it's not mine! What *I* had [before Carmen came] was a cold and sore throat!

The above is a perfect example of how healers experience the difference between the effects of somatic mimesis—the burning back pain of their clients, for instance—and their own aches and pains. What might sound like a heartless statement—"This causa that you have, you take it back with you because it's not mine!"—not only reflects this difference but also acquires a performative value. Meant to first identify a causa, this seemingly cold comment serves then to urge the victim to undergo a ritual exorcism for the purpose of lifting (*levantar*) the causa.

Unlike couples therapy, it is culturally much less common for couples (especially if one of the partners is still married to another person) to come together for a consultation with brujos. Presenting a unique situation, when a woman came with her lover (who was still married to another woman) to consult with Haydée, they signaled total trust (or at least the display of it) that neither one was involved in black magic against the other. Lauro, a man of about forty, suspected that his wife was holding him in the marriage with black magic. Magdaliz, his lover, seemed to have encouraged his suspicion and motivated him to come with her for a consultation with Haydée. Since this was the first consultation of the day, Haydée began with an improvised prayer as she always did to open her altar, asking God and her patron saint to help her heal Lauro because "he is a good man and has a good heart, though he's weak and people use him." After the plea was over, Haydée's first words to Lauro shocked him, Magdaliz, and me: "You are involved in drugs, which drugs?"

Showing obvious signs of embarrassment from such a direct accusation on his first consultation with Haydée, Lauro could hardly muster a response. After a series of probes and statements about him, which Lauro neither refuted nor affirmed, Haydée (implicitly confirming his suspicions about his wife) addressed all of us:

> He's been held [controlled, bewitched] in such a way that he can't even respond . . . [To Lauro] You gamble . . . [To me] I want water. [Sarcastically, to us] This man is engulfed in such a high temperature that I should need the firefighters to bring me water and splash it over me. [To Lauro] You are afraid—of what? But it [the negativity] comes from you!

Haydée's comment about the firefighters needing to put out the burning heat generated as a consequence of Lauro's causa, which was consuming him spiritually and materially (and was now also somatically sensed by Haydée), introduced a certain lightness into a heavy atmosphere.

Coger Muertos

"Catching the causa" of others (*coger muertos*, to catch the dead) means that the body of the brujo undergoes the effects of the bewitchment that had been sent to the victim (as in Eva's case) and embodies the muerto that was used to carry out the bewitchment in order to drive it away, thus exorcising the victim (Romberg 2003b:153–161). Coger muertos can only be done by expert brujos—those that have highly developed cuadros—and is the test that eventually turns novice mediums into powerful brujos. It is during the veladas held on the last day of the month that brujos deliver messages, one by one, for each member of the audience and, when needed, cogen muertos. In difficult cases, the audience might also be summoned collectively to help the victim of a causa—as is commonly done in espiritista circles—by holding hands and thoughts in unison so that their positive energies, so joined, can cleanse and heal the person in need.

During such a velada, Haydée, in trance, delivered several crucial messages given to her by the spirits for her audience. As a result of catching a few causas in the process, her materia (body) was overworked and in pain. As Haydée was lifting one causa, she said,

> [This woman] needs to be thoroughly cleansed . . . bring ice . . . I feel exhausted; I have a heaviness in my brain and body . . . Let's pray, 'Our Father . . . .' Bring the cleansing spray of La Madama! Now throw the ice cubes out on the street! Let's gather all our positive energies and unite our thoughts to help this sister who suffers so much for her children.

She asked for glasses of water with ice cubes to cleanse and cool the victims of causas and to cool herself. So great was the harmful effect on her own body as a result of the bewitchments she had lifted that after all the victims of causas were finally cleansed she immediately ordered Reina to rush her painkillers to her from the bedroom so she could resume the velada.

Reina also "caught the dead" at that velada while delivering the following message to a young man who was at this point already standing:

> [I see that] you're on the floor; you're cold. You were locked in a box, all dressed in black. [Voicing the man's thoughts she said,] I can't deal with this any more . . . [Talking to the evil spirit lodged in his body and sensing it in hers she said,] Go away! Repent! May God forgive you! Depart to the celestial mansions! [To the man] They [your enemies] gave you a water [potion] to drink.

Complaining of being nauseous [somatically reacting as a proxy for this man's causa], Reina choked a few times, then vomited a bit, after which she continued:

> [Speaking as if she were the man] I had a woman outside of my marriage . . . pray for me . . . I suffered a lot . . . [To the evil spirit] May God forgive you! Repent! May God forgive you! Depart to the celestial mansions! [Voicing the spirit] *Adios*, I leave now![12]

The Touch That Exorcises and Heals

In some cases causas are so strong that they need to be exorcised in a private ritual, usually by at least two brujos—one performing the exorcism and the other protecting the materia of the one who performs the exorcism. A couple of weeks after Armando and Haydée began consulting together (described in Romberg 2003b:176–183), she asked him to perform a ritual exorcism and healing for her son Eliseo. He suffered from extreme obesity—a problem triggered by the tragic death of his brother a few years earlier. At the stipulated afternoon, they met, together with Reina and two other clients who also needed to be exorcised, in Haydée's living room turned into a ritual space.

Below, following some contextual observations, is a long transcription of this exorcism that I offer—unlike previous ethnographic sections—almost in its entirety without any interlacing remarks. I chose this strategy to present as closely as possible a mimetic rendering of the event and allow for a minimally obtrusive reading experience and, hence, an appreciation of the phenomenology of this event.

When Armando arrives he is dressed in white, the sacred attire of santeros. Upon his arrival, Haydée, Reina, and Armando begin dancing to música santera around Eliseo to cleanse themselves and promote trance, while he stands motionless in the middle of the living room. Lowering his body and encircling Eliseo with undulating, snakelike movements and placing his open mouth near Eliseo's heart, Armando begins hissing a high-pitched, continuous "SSSSSS . . . SSSSSSSSSSSS," which I take to be evidence of his being possessed by La Cobra, one of Armando's protecciones who never uses words. La Cobra mimes a message around Eliseo's body, which Haydée interprets aloud, in a sad tone: "He'll die from the heart. [To Armando] *Luz a tu espíritu*! [May your spirit have light!]. [To La Cobra] But tell me this causa was in effect only until this day, because you have to help him—cleanse whatever negative there is within him."

> A.—[As if choking] GHGHGHGHGH . . .
> H.—[To Eliseo] He's cleansing you.
> R.—¡O, cará! May the peace of God remain here forever!
> H.—Open the cold-water faucet and leave it open . . .
> A.—Ay . . . Ay . . . Ay . . . [falls down to the floor and remains there motionless]

Haydée and Reina pray in litany: "Our Father . . . Hail Mary . . . On the mountain Christ died . . . Stop, fierce animal . . . Amen."

> R.—[Exhorting the evil spirit that pestered Eliseo] Go away, leave now! You are a spirit of light. Enough, enough of doing evil! Repent!

A.—[Speaking as if he were Eliseo] Ay, my heart aches. Ay, what a strong blow. . . . Ay!

Haydée and Reina pray in litany: "Our Father . . . Hail Mary . . . On the mountain Christ died . . . Stop, fierce animal . . . Amen."

R.—[Exhorting the evil spirit] Go and leave that materia in peace. Ask for forgiveness because it's enough, because this [bewitchment] ends here. You harmed enough, but this is until this day. Go away, because you are an evil spirit. Leave now!

H.—[To Armando, who stands as a proxy for Eliseo] If it hurts, toss it away. Toss away whatever hurts! Dispose of it now! Your heart aches. Don't sob! Don't suffer! God is always with you!

Haydée and Reina pray in litany: "Our Father . . . Hail Mary . . . On the mountain Christ died . . . Stop, fierce animal . . . Amen."

A.—[Sobbing as if he were Eliseo] Ay, Mother, I can't deal with it anymore . . .

H.—This [causa] was [in effect] until today.

A.—[Speaking as if he were Eliseo] My [dead] brother calls me. Ay, ay, I'm cold. They're taking me away, Mother, to the darkness. He's calling me. Help me, Mother . . .

H.—I always helped you. . . . [To me] Bring pieces of ice . . .

A.—[Moaning as if he were Eliseo] I'm in bed . . .

H.—You've already risen from the bed!

A.—[Moaning as he was Eliseo] Mother, heal my wounds [lacerations], because my wounds are yours. . . . Take away this burning, take away this pain . . .

H.—I always cure him, always help him.

A.—[Moaning as if he were Eliseo] My feet are burning, their flesh opens, Mother . . . [Begging] Ay, ay, Mother, please help me. . . . Mother, take this pain, please. Bring camphor, bring olive oil, and bring *altamisa*, please, Mother. Mother, I feel bad. Mother, take honey and pour it on my feet, hands, and head, because they [evil spirits] want to take them away from me. Mother, put white sacred powder on my feet and head every day. If not they will take me away. [Sobbing] I don't want to go. I'm afraid of [dealing with] life, Mother. Lift me, please. I don't have the strength to fight with this life. People laugh at me because I'm fat.

H.—That has been until today!

> A.—[Sobbing as if he were Eliseo] They laugh because they think I'm stupid. [Speaking as if he were Eliseo's dead brother] Mother, help me; drive me away from that friend of mine, because that friendship will be my end, will destroy me, will take me away.
>
> H.—He [the spirit of her dead son] doesn't know he's no longer alive. [Haydée shows the first signs of entering into trance.]
>
> A.—[Speaking as if he were Eliseo] Mother, help me!
>
> Cleanse me with the Seven Powers, please. Because, Mother, I can't take it anymore . . . [In pain] Oh . . . Oh . . .

Haydée and Reina pray in litany: "Our Father . . . Hail Mary . . . On the mountain Christ died . . . Stop, fierce animal . . . Amen." Armando, now possessed by the Indio, uses the third person to announce the arrival of the Indio while he rubs and cleanses Eliseo's body from head to toe.

> A.—The Indio is cleansing this materia, here with his mother. Here, please light a cigar for me. I'll give you what you need, because I'll cleanse you! Look, I always cleanse with my force and power. [He blows cigar smoke over Eliseo's feet.] Take this. These ulcerated legs . . . because this is until today. This cleansing . . . Take it so I can cleanse you. Pass it over your body. With these [spiritual] feathers I give you peace and happiness for your heart. Cleanse yourself over my body so I can send everything that is negative around you to the world beyond, where nobody can reach it. Because I'll cleanse this materia, because this cleansing . . .
>
> H.—Free him from evil spirits for me! Cleanse him with that smoke!
>
> A.—[To Eliseo] Come here, please [whispering in Eliseo's ear] get closer.
>
> H.—Give glory to God. May God illuminate you and take you to the celestial mansions.
>
> A.—May his materia come back . . .

Haydée and Reina pray in litany: "Our Father . . . Hail Mary . . . On the mountain Christ died . . . Stop, fierce animal . . . Amen."

> A.—[Voicing the evil spirit departing from Eliseo's body] JSJSJS . . . JSJS . . . From this chest I arose, because you helped me when I really needed it. And then I was left there with a black heart, covered with sweat. But I tell you that you drove me away and brought me

light, because I truly couldn't deal with him. But you with your spiritual light . . .

H.—[To the evil spirit] That's nice. May God forgive you and take you to the celestial mansions.

A.—Sambia, come cleanse this materia; it's destroyed. Cleanse this body so nobody can harm him and mess with him.

H.—So nobody can mess with him. Only I can, as a mother. May no son of a bitch in this world mess with him ever again! I, as a mother, I'm the only one who can. You [the evil spirit], you are already gone. You left already! [Blowing smoke] And here, have a drag yourself, to take with you. May God take you to the celestial mansions!

[To Armando] I, as a mother, thank you for what you have done. You have done a work of charity.

A.—Now the mother superior, Ochún, is coming [to possess me]. . . . I have to stay. . . . Thanks for cleansing this materia. Because here is where the burned ashes remain; all that was negative is left. [Possessed by Ochún] Light to your spirit and body! You need to thank God. But the only thing I want to ask you for is a glass of honey as an offering for me. And also give me some molasses for my forehead so I can leave. I want, please, that you honor me on my day. But I want it done truly in the right way, with a cape and crown. I want that service at the end of the year so all the goodness will return to our home. I will give you that new car. But it will be done as I want, not like you want! Because I'm your mother, and you can't govern me. I want you to spread some rivers at the feet of Ochún. I'll give you that trip to Havana, Cuba, because I'll be there, crowned. There'll be a service at the plaza and everybody will be there, all the three Juans [a reference to the legend of La Caridad].[13] You'll have the light. And you'll travel to Haiti. I want to see you there because you have to carry a message . . .

H.—I'm preparing your offering . . . [To me] Give me a napkin to wipe his face. [To Armando as Ochún, who possesses him] With your permission, I'll touch your face. Here you have honey, molasses, like you asked, so your materia can come back. [Now addressing Armando by his nickname] O, White Indio, pour the molasses.

Armando as Ochún then slowly rubs the molasses and the honey over Eliseo's feet, massaging them intensely. In reaction to Eliseo's apparent indifference to all that is being done to him, Ochún/La Caridad delivers the following warning:

A.—[As Ochún/La Caridad] Remember what I'm telling you. Do it for your mother, not for you. Because your mother is your light, and you're her light. And I tell you something else, please don't be ungrateful. Because the advice that your mother gives you, it's me [La Caridad] who gives it. And if you don't get away from that low-life guy who promises riches but is nothing more than a fraud, I'll give you no more opportunities. When I called you, I meant for you to come. Remember, I'm [La Caridad] the owner of this home.

H.—This is so!

A.—[As Ochún/La Caridad] I'm the light of this home. You shouldn't wish that I leave, because I'm powerful. I have the balls here, not you. And if you don't quit, I'll take your materia away [you'll die]!

Haydée and Reina pray in litany: "Our Father . . . Hail Mary . . . On the mountain Christ died . . . Stop, fierce animal . . . Amen." Armando gradually comes out of trance.

A.—Water, please. [Irritated, to Eliseo he says,] I will be honest and tell you the truth. The illness you have is really going to rot your legs. I saw this as clear as the water. And don't look at me as a man. Look at me simply as an entity of light. [As Ochún/La Caridad] Fill yourself with light so your mother will never have to suffer. And now goodbye, I have to leave.

H.—May God enlighten you, give you peace and rest and take you to the celestial mansions.

Haydée and Reina pray in litany: "Our Father . . . Hail Mary . . . On the mountain Christ died . . . Stop, fierce animal . . . Amen."

A.—Fresh water for these hands; the honey washes away with cold water . . .

H.—¡O, cará! May the peace of God remain here forever!

How best to convey the emotional tenor of this ritual, of a mother trying to save her son? Can this transcription evoke in any way its sensuality? Can it evoke the tension created by the cacophony of human and spirit voices interacting and by the somatic exchange between the spirits' active touching and caressing of Eliseo and his own surrender to their sensuous attention? A series of entities was involved in this exorcism—all possessing

Haydée and Reina with Eliseo, who died of heart problems in December 1999, three years after this picture was taken.

Armando's body—all of which we see reflected in the changes of posture, gestures, and tone of voice of Armando as each entity inhabits his body for a few moments. Might a recount of the sequence of these forces suffice to reflect the exorcism and healing Eliseo underwent? We see how the body of Eliseo, already consumed by evil forces, was first cleansed by La Cobra (as evidenced by the sounds and movements performed by Armando), who "devoured" the disease sent to his heart by a bewitchment. Haydée thanked La Cobra and wished, in espiritista parlance, "light" for this benevolent spirit that was helping her son. Joining this spiritual cleansing, the Indio—another of Armando's protecciones—applied his cigar's purifying smoke to Eliseo's visible and invisible wounds, which was accompanied by the healing powers of his feathers—another spiritual instrument of the Indio. And, lastly, Ochún (the African side of La Caridad and the patron saint of Haydée) possessed Armando, applied the healing effects of honey and molasses—her instruments and favorite foods—to Eliseo's legs. A combination of forces, the strength of the snake, the peace of the Indio, and the sweetness of Ochún, work first to cleanse Eliseo's causa and then to heal him. This order follows the order of spiritual healing but still is not enough to convey the drama of the exorcism and healing of Eliseo.

The actions around the main characters also evidence the gravity and meaning of this ritual. Haydée, for instance, requested ice cubes to cool his negativity and asked that the cold-water faucet be opened to drive away (as would the flow of a river were this taking place in the countryside) all the negativity lodged in Eliseo's body. The dialogue that developed between Eliseo's mother and various entities, as well as the Lord's Prayer, Hail Marys, and the folk prayer "On the mountain Christ died" prayed in litany, added to the dynamic flow of spirits—evil and enlightened—and the blurring of boundaries between profane and sacred realms.

From the experiential perspective, though, just imagine entities having their hands stroking your legs with honey, a mouth mockingly biting your belly, waves of their breath and smoke blown onto your feet and ears! These otherworldly motivated gestures, I guess, must have deeply touched Eliseo, who stood motionless and speechless throughout the ritual. Consider how Eliseo must have felt when Armando voiced in sobs Eliseo's innermost thoughts, shame, and fears. Perhaps, in Csordas' apt phrase, he experienced for a flash being within the sacred order as "another myself" (outside the social order), which, in a radical sense, is "not myself" (1990:37).

At the end, I noticed that Eliseo swallowed his saliva in a long gulp and twitched his eyes longer than usual while letting out an almost imperceptible sigh of relief. The pressure of the exorcism, the pain at seeing his mother's anguish, and his own hidden fears and shame—all finally released.

Chapter Six
SPACE

El Yunque

Basi, the botánica owner and espiritista with whom I lived for several months, insisted I meet Ken and Mora, a married couple working together as healers. Basi and her teenage granddaughter who lived with her had participated in a series of workshops on the beach that Ken and Mora conducted about healing, cleansing, and meditation techniques. The flyer she gave me with the address and phone number read as follows: "Ken [his last name]: Magnified Healing Master Teacher" (in forty-eight-point italics) and on the next line "Reiki Treatment: Balancing of Inner Self." I called him and met with him and Mora, a santera-espiritista, at their home, where they worked jointly. After conversing with them a few times and learning about their eclectic style of healing, which included other systems in addition to Reiki, I came to the decision that I would like to get initiated in Reiki since it seemed the most doable for me at that time. I liked the fact that Ken and Mora specialized in different systems and yet were able to highlight their similarities and thereby work jointly.

Perhaps this eclectic environment suited both my curiosity and my fears of the initiation process. It was clear to me that I wished to personally experiment with some formal spiritual initiation but also that I was apprehensive of engaging in a too-demanding healing system. Unlike other opportunities I had during fieldwork for getting initiated, for instance, in Santería, initiation into Reiki—a self-healing system—felt more appropriate to my lifestyle; it would allow me a direct experience with an initiation ritual within a healing system without the demands of a totalizing lifelong commitment, which Santería would have required of me.

On the chosen day, Ken, Mora, and I drove early in the morning to the Yunque in my car. My ritual would take place in the middle of an especially well-chosen clearing in the rain forest on the bank of a stream whose water flowed from a single, small cascade and continued down into a creek, finally flowing into the sea. It was an idyllic place that remains imprinted in my memory, chosen, according to Ken and Mora, for its strong spiritual energies—similar to Tonio and Haydée's references to the Yunque, the abode of the spirits.

The chosen clearing in the Yunque.

Ken assesses the place for my initiation.

Mora conducts her private ritual.

As we settled down in the clearing, Mora began to perform a private ritual; having approached a huge tree, she uttered some prayers beneath it while holding a coconut between her palms as if it were a baby. She walked to the bank of the stream, sat down, poured honey on and around the coconut, and gently deposited it into the water. In this manner the sweetened coconut was sent away to be carried downstream toward the sea. Mora then poured the remaining honey over her head and shoulders. As part of what appeared to be an offering and cleansing ritual, Mora immersed herself in the water, allowing her body to float and drift, drawn only by the mild current.

While Mora was getting out of the stream and drying herself, Ken asked me to sit on a rock with my palms open to the sky in order to be cleansed. While I was engaged in my own ritual, Mora took over my role, grabbing my camera and documenting what was going on.

As Ken began pouring honey into my mouth and over my face, hair, and body (I happened to be wearing a bathing suit this time, unlike that other time at the toque), he asked me to taste and feel the healing sweetness of honey and to absorb the cosmic energies of the Yunque. He did not mention Ochún, but she came to my mind, especially how she had claimed me as her child at the toque. And then, just as with Mora, Ken asked me to immerse myself in the stream and to get as close as possible to the cascade in order to receive its cleansing energy. "Just relax in the water a while," he said. As I floated aimlessly, I became especially aware of all my senses, of my body in contact with the water, the rays of light entering through the

Mora drifts in the stream.

Ken pours honey over my body and in my mouth.

clearing, and the movement of the water touching my hair and different parts of my body. I began to swim gently toward the cascade, soon coming to rest upon a rock just beneath the invigorating mild stream of falling water, sensing a sort of powerlessness against the weight and uncontrolled abundance of the water that embraced me.

It was a strange, mixed sense of bliss and anxiety, the unsettling feeling of lacking control over my body as an external force took hold of it, not unlike the exhilarating sensation of one's body reacting without any conscious command during the dramatic drops of a rollercoaster after making the apex of its ratcheted ascendancy. And yet my mind was free to wander. I do not have a sense of how long I drifted in the water, but as I approached the bank and came out of the stream I felt very cold, partly because the bank by then was in total shade, but also, I think, because I had stepped out of a womblike state of peaceful, introspective solitude into the world again—it was a kind of induced rebirth.

I drift in the stream.

It was the closest state I could identify with anthropological accounts of initiation rituals, such as those of Victor Turner in his now-classic *The Forest of Symbols* (1967), in which the symbolic becomes real, orchestrated cultural intentions create individual sensual transformations, and these sensorial transformations induce and become the signs of another implied and socially desired transformation—in sum, the "orectic-emotional" nature of symbols, in Turner's terms, elicit psychophysiological or biopsychical transformations that correspond to desired social, "ideological" outcomes (43). Noting the ritual process of the Ndembu of northwestern Zambia in south-central Africa, Turner concluded: "Norms and values, on the one hand, become saturated with emotions, while the gross and basic emotions become ennobled though contact with social values. The irksomeness of moral constraints transformed into the 'love of virtue'" (30). Since mine was an individually tailored ritual, the ideological pole of this process seems to have been defined more by a *sui generis* desire than by social values or moral constraints. Participation in this type of ritual was my conscious choice, following a desire for self-fashioning—not defined by social constraints as in the Ndembu case—similar to that of many in today's world who opt for a certain way of life out of a construed sense of extreme, autonomous selfhood and a set of self-created lifestyle choices (Giddens 1991). That is, the social and moral values of my ritual, of their orectic or emotional aspects, were not givens; they were not predetermined, as in accounts of traditional rituals. Feeling different at the end of this first part of the ritual but not yet aware of the significance of this difference, I covered my chilly body with a towel and sat down on a nearby rock waiting for the next phase of my ritual.

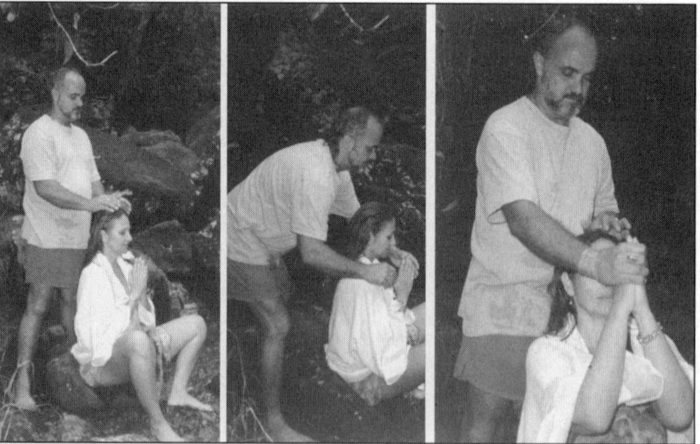

I am the object of Ken's magic passes.

At the foot of a wide-branching tree I sat with my eyes closed while being the object of Ken's magic passes of his healing energies over my body, which I was able to see only a week later, when the photos Mora had taken were ready. I remember sensing various temperatures in my body and lights in the back of my mind evoked by Ken's words depicting variously colored, spiritually meaningful landscapes, which I gather were uttered while transferring his healing energies over various parts of my body. Only at the end of the ritual did I learn that these magic passes had been aimed at transferring Ken's spiritual knowledge and healing powers to me through manipulations of my aura (without actually touching my body), accompanied by depictions of idyllic landscapes, each with its particular images, colors, temperatures, odors, and sensations. After some time, which I cannot really pinpoint precisely, and still with my eyes closed, I felt Ken's hands holding mine; he was asking me to verbalize the sensations I was having. I remember being in a peaceful mood, in total contact with and at the same time distant from the world around me. Perhaps this was one of the moments I recall of being in a state of blissful harmony, to use a common cliché for such feelings. Unlike the Ndembu and many other such cases, the emotional-physiological (orectic-emotional) impressions I had were saturated not with irksome social norms and values but rather with emotional-moral sensations attached to imaginary landscapes informed by my own previous experiences of what harmony and well-being meant and anchored in the eclectic spiritual lingo of Ken and Mora.

At the end of this experience, I was given instructions in how to recall the sensations I had just experienced in these surroundings at any time I wished, how to recall them in order to meditate, cleanse, and heal my aura

Ken instructs me how to recall the images I had.

via the various imaginary landscapes I had just experienced for the purpose of achieving the first level of Reiki. This first level would also enable me to apply my newly acquired self-healing technique to my children (but not to anyone else at this level). If I continued practicing these cleansing and recalling techniques for my own aura, I could cleanse my children's auras and heal them of minor ailments by placing my palms close to their bodies, thereby transferring to them my own recently acquired healing energies.

It was not easy to leave. Walking toward the parking lot, I felt still connected to the cosmic presence of the Yunque. And as we were walking away from the shady forest with smiles and well-being on our faces, we felt the warmth of the afternoon's sun and decided to stay there for a little while longer and absorb its rays. Ken and Mora took this opportunity to teach me how to perform a yoga-inspired "Salute to the Sun" and "The Buddha Smile." These yoga gestures involve not only conscious movements of our bodies and directed thoughts but also the invocation of various spirits and cosmic forces and our expression of gratitude.

Ken and Mora conduct farewell offerings.

When we left the Yunque I was in an exhilarated mood, extremely content about what I had just experienced but also extremely hungry; it was already mid-afternoon by then. Apparently we had been away for five or six hours. Mora had to return home for a client, but Ken and I went to have some lunch at a restaurant by the sea, a perfect place to continue our conversation about my ritual and his work as a healer. We chose something to eat and waited impatiently for our food as we conversed about my experience at the Yunque. We waited and waited, but the food was not coming out.

After an hour or so the waiter, quite distressed, announced that what we had ordered was not available any more; the provisions of the seafood we had ordered had just been unfortunately exhausted. He suggested an alternative dish, which I reluctantly yet also impatiently accepted, since after an hour of waiting I was beginning to feel sick from hunger. "I'll take the veggie burger," I mumbled coldly. To my utter surprise, Ken calmly refused to order something else, opting to eat nothing instead. Of course, I asked him why. After all, he was as hungry as I was. But he said he did not fancy anything else and was content with the situation, even though I insisted several times, as his host, that he choose something else. I watched him calmly continue talking about his work as a healer, his life history, and my research project. Another thirty minutes passed, during which I have to admit I felt increasingly mortified that Ken refused to eat anything. When the waiter finally returned, he brought my veggie burger—and the seafood Ken had initially ordered!

Clarifying for us this sudden change, the waiter explained that the cook had just received another extremely late shipment of seafood and had immediately set about preparing the dish Ken had ordered. I was amazed, but Ken was not. Somehow he got what he had sought without getting irritated and anxious as I had. Instead of becoming frustrated by the lack of professional expediency of the waiter and, by extension, of the quality of the restaurant, Ken told me he had been "thinking about the cook, sending him good energies, opening his path, encouraging him to labor in a harmonious atmosphere." Ken's reaction, I felt, was consonant with his being, with his life's project, and eventually with what he was trying to teach me from the moment we had first met about the cosmic, energetic connection we have with things and others. It was, for me, an embodied way of learning. Similar to other experiential lessons I had while interacting with other healers, this vivid parable afforded me a memorable revelation, a far cry from the kinds of esoteric knowledge advocated in written sources. How fitting, I thought, his approach was to his particular career as a healer.

Assuming this cosmic, energetic connection, healers of various systems in Puerto Rico revere sacred spaces and landscapes such as chapels, altars, the Yunque, the river, and the monte for their magical potential. Because they are thought to be the abode of powerful entities and spirits, being in these spaces allows healers of various traditions to draw on their powerful energies. But rather than characterizing one single religious tradition, these energies conflate the kind of lingua franca I suggested at the beginning that incorporates the beliefs of the three great religious streams of Puerto Rico—the Taíno, the Catholic, and African ancestor- and deity-worship traditions. Special care is therefore given to the performance of rituals in these sacred places—both feared and venerated—marking their extraordinary nature and assuring their additional blessings.

Each such landscape embodies a particular cosmic force, following a creolized moral-religious geography generated through centuries of colonial Catholic rule, the embodied memories of slavery, and an idealized, pastoral Africa (Romberg 2007). Following the religion of the orishas and Spiritism, for example, the sea is the dwelling of Olokum and Yemanyá; the river, of Ochún and La Caridad; the monte, of the guerreros Eleggua, Ochosi, and Ogún as well as the Indios; roads and markets, of Eleggua and Babalú Ayé; and the cemetery, of Oyá as well as Papá Candelo. For brujos, the sea is the place for cleansing negativity because its strong, salty waves purge and drive it far away; rivers, on the other hand, are the places for empowerment because their "sweet" waters can heal and protect, as in Christian baptizing practices, a person from misfortune. The monte is the place where the warrior spirits are summoned for protection, for fighting all sorts of legal, love, and family problems; it is also the place where healers go for remedies for health problems. Roads and markets are the places where critical decisions, decisive paths, and dilemmas are solved, as well as bewitchments broken. Cemeteries are the abode of the muertos, some of which can be recruited (as in Palo) for the performance of trabajos malos. (Again, these are always done as retaliation.)

In the same way that certain spaces (homes and places of business, for example) may host negative or evil energies, anyone sensitive enough would feel such energies simply by being in these spaces, just as they would feel the negativity emanating from some people. Like cleansing rituals performed for the body, such spaces can also be cleansed and influenced at a distance through the healer's thoughts. This is what Ken did when he visualized a harmonious atmosphere at the restaurant, helping—as he suggested—the supplies to arrive and thereby "opening the path" for the cook to perform his job as expected. In most cases, however, special cleansing rituals are performed in situ to lift any spells cast over homes or stores and thereby to protect the actual place and its owner from the assumed disabling effects of such bewitchments.

The House and the Business

Rosalía, a woman of about forty, comes to consult with Haydée for the first time, and as soon as she is seated, Haydée says,

> —Your son is fifteen . . .
>
> —Seventeen.
>
> —He has a car?
>
> —No.
>
> —But he rides in a car with his friends. He's not bad. Do you want to cut [the cards] for you or your son?
>
> —For everything.
>
> —Cut them in three.

During the divination session, different aspects of Rosalía's life and relationships come to the fore: her son lives with her first husband, her mother is sick, her current marriage with Juan is deteriorating for no apparent reason, and she and Juan own a house and a heavy-machinery store. After a half-hour or so has elapsed, Haydée says,

> —You don't believe in this.
>
> —If I didn't, I wouldn't have come. I believe.
>
> —Then it's your husband who doesn't believe.
>
> —It's my husband.
>
> —He's the one who cuts [limits] you—ha, ha, ha! What is he afraid of?

To Haydée's series of questions, Rosalía answers that her husband is always in the store with her, that he does not do drugs, and that the problems they have are because of the kids (namely, Rosalía's adolescent son from her first marriage and the two younger boys from her marriage to Juan). The adolescent son, the one who lives with her ex-husband, especially worries her; she often goes to school to check on him. Haydée asks,

> —Do you owe money for the machinery in the store?
>
> —No, we own the machines.

—You're very responsible; you pay your debts. You love your husband, but you're becoming distant. It's the envy that people have for you. . . . Isn't your store going down?

—It is . . .

—And it's going down fast. If you don't open your eyes and cleanse that business, you'll have to close it and eat your machines. Forgive me for talking to you like this. There [at the store] it's you who decides everything.

—Yes, I do.

—The space is rented, right? If you don't open your eyes, it's going to be emptied. You have to cleanse that store. You'll shed many tears for that store, you know? You have to cleanse it! Your problem is the store, not your oldest son (because he's with his father), it's not your husband; it's your store. Your ex [husband] is attentive to your store; he wants to hit you where it hurts the most—your store. He holds such a big grudge against you that he wants you to suffer for your son in your flesh. He doesn't care about what that child does. That's very wrong. How mistaken he is! He'll say you're a mother who doesn't care for her son . . .

—Exactly. Yesterday he [the ex-husband] came to the store, something he never did before.

—For your husband to see him. He'll make demands . . .

—He's demanding the house, for his part.

[. . .]

—You have Santa Bárbara: you get angry and then cry. Don't deteriorate; don't cry. They [the spirits] say the store will shine, but you need to do something about that store with the *quita-maldición* [un-curse] plant. Who cursed it?

—I try to *echar pa'lante* [go forward]. A santera told me, "Go to Haydée and give her many regards from me."

—Ah, that's Sabrina, the santera who gifted me with La Mano Poderosa [an icon].

Haydée starts reciting and writing the ingredients for the cleansing trabajo, which she will perform at the store itself:

—I want quita-maldición; you'll get them in water form at the botánica. This store has been cursed, you know?

—Now that you tell me, I realized, once not long ago, when I found something ugly with the name of my son's father inside.

—I want patchouli—in stick. Montana [the botánica] has it in a big pot with the plant inside; Magnet Water—for attracting clients; Flowers' Water; Madama Cleansing, Always-Alive Water—so the store will be always alive; Prayer of the Santa Camisa; Prayer of the Store; a jar of honey with the honeycomb inside; and I want two horseshoes—because there aren't four corners [in the store]; I want Blessed Water—two jars; Seven Powers Shield [*resguardo*]—for that store.

Haydée repeats all the ingredients aloud and ends by saying,

I'll put this store to work in time, to sell all the machinery, because nobody enters that store now. It will cost you ninety dollars. If you want your store, you need to make a sacrifice because, remember, if one is not willing to make a sacrifice, he will not have what he wishes for.

Rosalía agrees, saying, "This is so." Haydée also recommends the performance of a trabajo for the ex-husband to neutralize his envy and prevent him from sowing the seeds of envy in their son.

After less than a month Rosalía comes again to see Haydée, who is now in bed recovering from a minor surgery. "The store is going very well since the day you came [to the store to cleanse it]," she tells Haydée. "Thanks to you, everything is going very well. We're renting our machines, and many people come to the store. Before, nobody used to come in." Haydée reminds her that when she came to cleanse the store Juan expressed his desire to come to consult as well. Rosalía and Haydée plan a cleansing for Rosalía's home and a trabajo for her ex-husband. Rosalía will bring Juan as soon as Haydée resumes her consultations.

As promised, a few days later Rosalía comes with Juan, a man in his forties, to consult with Haydée. In consultation he hears the following warning:

They [the spirits] say that you have to get ready because there will be a problem hitting you and your wife, like somebody asking for money, related to the courts. Remember that your wife's problems are yours too. There is somebody who, motivated by sheer vengeance, will initiate a court case against you, and there's going to be a discussion between a man and a woman, not between two men; I mean that if it's between your wife and somebody making demands on her, let

> her be the one to solve it. Make sure you don't intervene. You have a firearm, right? Where do you have it? In your house? Be careful. Is it registered?

As the man answers affirmatively to all her questions, Haydée adds to the warning.

> Beware of that firearm being used for causing harm, because it's your life that will be doomed. I have to cleanse your house! [Turning another card of the deck, Haydée continues.] They say that in front of your store somebody has been *tirando* [throwing bewitchments]. You need to protect it with *brazo fuerte* [vernacular for the tártago plant]; I will give it to you as a gift—I have one outside—so you can plant it. You'll make a hole [in the ground] and will say: "I'm not planting tártago; I'm planting brazo fuerte so my store will be protected." They say that San Miguel is always with you *cortando* [cutting bewitchments]. They say you shouldn't worry; sometimes you get desperate because you have to pay some bills and money doesn't come in.

After concluding that he as well as his home and store need to undergo some cleansing rituals, Haydée says with enthusiasm:

> As soon as my doctors give me the OK for my foot [recovering from surgery], I will go into the river and the sea with you. I will go also into the cemetery if needed, at any time, because I'm a bruja espiritista; I am not [just] an espiritista; I'm a bruja who does espiritista work. When can we do the cleansing of your home and store? Where do you live?

Learning that the two places are close to each other, Haydée shares her plan aloud:

> We could do them both the same day, but it has to be early in the morning so Nana will be able to look after the people [waiting to consult]. Two things, then, are pending: your cleansing at the sea and river and the cleansing of your home and store. The dry coconut and the butter of *corojo* are for your home and store;[1] I'll arrange it with your wife; first we do one and then the other. That day you open the store, then we first go to cleanse the store, and then we go to cleanse your home. Because I need to break that coconut at a

> crossroad, you know, my friend?—of four roads; both coconuts, you know? It's not easy.

Juan, overtaken by the details of this kind of feat, asks,

> —In the very middle of a crossroad?
>
> —[Eagerly] I get out of the car, and whether someone sees me or doesn't (*me vea quien me vea*), I do it. Is that so or not? And [believe me] no one sees me, ha, ha, ha! Cars stop, but when they see what I'm about to do, [speaking in a slower cadence] they don't look at me—and that's the beauty of it! Further, as they get scared they swerve from their path in order to avoid driving over whatever I leave there, whichever [negativity] I gather from you, your home, and store.

Coconuts are used for cleansing spaces. A story I heard about Mr. Coconut from one the babalawos I befriended may explain this. As far as I can remember, the story goes like this: Coconut in the old times was very proud, all white, the favorite of the gods. But a poor man once knocked on his door for help. Seeing him in rags and dirty, he refused to help him. God (Olofin), who had disguised himself as that beggar, punished Coconut for his pride and arrogance and ordered him to roll forever on the earth, gathering on his skin all the dirt of the world. That is why, the story concludes, the outside of the coconut is brown and only the inside still white. Perhaps following this story, coconuts are therefore rolled in the spaces that need to be cleansed so they can gather the negativity and bewitchments lodged in houses and stores. Breaking these already polluted coconuts afterward at a crossroad ends the cleansing ritual.

Lena, a short redhead of about thirty, came to consult with Haydée. Her messy hair tied carelessly at the back of her neck, her sloppy clothes, and her unsure demeanor inspired compassion—at least in me (and I suspect also in Haydée). By and large, Haydée's revelations offered, in more ways than one, strategies through which Lena could take control of her life—apparently this was what she needed the most. At one critical point during the divination Haydée asked,

> —How is your business doing? On the floor! You're alone with your father; clients don't come. Your boyfriend? Also going bad! Who's cooking [in your eatery]? You forget to put on perfume, to spray the

scent of white lilies, to put a horseshoe. . . . You've cried for Manuel [the boyfriend] these days, but he's distant; he's not coming back because you and him, your backs are turned against each other. Who takes care of the eatery?

—My father and I. Before, a woman used to serve a little . . .

—Ah, that woman *tumbó* the canteen [made it fall, bewitched it]. [She rings the bell as a comprobación.] And you know that! If you don't react quickly, you'll lose your business. . . . Is that woman from Puerto Rico?

—She's the mother of my sister-in-law—of the one who doesn't want to leave my house. My brother convinced me to take her since she has experience . . .

—Experience in what? She ordered the making of a brujo [black magic]; she's the one who bewitched your eatery. And you've let your brother—who wanted to be nice to his mother-in-law—direct you! Now you need to raise that eatery. Bring me what I tell you.

Haydée begins reciting and writing the ingredients:

—The first thing is a leaf of higuereta—do you know what that is? You need to step on the name of that woman, which is?

—Siquita.

—So Siquita will shed the tears you've shed. Siquita shouldn't play with the bread of people. And if you thought you'll raise your restaurant and then ask her to work for you again, don't come back here again! I will raise your eatery for you. I'm your bruja, and you know it.

Many other aspects of Lena's life come to the fore. Her complicated relationship with her brother is one of the issues. He and his wife came, uninvited, to live with Lena and her father. He has an apartment but does not use it. Manuel does not approve of this; that is why, according to Haydée, he has been distant.

What do you prefer?—to sacrifice your relationship with Manuel because of your brother? If I saw that my brother bothered me, I would get rid of him. Because [the spirits tell me] "You're too willing to give but not to receive." But we'll step on [control] all of them. You need to spit on a higuereta leaf as you think about all those you want to step on and then throw the leaf in a busy road so everybody

> will run over it. . . . You need to look after your *habichuelas* [beans, business].

After writing all the ingredients of the propitiatory trabajo planned for the restaurant, they set up a day in the late afternoon, when the eatery closes, to perform it.

Later in the consultation, Lena hears Haydée warn her again about Siquita, who "will try again to destroy your business"—especially now, after Lena had to suspend Siquita after the business weakened. Haydée then reveals a sad detail about Lena's father:

> —He's going to leave [this world], but you need to go on living.
>
> —[Sadly] I don't have anybody else . . .
>
> —[In a comforting tone] And who are we [Reina and Haydée]?
>
> —He will not see the grandson I want to give him?
>
> —I was going to give you a recipe for you to get pregnant with *higuera* [fig] leaves, almond oil. You didn't have a pregnancy yet, or an abortion, right? Your uterus is virgin. I have three women who got pregnant with this trabajo.

As Haydée mentions the ingredients that will help Lena conceive and have a baby, she also writes them down. She hands the recipe to Lena and, before Lena departs, adds: "Your father knows that he's going, and that makes him sad. Remember, here you have two friends."

At a velada held at Haydée's a few days later, Lena received further revelations about her father first from Reina, then Haydée:

> R.—There will be a denouement this year. Even if you kick and cry, he'll die; you need to get mentally and physically ready. He has lived for far more years than you.
>
> H.—I lost my mother, and after two months my son was murdered. Your father doesn't believe [in God or the saints]. You say to yourself, "Without him I can do nothing." He lives with you, and one day you'll find him dead. The world will not end. Pray the Oración del Necesitado [Prayer for the Needy]. I don't know why They give it to me. . . . Don't cry.

The day for the propitiatory trabajo arrived, and Haydée, Reina, Chelo (Haydée's housekeeper's daughter), and I drove to Lena's eatery in the industrial area of Cañones, about a half-hour from Haydée's. First the

Propitiatory trabajo for Anita's store.

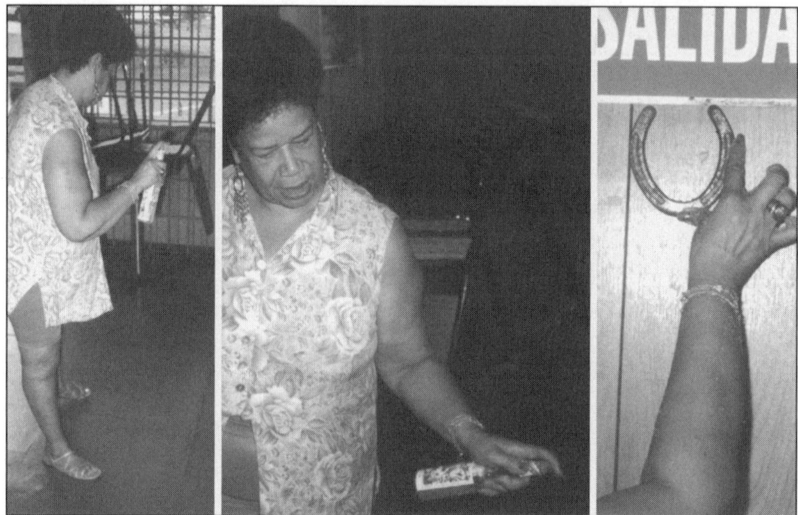

Haydée cleansing and blessing the store.

pumpkin that Lena had bought in advance for this trabajo was prepared with all sorts of magical powders. Then the whole space was cleansed with the aerosol of the Madama and blessed (baptized) with drops of Florida Water sprinkled on the floor and entrance to the eatery. Finally a horseshoe was hung on the wall right in front of the entrance to attract clients.

A series of prayers was selected from a Spiritist prayer booklet, *La Fé en la Oración* (Faith in Prayer), for this particular occasion, all of them bought by Lena as separate prayer sheets at a botánica. They summoned a combination of Catholic saints, orishas, and Spiritist entities to help protect and bless Lena's business and guarantee the success of the trabajo with the pumpkin. Finally, Haydée asked Lena to deposit the empowered pumpkin on a corner behind the counter and "think strongly" about the good things she wished for herself and the eatery.

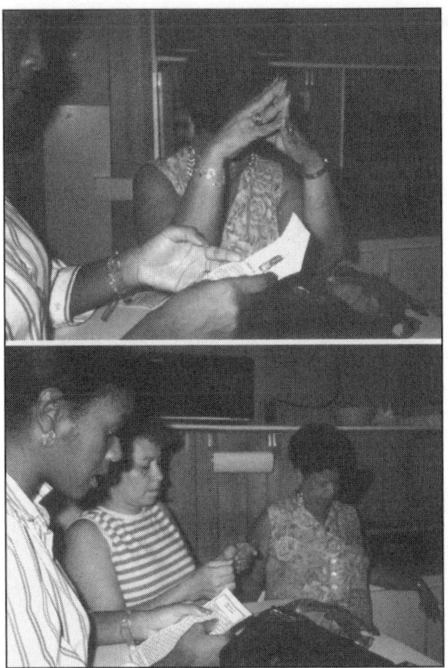

Haydée, Chelo, and Lena invoking santos and entities.

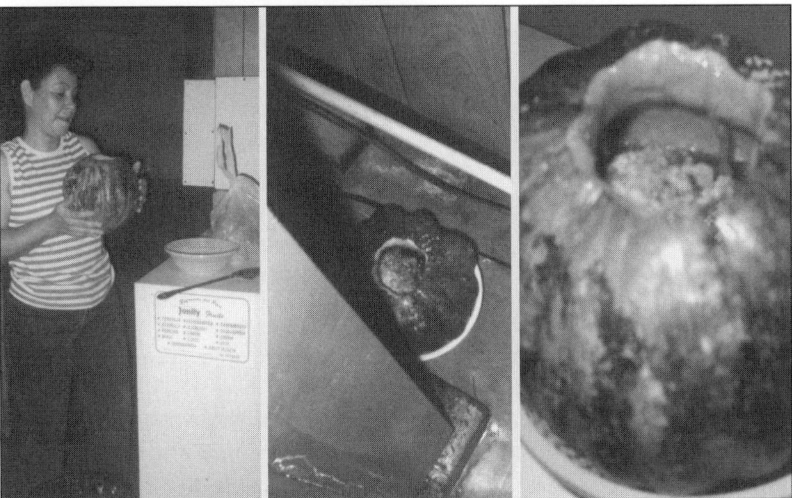

Lena "thinking strongly" about her wishes.

Roads

The notion of *camino* (road, path, course) is key to spiritual discourse, magic, and healing in West African and Afro-Latin religions, for it signifies a given personal destiny as well as the choices one makes in the course of one's life—choices that may encourage or hinder personal development. One may have his or her path closed, darkened, entangled with obstacles; trabajos are performed to have it opened and sweetened. For instance, Haydée revealed to a woman that her husband was having an affair with an addict, saying, "I see dark and murky caminos; it's a woman. These are dark caminos—that woman is an addict. If you bring him here, I'll make him cry."

Within Santería the notion of camino is also important, for each orisha has many caminos or paths resulting from their particular experiences depicted in their various patakis, which also correspond to the different configurations of signs (*odus*) of divination. Following the key metaphor of the camino for the spirit and one's life, the idea of the crossroads occupies a central place in Santería, signifying, for instance, the dilemmas one may face during the course of one's life in making life-changing choices. The crossroads is one of the symbols that characterize the caminos or faces of Eleggua (in this case, the trickster side of this orisha). Eleggua stands at crossroads between this and the other world; he also controls—and occasionally plays tricks with—the caminos of travelers.

Altars

The private rooms where brujos receive clients, sometimes accompanied by family members or friends, are their altars, where they perform divination and all sorts of cleansing, magic, and healing trabajos. In this space they display their own protecciones—santos, Spiritist entities, or orishas—with their candles or any kind of special offerings, and by them they place the trabajos they have performed for their clients. These usually stay for nine days before they are taken somewhere else—depending on their nature—and deposited in such places as cemeteries, rivers, forests, or the sea.

Before clients need to reply to important court or Social Security letters, these documents are sometimes placed under a specific santo for protection and empowerment on special shelves located in the altar. The idea is that all that is stored in the altar will profit for the duration of the safekeeping from the energies, thoughts, prayers, and pleas that its owner is granted by his or her protecciones.

Trabajos at an altar.

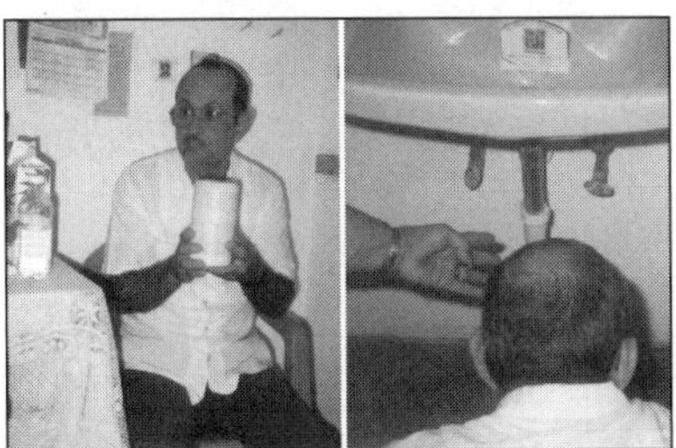

Trabajos are kept and further empowered at home altars.

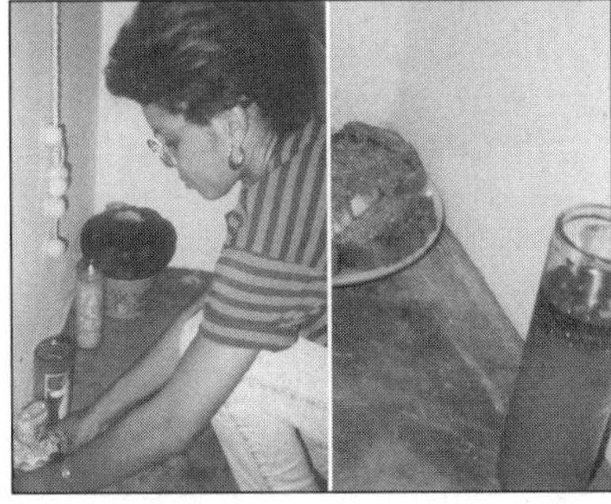

Usually another, more spacious room, marquee, or enclosed balcony or porch (*marquesina*) is assigned as a waiting room. Although it is not formally a ritual space, it actually could be so used. Careful attention is given to this space, especially as a spiritual parlor that precedes and sets up the right mood for the consultation in the altar. Haydée had a running fountain in the marquesina and placed La Caridad, her patron saint (and therefore "owner" of her house), in front of it to secure La Caridad's blessings and protection, which Haydée summoned by regularly making offerings to her. One morning upon arriving to work with Haydée, I saw fresh flowers floating in the fountain. "I tossed them there," Haydée explained, "to thank

Entities and santos empower trabajos left at altars.

After a trabajo is made, it is blessed by the brujo and entrusted to a santo by the client.

my santos for waking me up today with good energies and strength after my operation." Dropping flowers and herbs in the fountain on a regular basis cleansed it of any negativity gathered there from her clients. It is as if the natural space of the river, the mythical abode of Ochún/La Caridad had transposed itself to the waiting room, allowing Haydée to make an offering (*dar un servicio*) with candles and flowers for her patron saint in a conveniently accessible surrogate abode.

Over approximately three months, Haydée transformed her living room. She had one of its walls knocked down to enlarge its space, and in this new space she arranged a private altar, a kind of "private chapel, a place of meditation and communion with La Caridad," as Haydée described it. Haydée had made a promise to her patron saint that she would have a beautiful altar in her living room. She had a clear idea of how it should look, envisioning it having different-sized icons of La Caridad that would be adorned every day with fresh flowers and encircled by a group of lit

Haydée's new living-room altar.

yellow velones dedicated to La Caridad. The space was carefully designed according to a mental religious template that specified the place and size of each element and the relative distance between each item to the sides and from top to bottom.

As with many other aspects of their various rituals, brujos constantly make subtle changes in the construction and arrangement of their altars that result from practical constraints as well as spiritual dictates. New opportunities afforded by the latest communication and reproduction technologies and the increasing commodification of ritual paraphernalia are carefully weighed and made to fit the spiritual needs of their living conditions. I have already noted the impact of migration, consumerism, and new technologies in extending (in both space and time) the possibilities for spiritual empowerment of brujos (Romberg 2003b, 2005a, 2007).

Similarly, practitioners of Santería in Miami and Vodou in New York make all sorts of changes to traditional rituals that depend heavily on the flora and fauna of rain forests in the case of Santería and to a peasant lifestyle in the case of Vodou in order to adjust to their new environments in American urban centers, as depicted so vividly by David Brown (1999) and Karen McCarthy Brown (1995a,b, 1999), respectively. Imagine a practitioner making libations to his or her *loas* (Vodou deities) or orishas in an altar-room on the thirtieth floor of a highrise building. New York City Vodou practitioners may discover an oak tree in a public space such as Central Park as a surrogate ritual pole (*poto-mitan*) that connects this world with the underworld of the spirits for the performance of a private Vodou ritual (Kramer 1985). What could be the meaning of the traditional yearly festival in which families offer harvested yams to the loas in gratitude for their protection, once their lives no longer are connected to agriculture nor dependent on family relationships? (K. Brown 1999). These are just a few of the dilemmas practitioners face once they migrate with their santos, orishas, or loas to new environments. Urban healers often have to grow their own healing and magic plants at home in individual pots or in secluded gardens if they cannot obtain them in their natural environment or purchase these plants, dried and in the form of emulsions, in botánicas.

In addition to modifications due to environmental constraints, altars change according to the rituals their owners perform. As such they reflect the dynamic iconographic tension between old and new icons, ideal and substituted images, immanent needs and immaterial desires. Since the passing of time is best determined when it is materialized in some way or another (Appadurai 1986), altars may provide frames of reference for tracing such passage.

Haydée holding a branch of pazote.

Altars change in response to the rituals performed.

One of the main purposes of the exhibition Face of the Gods: Art and Altars of Africa and the African Americas, curated by Robert Farris Thompson in 1993, organized by the Museum of African Art, New York, and shown in 1994 at the University of California, Berkeley, was to display the aesthetic-religious significance of altars. As forms of communication between humans and the spirits, altars are the means by which humans appeal to and summon the spirits as well as where they make offerings to them. The 1994 Berkeley program guide explains that the exhibit "explores the altar as a focus of ritual and artmaking, and also as a riveting visual and spiritual document of the enduring impact of African religions on both sides of the Atlantic Ocean" (*Face of the Gods* 1994, n.p.). According to Thompson, "The vernacular term altar in Yorba and Ibo and many West African languages is 'face of the gods.' You can't pray unless you know where the face of the gods is. The face is the altar, and it is important to align your face with that face." In contrast, an altar is imagined by the Congo of Central Africa, "as a 'crossroads' or border between the worlds" (ibid.).[2]

Altars manifest the ritual eclecticism of brujería.

Trabajos

Magic is in the details. If one follows closely the making of trabajos, as I have tried to depict here, one can sense the kinds of techniques upon which magic depends and, ultimately, how its purposes are carefully engineered through spatial relationships as well as topographical locations. As a language composed of synonyms, magic works depend on a repertoire of ingredients and possible substitutes—an elasticity particularly handy in times of migration. As shown, trabajos also depend on spatial mimesis, by means of which particular arrangements between ingredients manipulated by brujos are meant to mirror the desires of humans: tying proxies of lovers unites their human spiritual doubles; placing an object that belongs to one individual over an object that belongs to another person places the first person over the second on a parallel spiritual plane. Once human desires are replicated on a spiritual plane, they need to be successfully reflected back (according to the law of resemblance) on the world of humans.

Wendy, a fashionable blond woman of about thirty, writes her full name on a piece of brown paper and places it in the air facing another piece of brown paper on which she had just written her husband's full name. She then hears Haydée say, "Just as your names touch each other—one in front of the other pressed together, as if kissing one another—you and José will

A trabajo that "separates" and a trabajo that "unites."

become fused [on a profound level]." Commenting reflexively on what she is about to perform, Haydée continues, "This trabajo for uniting couples is very beautiful."

Haydée carefully opens, one by one, small sachets containing several magical powders and pours them inside a four-inch-diameter goblet placed over the pieces of folded papers with the names written on them. She states, "I'm uniting the five senses of José to the five senses of Wendy. This is for uniting a couple. He wants to stay with her, but she is a pain in the neck." The various colored powders—violet, blue, yellow, green, red, each serving a purpose on the amorous plane—are topped one over the other, creating an irregular, fluffy rainbow at the bottom of the goblet. "Look, Wendy, how this works. I'm going to pour the azogue now; [in a rhyming phrase] *para que José corra y corra nadie lo socorra* [so that José may *run* and *run* and nobody helps him] until he arrives to Wendy's feet. Look, look how the azogue *runs* through the powders." Then the climactic moment of this trabajo arrives: tiny shavings of gold and silver, the symbols of happiness and wealth, are showered over the mercury moving aimlessly (running) between the rainbow powders of love.

Clearly seduced by the looks of this trabajo and expressing her esthetic satisfaction at its making, Haydée asks Wendy to take it and put it in one

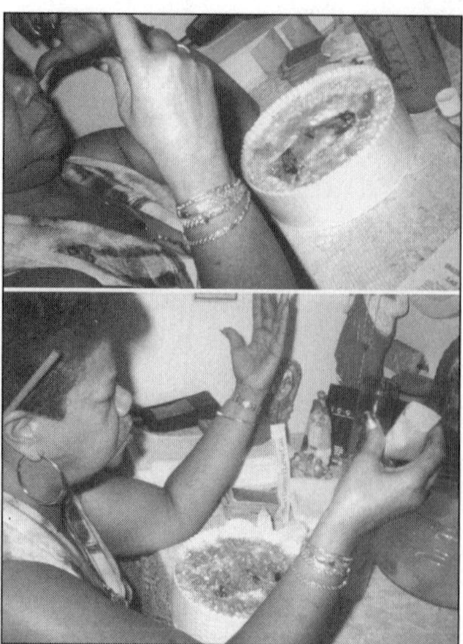

"This trabajo for uniting couples is very beautiful."

corner of the altar on the floor and, next to it, place a lit velón (which will burn for a few days) dedicated to San Aparicio. This is the time for Wendy to make her petitions: for a happy home, for love, for a strong relationship, for an atmosphere of peace and unity in the home, for living with the children in a united, happy family. Even after the velón has completely burned out, the trabajo will stay there for nine days, during which it will be empowered by the positive energies lingering in the altar.

After Haydée reprimanded Elena, the woman who worked at a fast-food restaurant, for not following her advice from an earlier consultation, Elena now sat, embarrassed, during a second consultation awaiting a solution to her problems at work. Regarding those who wanted to get rid of Elena at her job, Haydée said:

> —We should *ensalchichar* [stuff in a sausage casing, restrain] these people. If not, you'll be left without a job. How many are those [who hate you]? Who is Ariana?
>
> —The manager.
>
> —She's good with you, apparently. What are you, a cashier? A cook? I see you with money. I hope people will not say that. . . . Don't cross your hands [and cut off the revelation]. But they *will* say that you took money. [She shifts the topic.] The man you have is a good one, [but] you don't want to get married. Why do you feel aggravated, as

> if everything bothers you? You are restless. . . . Is he [the lover] already married?
>
> —No!
>
> —You've cried because of them [at work]. They said you've taken [stolen money]. They want to get you out of there. They [the spirits] say I need two bottles of benzene, and this has to be done right away. There's somebody who shows you two faces. I need a black wax doll because that doll will be named after those bitches and assholes; black pepper in grain, salt in grains . . . and a man's black handkerchief. I'll charge you fifty-five dollars for this trabajo because I have to prepare it here, and then I have to go into the cemetery, I need to *joderme* [be fucked, endanger myself] and go with you to bury this trabajo.

This time Elena did come after a few days with the ingredients for a trabajo, which Haydée performed and then took with Elena to the cemetery to bury, leaving it for the muerto who would take charge of the trabajo from that point.

Sacred Landscapes

Cemetery

One of the distinctions Haydée made early in our relationship was that she was an espiritista-bruja, directly referencing the kind of trabajos she made: "The cemetery is a bruja thing; tying [a type of magic] is an espiritista thing. If I need to save my clients, I bury lizards, snakes, scorpions, or whatever—ha, ha, ha!—and ask the muertos, as the palero does, to deliver the trabajos." The cemetery is where trabajos malos are generally taken—but not all of them, as in the case of Fernanda.

When she came to see Haydée, Fernanda was extremely worried about her untamable adolescent son. Haydée suggested performing a trabajo to put her son's "back against the backs" of a bunch of hooligans he was hanging out with:

> This trabajo will set them apart. We have to break that friendship. Your son is a good guy. He doesn't drive his friends mad, only his mother. He has to get away from these good-for-nothing guys. We need to win over the enemy, that is, make them go one way and your son another. Your son will not be able to go out with them tomorrow night if he wakes up ill tomorrow. But we can't take this trabajo to the cemetery. We can't put your son in the cemetery. This one will

> go to the monte instead. If it doesn't rain after nine days, we'll go up there. Until then it will stay here, and only then will we take it to the monte.

On another occasion, an impromptu procession of three cars—bearing five clients, Haydée, Reina, and me—left Haydée's house about two in the afternoon. We were heading to the cemetery of Loíza. We stopped on our way to buy flowers for Haydée. When we arrived, we parked and entered the cemetery as a group, each of the clients, all women, carrying in plastic shopping bags their trabajos, which had been performed days earlier at the altar and left there until that day. Haydée moved ahead of all the other women, and I accompanied her. She stopped at a grave, read aloud the name of the woman buried there, on top of the tomb arranged the flowers she had brought, and began praying. As she was praying, a cemetery guard passed and greeted her. She nodded and continued praying. As soon as he went away, Haydée explained to me that she always brings flowers for one of the graves in order to mislead the guard, who, seeing her pray for a supposed relative, would leave her to herself. That's what she needed to successfully conclude the trabajos she had performed for her clients.

The group moved along the central path, following Haydée, who turned right at one of the middle rows, then to the left for a few steps, then right again toward a section that seemed to lie at one edge of the cemetery. There the women were instructed to kneel behind the tombs and without

Haydée leaving flowers and burying trabajos at the cemetery.

much fuss take their trabajos out of the bags and quickly bury them in the ground. During this burying of the trabajos, Haydée and Reina prayed the rosary—as ordinarily is done at burials. As soon as the women finished their surreptitious labor, they joined Haydée and Reina in a few more repetitions of the Lord's Prayer and Hail Mary. Just before leaving the cemetery, Haydée knelt abruptly beside one of the tombs and buried a few coins. "To pay for the services of the muertos; you always have to pay the owners of the cemetery," she whispered to me as she got to her feet.

The Sea

The sea is a complex site in the spiritual imaginary of brujos, symbolizing a place of no return that can be used for ritually opposing purposes such as for cleansings and for bewitchments. Haydée often defined her unique spirituality in relation to her attraction to the sea as a place of solace.

> When I want to cleanse myself I have to go to the sea to cry . . . The sea is my place of refuge, where I cry, because I cry in my home but deposit my tears in the sea. I always tell my Caridad, "Gather all my tears and take them to the bottom of the sea." Because La Caridad is the patron of the sea; she's the one who manifested herself [according to legend] to the [three shipwrecked] fishermen. [To me] I don't know if you know, she's the one who stopped the waters so they could pass by. That's why she's the one who gathers my tears. The more I'm overburdened, the more she rescues me. Because when I wish to fall on my bed to die, she leaves me there, one, two, three days to feed my matter—she knows that my body needs it. Because I'm one of those people who looks for a refuge; I don't like to cry in front of anybody—the only ones are Reina, my partner, and my son, but I don't want my son to see me suffering. I lock myself in my bedroom and cry and plead to my God and my Caridad that if I have offended anyone that they allow me to reach that person and ask for forgiveness. But if I haven't wronged anybody, then I ask that the person who offended me will be driven toward me, and I leave everything in God's and my Caridad's hands. . . I go to the river to cleanse myself with its sweet water after the salty water of the sea.[3]

The sea, imagined as the infinite elsewhere below the waters, repository of our sorrows, is also the endless void from which bewitchments cannot be undone. Harming people this way is often recalled as "having one's

Haydée releases a pigeon after it was magically prepared at the seashore.

name thrown into the sea," which means that the person's spirit has been thrown to the bottom of the sea—that is, an object that embodies the person's spirit is tossed while his or her name is invoked. With it, the person's plans and desires also sink and forever remain unmaterialized. Notably, the connection between salt and bewitchment appears in the vernacular expression *estar salá* (to be salted, to be cursed). Even though reports date back to ancient times of salt's use as a protection against witchcraft in many different areas of the world, *estar salá* suggests its use as a vehicle for as well as a state of bewitchment. I have not been able to find any evidence of the link between this vernacular expression and the transatlantic slave trade and slavery practices in the Americas, but if one takes into account the grim memories embodied among surviving kin in the Americas of the sea voyage and the excruciating pain produced by the fairly common rubbing of salt on the open wounds of slaves who were tortured, a possible explanation for the connection between salt and being cursed may be safely entertained.

The River

We are standing at the side of the road, going up the Yunque, one of the few spots where the river appears just a few steps down from the road for a few yards before disappearing behind some rocks and heavy foliage. Haydée explains,

> When the river is too high [*crecido*], like in these days, I can't perform cleansings here. Usually I cleanse my people here [pointing to a spot in the river]. I throw their old clothes here, so that the river flushes them out to the sea. Then, here is where they receive the blessing, with the water, good water, good and clear, like God baptized Jesus in the Jordan River. This is the Guzman River. It takes the [old] clothes, everything that's bad, to the sea. This river, like all rivers, ends in the sea. This is lovely. When I cleanse my people, the water reaches their arms up to their chests, and after that I cleanse myself. You can see how the current flushes away pieces of bamboo; all the debris is washed away. God brought me here. They [the spirits] brought you to my home; they take me to where I need to go. God's mysteries are only known to Him. That's why I feel happy.

"Usually, I cleanse my people here."

El Monte

One afternoon, a few clients came to fetch Haydée to deposit their trabajos in the monte after the trabajos stayed in the altar for the prescribed days. I drove with Haydée, Reina, and María, a friend and a habitué at Haydée's. While driving to the monte Haydée explained to me,

> Some trabajos, the malos, go to the cemetery. Those that go to the monte are those that unite couples with the help of Santa Inés del Monte Perdida [Saint Agnes Lost in the Mountain], San Salvador de Orta [Saint Salvador of Orta], La Virgen de Covadonga [the Virgin of Covadonga], and the Seven Powers. We pray for them, for example, when we take trabajos to the river—such as the goblet with a bride and groom—so that they'll stay in the monte. Those that go to the cemetery, you have to know how to make them and then manage to dig them in the cemetery unbeknownst to the local gravedigger. Those who don't know how to perform trabajos malos shouldn't make them.

As we drive through the Yunque, the women get very excited, making comments about the wonders of that landscape. We stop along one of the curved paths near the bank of a creek and park under a big tree, the roots of which descend a few meters beneath us. While the women begin descending carefully through a walking path toward the banks of the creek, Haydée instructs first the younger one: "Cathy, insert these dolls [wax proxies for Cathy and her boyfriend tied together] under the tree and ask whatever you want." Then to Lillian, who in the meantime disappears down the path, Haydée says, "You, too, plant in the ground your trabajo and plead. I will also make petitions for you from here." Interestingly, any broken santo should always be buried, according to various brujos, near a tree in the monte by its owner, who needs to light a candle while commending the santo back to the land of spirits. It is as if the spirits of the monte are not only warriors who fight, if needed, for seemingly impossible-to-win situations and protect and heal humans but also contain and reenergize any santo that returns to its abode.

One morning as Haydée, Reina, and I went shopping for food, we encountered a young couple walking a baby in a carriage. They greeted Haydée warmly, kissing her several times. The young man kissed her hand as well and said, "I had this baby thanks to what you did for me. He is yours." Haydée replied, "It wasn't what I prepared; it was God." As they

Spirits of the monte are entrusted with trabajos meant to unite lovers.

bid farewell, Haydée told me that this married couple had been unable to conceive a baby "for two or three years because he was bewitched with impotence by the angry mother of an ex-girlfriend." Haydée had conducted a ritual in the Yunque for this man, together with his wife and her mother, where the spirits of love that inhabit it were invoked as Haydée first cleansed him and then "poured invigorating libations on his penis." I was quite astonished that this very intimate ritual had been performed in front of his mother-in-law, but Haydée said it was necessary that she witness this ritual. Obviously, the ritual was a success, and Haydée was very proud about it.

Indeed, the Yunque is the place where brujos conduct rituals aimed at effecting personal, life-course transformations—of the kind Arnold Van Gennep identified as "rites of passage" (1960 [1908]). Haydée performs spiritual weddings in the Yunque. "Instead of a judge conducting the wedding ritual, the bride and groom are married in front of God. Whomever God unites, human beings can't separate," she said. I attended one such spiritual wedding (described in Romberg 2003b) that included another ritual performed to "hide" the groom from his persecutors. When young men get involved in minor illegal activities and then under the pressure of their parents or close relatives repent and decide to abandon their former way of life completely, they might seek the help of brujos with the hope that they will help them hide (spiritually) from the eyes (and bullets) of their previous associates. During divination Haydée advised Juana, Larry's mother, to send him away from Puerto Rico because she had a vision that he would be shot in the back. "He has a beautiful cuadro," she told Juana, "and he needs to develop it in the next velada. His cuadro needs to talk; it can't remain mute." Haydée promised Juana that she would spiritually "hide Larry in the monte today until he can leave Puerto Rico. It's better to have your son living in the *carajo* [shit] than buried in the cemetery. I will hide him and protect him." I cannot explain why, but I became very emotional at hearing Haydée—a mother who had lost two of her own children—speaking like that to another mother; it felt as if I, too, as a mother, was being addressed.

The monte in general and El Yunque in particular hold unique places in the imaginary of practitioners as sites of safety and shelter, perhaps as a result of their role among maroons in colonial times. Mountains are where ancestor warriors have protected from time immemorial those who hide in their forests. The monte is where brujos fly in their nightly incursions, frighteningly igniting the collective imaginary of fervent Catholics and Protestants, in search of remedies for their clients, even though, as Haydée once told me on our way to the Yunque for a trabajo, "when I fly over the Yunque nobody can see me." I remembered the "On the mountain Christ died" that she typically delivered after the Lord's Prayer, as Haydée was explaining to me that upon disincarnating, brujos join the spirits of other brujos hovering over the Yunque in order to influence the living; this also reminds me of Tonio's wish to fly over the Yunque. But then with her usual cheekiness, Haydée jokingly added, "Until that time arrives for me, let's stop on our way up to the mountain of the Yunque to buy a roasted chicken. I'm starving." Later, as she opened the delicious-smelling food in the car, she said, "This is how we brujos are," and we continued driving up the mountain with merengue rhythms playing loud on the radio. Parting the chicken into pieces on her lap, she handed a piece to Reina and one to me and—savoring a piece herself while singing and moving her upper body to the merengue tunes—said, "When we have to work la obra espiritual, nothing stops us, ha, ha, ha!"

Epilogue
A FAREWELL TRABAJO

Before leaving Puerto Rico in December 1996, I asked Haydée if she would address a letter to my dissertation committee granting me permission to publish any or all of the photographs, tape recordings, and videos I had compiled while working with her. She happily agreed to my request but, in keeping with her usual spiritual entrepreneurship, suggested that we combine the writing of the letter with the fashioning of a protective and propitiatory amulet for me, the two thus becoming a kind of farewell trabajo. Notably, I had never asked her, out of concern for my work with her mixed with fear of what might be revealed, to conduct a divination session for me. And now I reluctantly became the protagonist of a trabajo. Following her instructions and feeling quite odd, as if acting on a script that was not meant for me, I purchased seven twelve-inch-long, thin strips of colored ribbon—each indexing one of the colors of the Seven African Powers—and seven small, jingling bells at Basi's botánica and brought everything on the stipulated day.

It felt strange sitting for the first time on the assigned chair for clients beside her table in the altar. Reina was also there, occupying my usual position seated behind Haydée, taking pictures (always my role) of the whole ritual about to begin.

In a bureaucratic posture, Haydée writes the letter, spelling aloud its content as I have seen her doing so many times before when writing magic recipes for her clients. She asks Reina to bring her some honey, which she then pours on my extended open hand. She licks the honey and asks me to lick it too. Then she asks me to give her the ribbons and bells and begins to carefully tie a bell at the end of each colored ribbon.

I observe quietly, as I had seen clients do. After all the bells have been attached, she knots the ribbons together, jingles them above her head several times, places them on the table, pours honey on them, and wraps everything in aluminum foil, securing the packet with masking tape. I feel I do not need to ask her what the bells tied to the ribbons are for. She offers the little wrapped, two-inch by two-inch metallic packet to me and wishes me good luck. We raise our arms in "spiritual communion," as we

Haydée writes a recommendation on my behalf.

Haydée and I seal our spiritual bond with honey.

did many times before to mark our spiritual bond and, this time, also her good-luck wishes.

This was a special trabajo I had never seen her perform before. I think about the meaning of this amulet, which to this day I keep in one of the boxes where I store my research materials. The rainbow colors of the Seven African Powers come to mind as well as the jingling sound the bells made when she wiggled them gently over her head. Perhaps she once again *brujeó* (witched), as she had many times before, that her spiritual work (and my work documenting it) vibrate and resonate via the magical mimesis of color and sound throughout no less than *todo el cosmos*—the entire cosmos.

Notes

Introduction

1. The names of some places and people have been altered to protect their privacy. All translations from Spanish and all photographs in this book are mine.
2. Although it is theoretically relevant to read the healing practices of brujos through their different gendered and racial positionalities, this reading is foreign and even contradictory to the ways brujos enact and interpret the significance of their work. To impose this sort of theoretical contextualizing framework would defy their take on what they do.
3. This important shift was brought about by the economic boom of the island between World War II and the 1970s, prompted both by the 1950s development program Operation Bootstrap ("industrialization by invitation"), which, among other effects, raised the average incomes of Puerto Ricans 1,000 percent—with annual personal income rocketing from $118 to $1,200 (Wagenheim and Wagenheim 1994:183–184)—and promoted the various forms of federal aid for Puerto Rico administered by specialized state agencies under the system of welfare capitalism.
4. I borrow the notion of intertextuality in an inclusive way, in reference not just to texts but also to the various symbolic and gestural sources of empowerment embodied in ritual.
5. I was often put on the spot by healers who asked for my own interpretations of their dreams and visions (see Chapter Two), assuming—mistakenly!—that I was developing these competencies in the course of my work with them, that is, learning to let the spirits talk through me. Of course, it is also possible that they were testing me to assert their own mediumship powers.
6. See, for example, Csordas 1990, 1993, 1996; Desjarlais 1992, 1996; Rouch 1978; Stoller 1989a,b, 1995, 1996, 1997; and Taussig 1987, 1993, 1997, 1998, 1999.
7. The English orthography is *orisha*, the Yoruba is *òrìṣà*, and the Spanish is *ocha*.
8. The difficulty of falling into trance is widely reported. See Rouch 1971 and Stoller 1989a.

9. Consider also the contradiction in the aphorism "Superstition brings bad luck" (Raymond Smullyan 1983, quoted in Eco 1989:v).
10. Jay Ruby notes (1980:9) that according to David Efron (a student of Franz Boas who also researched gestures in a cultural context), the phrase "motor habits" was coined by Boas in his *Primitive Art* (1927:315), not by Roman Jakobson as some have suggested.
11. Moving beyond purely subjectivist takes on the role of imagination in ritual, I here assume "imagination" (or *imaginaire*, as it is also termed in French scholarship) as a social practice and a constructed landscape of past and present aspirations (Appadurai 1996:31), as well as a joint intersubjective production (Murphy 2005). See also Crapanzano (2004) about Sufi imagination as a bridge between inner and outer consciousness.
12. For a review of performative approaches to healing see Bell 1998, Csordas 1996, Laderman and Roseman 1996, and Tambiah 1968, 1985a,b.
13. I am extending the linguistic sense of "deictic," a term coined by Charles S. Peirce from the Greek *deiknýnai* and developed by others such as Michael Silverstein (1976), to indicate nonlinguistic, contextually sensitive, gestural behaviors performed in ritual contexts.
14. Suggestive of the often "cacophonous and humorous dialogue involved in fieldwork" (Weiss 1993:187), this reframing was one of the many ways in which subtle but not so innocent power relations were manifested during my fieldwork, as will be evident throughout this book.
15. See Jay Ruby on the various uses of photography in early anthropological research (2000:53–54) and Michael Taussig (1993) on the fascination with and fear of the mimetic faculty of new technologies of reproduction in general and of the camera in particular in anthropological and colonial encounters.
16. My textual presence and authorial voice (Hazan 1995) is rather eclectic, as will become apparent, shifting among those of the scholar, storyteller, insider, novice, advocate, and chosen witness (Jackson 2002, Stoller 1994).
17. On several occasions the authenticity of one healer's possession (not necessarily his or her healing powers) was confidentially discredited by another in my presence.
18. Elsewhere I have addressed the "public relations" role that my taking photos of every ritual and gesture played in my particular relationship with Haydée and the centrality of photos in today's competitive spiritual field for practitioners at large (Romberg 2003b).

Chapter One

1. I recently learned that these are the three theological virtues recognized also by Masons.

2. Until May 22, 2006, more than ten years after I heard Tonio mention Oilatum for the first time in my life, that name had remained in my manuscript with a question mark. Unsure whether I had heard him correctly, I had not been able to trace its correct spelling and meaning. Imagine my amazement when I see at my neighborhood pharmacy a packaged soap bar labeled "Oilatum." After more than ten years I finally can trace this soap's history and reconstruct its possible uses among brujos in Puerto Rico. In 1847 the Stiefel family, in Germany, began manufacturing soap with active medicinal ingredients for the treatment of skin problems. Perhaps it had already by then been introduced in Puerto Rico via Spain. In any case, in 1910 some of its products were introduced in the United States, and right after WWII, the entire business—manufacturing and distribution alike—moved to the United States. Its products are now sold in more than 110 countries, among which, of course, is Puerto Rico.
3. In the glossary of *El Monte* (1975:539), Cabrera provides a few stories about the *ruda* that parallel Tonio's account. "Brujos hate it: it's their worst enemy. '*Mata que mata brujo*' [Plant that kills magic works]."
4. Similarly, according to Steven Feld (1990:218), the Kaluli of Papua New Guinea assert that birds are the spirits of their deceased, the *ane mama*, or "the 'gone reflections' of Kaluli who have left the visible world upon death and reappeared . . . 'in the form of birds.' . . . 'Becoming a bird' is the passage from life to death." Malinowski notes (1935:39) that among the Trobriand Islanders, flying witches can assume the shapes of fireflies, night birds, or flying foxes. Tungus shamans speak of bird flights and tattoo their bodies with birds. In Songhay the great Sohanci sorcerers, Stoller tells me, "become" vultures and desert hawks in order to fly from one place to another (personal communication 2006). See also Rosalind Shaw (2002) for the nocturnal predatory nature of Temne flying witches.
5. Among Songhay sorcerers there is a similar competition: "They compete among themselves like gunslingers. They are children of fire, which can never be contained" (Stoller, personal communication 2006).
6. Similarly, Songhay witches fly in the night, but they are said to leave their skins on hooks and fly off (Stoller, personal communication 2006).
7. *Mabí* is a Taíno word for the drink made of its fermented bark and leaves often referred to as a creole beer. Based on its effervescent properties, the aphorism *subir como el mabí* (to raise like the mabí) suggests progress in business or a job.
8. Robert Farris Thompson (1983, 1993, 2005) has traced and recorded how certain elements of African expressive culture were incorporated in the dance, music, material culture, and worship of the African diaspora. See also Gundaker 1993.

9. About the "vertigo" and "horrific comedy" of members of dominant groups apprehending their own reflection in the representations of subjugated groups see Taussig 1993 (236–249) and Stoller 1989a (147–163) and 1995 (158–161).
10. In Nigeria, Changó is known as Shango and in Niger as Dongo; in both places he is an orphan spirit of mercurially dangerous disposition. Born in the Nupe region of the middle Niger River, he is the deity of thunder, who leaves death and destruction in his path—unless human beings pay him his due. (I thank Paul Stoller for this information in personal communication.)
11. Here I am inspired by Stoller's suggestion (1995, 1997) that colonial memories are embodied in spirit possession.
12. After learning from Paul Stoller that facing palms toward others is a widespread form of greeting in Africa, I would like to think that in the photographs of Tonio's hands he was not only complying with my request on the last day of my stay in Puerto Rico but in a way also saluting me and now you, the reader, farewell.
13. A few months after Tonio's death, I read a first draft of this chapter in his honor at a session convened by Haim Hazan for the Thirty-fourth World Congress of the International Institute of Sociology on Multiple Modernities in an Era of Globalization, in Tel Aviv, Israel, July 11–15, 1999.

Chapter Two

1. Notably, the "Greeks did not speak of *having* a dream but invariably of *seeing* one," which suggests "the belief in the 'objectivity' of the dream, in its independent existence 'outside' the dreamer" (Kilborne 1981:167).
2. The complete name is La Virgen de la Caridad (the Virgin of Charity, Our Lady of Charity) or La Virgen de la Caridad del Cobre (the Virgin of Charity of Cobre), the name given to her in Cuba and often shortened to La Virgen del Cobre. Gold and yellow are associated with her.
3. For comprehensive reviews by social scientists of the literature on dreams see, for example, Kilborne 1981, 1995; O'Nell 1976; and Tedlock 1987a,b, 1991, 1994.
4. Crapanzano notes (2004:57) that *barzakh*, the centerpiece of the Andalusian Sufi philosopher Ibn al-'Arabi (1165–1240), refers to in-between states that resist definition, like those of dream. In the words of Moulay Abedsalem, "The dream is between waking life and sleep" or "little death."
5. While recreating the conditions of preindustrial sleep, "Dr. Thomas Wehr and his colleagues at NIMH [National Institute of Mental Health] found that human subjects, deprived at night of artificial light over a span of several weeks, eventually exhibited a pattern of broken slumber—astonishingly, one practically identical to that of pre-industrial households. Significantly, the

intervening period of 'non-anxious wakefulness' possessed 'an endocrinology all of its own,' with visibly heightened levels of prolactin, a pituitary hormone best known for permitting chickens to brood contentedly atop eggs for long stretches of time. In fact, Wehr has likened this period of wakefulness to something approaching an altered state of consciousness not unlike meditation" (Ekirch 2001:22).

6. In his work on dreams in Sambia, Papua New Guinea (1987), Gilbert Herdt focuses on the dialogic context for dream reporting, identifying three major contexts for the circulation of dreams: public, secret, and private.
7. See also Crapanzano 1980, 1992.
8. Stewart also notes a common theme: the image of a wide field, which provides the context within which beneficial actions take place or where reassuring omens are received. The field does not have a meaning in itself, however, except as being the background "against which other meaningful symbols such as the egg or the coin are found" (1997:887).
9. Freud draws parallels (1994 [1911]) between myths, legends, works of fiction, and dreams in developing his theory of "typical dreams," arguing that myths, fairy tales, and legends, as well as some poetry and theater, reflect universal unconscious wishes, those that appear in dreams. These dreams are easily recognized. Malinowski in his *Sex and Repression in Savage Society* (1927) contests Freud's claim about the universality of the Oedipus complex, showing that it takes another form among the matrilineal society of the Trobriand Islanders (which is also reflected in their folk narratives), wherein the father is the benevolent figure and the mother's brother is the disciplinarian.
10. Stewart found that some dream narratives resembled one or another folk tale, but "the familiarity of the story did not diminish its credibility as a personal account of a private experience in the way it might for us if an acquaintance narrated a dream that, for example, closely corresponded to the Little Red Riding Hood story" (1997:879).
11. Similarly, Siegfried Nadel noted that for the Nupe of northern Nigeria, "the body of the newborn carries the mark of the ancestral element which is reincarnated within it" (Nadel 1954 cited in Augé 1999:27).
12. Notably, Moroccan fellahin recognize "the existence of false dreams, which they say, are caused by the devil, Shitan" and which occur most often not among pious men (Crapanzano 1992:241). Since dreams are affected by the condition of the dreamer, the dreamer can influence his dreams. Therefore, an individual can take certain measures to promote good dreams, such as sleeping on one's right side, refraining from sexual intercourse, and praying before going to sleep (242–243).
13. If indeed dreams and religious experiences each constitute a "finite province of meaning," following Schutz (1962), they each embody a particular

reality guided by its own distinctive logical, temporal, corporeal, and social dimensions. Movement between the provinces then becomes paradoxical only if one conceives of these provinces as separate ontological realms. For espiritistas, however, these are interconnected realms of experience and meaning.

14. Whenever speakers say "they" during divination, they mean "the spirits," and I signal this by capitalizing it, also in mid-sentence, as "They."
15. *Bozal* refers both to unbaptized, "unseasoned" African slaves brought to the New World, believed by the planters to be the coarsest of all slaves, and the particular speech they developed. See Armin Schwegler 2000, 2006 for excellent, detailed studies of bozal Spanish (*lengua congo*, characterized as the product of the convergence of various Bantu languages on Cuban soil) as it is spoken in Palo ritual practices in Cuba.
16. I have asked a young Yoruba speaker who is not involved in Santería to translate these Yoruba words used in Cuban Santería for me. Interestingly, the only words that have a slightly different meaning in vernacular speech are *ojiji*, which might mean "surprise"; *emi*, which means "me"; and *okan*, "one."
17. See Jean Rouch's discussion (1978) of the self and its doubles as they enter and leave the body during possession, magic, and sorcery rituals, their effects on the filmmaker-observer, and their weird presence during playbacks.
18. This is such a recurrent phenomenon that it would be impossible to mention all of the cross-cultural cases.
19. These types of nightly activities have been observed cross-culturally in both European and African contexts.
20. Ifá is the highest system of divination performed, using sixteen palm nuts (*ikin*) and small objects (*abira*) as symbols of specific alternatives and making marks (*odu*) on a wooden divining tray (*okpon*). Another system is the *dilogun*, performed with sixteen cowry shells; another is the *okpele*, or divining chain, made with half-pods; and the simplest system is *obi*, performed with four coconut halves to answer only yes/no questions.
21. Although scholars distinguish between trance and possession (see Firth 1967:296 and Douglas 1996:79–80), I use these terms indistinguishably here due to the nature of my ethnographic materials.
22. Discussing classic anthropological research, Kilborne traces the role of collective representations (1981), especially in what Jackson Stewart Lincoln termed "culture pattern dreams" (1970 [1935]).
23. Contrary to my experiences, Michael Jackson notes that his Kuranko informant of northeastern Sierra Leone was very interested in comparing dreams and dream interpretations with him. Indeed, Jackson recorded his own and his informant's dreams with the hope of gaining a dialogic

perspective on Kuranko dream interpretations (2002:271).

24. Making the researcher's own dreams public is not a new practice. Psychiatrist and anthropologist W. H. R. Rivers' description of one of his own dreams, which he labeled "Presidency," was published in *Conflict and Dream* (1923), a posthumous volume of his work. Adam Kuper years later (1979) subjected Rivers' "Presidency" dream to his structural analysis together with a dream by a Plains Indian published by George Devereux (1969 [1951]). More recently (1991), Nadia Serematakis addressed her own dreams in the field.
25. Unlike Jackson, who self-assuredly interpreted the dreams of his Kuranko informant (2002:271–274), I was hesitant to offer my interpretations when dreamers were disturbed by their dreams because I often felt that they might not coincide with the dreamers' Spiritist expectations and interpretative frameworks.

Chapter Three

1. Several anthropologists of ritual have engaged Austin's argument, among them Fredrik Barth (1975), Bruce Kapferer (1986), Roy Rappaport (1979), and Stanley Tambiah (1968, 1985a,b). Notably, predating Austin's linguistic-legal approach to performatives, Malinowski conceptualized magical words from a performative perspective, coining the phrase "verbal missile" to convey their pragmatic efficacy (Tambiah 1990:74). See also Deborah Kapchan 1995 for a discussion of the performative move in folklore and the social sciences.
2. In some religions, not only are the words sacred but also their performance. Religious experience is encountered during worship through song and movement as well as through discourse. In the historical black church, for example, worshipers participating in the "ring shout" transformed biblical messages and stories into movement. "The dancers or 'shouters,' as they were called, would form a circle, and to the cadence of a favorite shout song or 'running spiritual' would begin a slow, syncopated shuffling, jerking movement 'bumped' by the handclapping or body slapping of those waiting on the sidelines" (Lincoln and Mamiya 1990:352). Albert Raboteau notes, "Exodus became dramatically real, especially in the songs and prayer meetings of the slaves who reenacted the story as they shuffled in the ring dance they called the 'Shout'" (1995:33).
3. I transcribe parts of this ritual in stanzaic form to convey their poetic rendering.
4. Notably, I found a similar folk prayer (*alabado*) transcribed and translated by folklorist Juan B. Rael in 1940 as it was recited by a seventy-year-old resident of Cerro, New Mexico. It is a part of the collection Hispano Music and

Culture of the Northern Rio Grande in the Library of Congress' American Memory.

5. This expression indicates the presence of the spirits.

6. When rituals "work," Turner argues, "the exchange of qualities between the semantic poles seems . . . to achieve genuinely cathartic effects, causing in some cases real transformations of character and of social relationships" (1974:56). As a result of ritual, "people are induced to want to do what they must do. In this sense ritual action is akin to a sublimation process. . . . Paradigms in ritual have an orectic function of impelling action as well as to thought." Relevant here is the distinction Turner makes between a cluster of significata that refer to the moral and social order, or the ideological pole of symbols, and a cluster of significata that refer to the natural and physiological level, or the sensory pole (related to the orectic function), which "may be expected to arouse desires and feelings" (1967:28).

7. It was first published in *Impulse, Annual of Contemporary Dance* (1951).

8. The power of iconic communication is addressed by Bateson in his discussion of "primary processes" in dreams and their relation to artistic style when he notes that in "iconic communication there is no tense, no simple negation, no modal marker" (1972b:140). James Fernandez seems to give icons a comparatively important function in expressive culture for their emotion-eliciting value, arguing that according to the situation, a token can be a "sign-image, pregnant with felt but unconceptualized meanings; a symbol, possessed of fully conceptualized and often articulated meanings; or a signal, whose meaning lies in the orientation it gives to interaction" (1974:120).

9. See J. David Sapir 1977 for the connection between metaphors and riddles.

10. From one of Sternberg's classic films, *Morocco* (1930), to contemporary commercial and artistic films and comic books, the image of falling pearls has become a key symbol, recurrently referenced and quoted for strong emotional states and tragic events. In *Morocco*, Marlene Dietrich snaps the pearl necklace given to her by her rich suitor, Menjou. The string is caught in a chair, and the pearls spill over the floor as Dietrich rushes out of the room in search of another man, her true love. In Mehrjui's postrevolutionary Iranian film *Leila* (1996), in anger the main character breaks the pearl necklace her mother-in-law gave her as a subtle form of bribery, and the camera cuts to successive closeups of the pearls falling into the bathroom sink and onto the floor. In *God's Hands* (1998), a big-wave riders' story, pearls fall on a seashell in slow motion. In Matthew Barney's artistic film *Drawing Restraint 9* (2005), pearls sensuously fall out of a diver's mouth. And in the comic-book series *Batman: The Long Halloween* (1996–1997) about the death of Batman's parents, the murder of his mother, Martha Wayne, is dramatized

by the image of her string of pearls being torn from her neck and falling into the gutter.

11. Compare this with the "dual meaning" of photographs in a center for the aged in London, where some individuals, according to Haim Hazan (1986:309–310), wished to be photographed only under certain conditions. Faced with "the self-contradictory meaning of photographs," they rejected any form of self-objectification, even as they desired to be visible in society.
12. Cabrera notes that azogue acts as a stimulant that by its movement makes the *nganga* (*prenda*, or cauldron where spirits of the dead are kept by the palero) "beat continuously like a heart" (1979:145).
13. Although powerful brujos do manage evil forces, they claim that they do so only as retaliation to evil wished or summoned to harm their clients. As I discuss extensively elsewhere (Romberg 2003b:109–171), brujos espiritistas see their work not as bad or evil but as the result of godly gifts and, as such, guided by the life of Jesus and the ethical tenets of Spiritism.
14. According to Robert Farris Thompson, the prendas or ngangas that Cabrera mentions are connected—by way of the effects of slavery in the Americas—to the *minkisi* (singular *nkisi*), magical objects of the Bakongo in Africa (1983:117–125).
15. The Dominican popular musical genre merengue is as pervasive in Puerto Rico today as Puerto Rican salsa music.

Chapter Four

1. See for example Classen, Howes, and Synnott 1994; Desjarlais 1992, 1996; Howes 1991; Laderman and Roseman 1996; Rouch 1971, 1978; Stoller 1989a,b, 1995, 1996, 1997; and Taussig 1993, 1999.
2. In the course of the following months, both he and his wife, Lorena, became familiar with personal details about my background.
3. This could be seen as an independent addition to Mauro's own genealogy of religious ancestors—babalawos in his lineage—whom he recalls, not unlike healers do in West Africa, at the beginning of certain rituals.
4. The same kind of exchange exists in various magic and healing and magic traditions the world over.
5. Bascom documented (1969) the hundreds of myths that compose Ifá in a unique volume, with transcriptions in Yoruba as given to him by Yoruba babalawos during 1937–1938 and then translated to English.
6. Though I ended up focusing on espiritismo and brujería in my dissertation and book (Romberg 2003b), I am forever grateful for what I learned from Mauro and Lorena.

7. The latter two conditions correspond to what Labov termed the "interpretable" and "reportable" aspects of verbal behavior (mentioned in Hymes 1975).
8. See, for example, how Dan Sperber (1985) and Edward Evan-Pritchard (1976) have addressed the ethnographically "fantastic" and "apparently irrational," respectively. A more recent discussion by Stoller (1998) illuminates these theoretical and experiential dilemmas.
9. Ervin Goffman refers (1981) to the implied change in the status of addressees in speech as a change of "footing," by which he suggests "a change in the alignment we take up to ourselves and the others present as expressed in the way we manage the production and reception of an utterance. A change in our footing is another way of talking about a change in our frame of events." Indeed, "participants over the course of their speaking constantly change their footing, these changes being a persistent feature of natural talk" (128).
10. Testing Searl's speech act theory in ritual contexts, John W. Du Bois shows (1993) that certain mechanical oracles (decided by random technologies), such as those among the Azande and the Yoruba, produce speech acts that afford meaning without intention.
11. Here I follow Mikhail M. Bakhtin's work on speech genres (1986:60, written in 1952–1953), in which he develops his conception of language (in contrast to de Saussure) as living dialogue. Speech genres determine those relatively stable types of utterances defined by a particular thematic content, style, and compositional structure, all of which depend as a whole on a particular sphere of communication.
12. Similarly, the musical accompaniment in Chinese opera has the role of punctuating the spoken parts. The head percussionist conducts the accompaniment and, like Santería drummers during possession rituals, coordinates the development of the dramatic action. The various gongs are used to coordinate the action as well as the position and personality of each character as the plot develops. The large gong is used for serious, exciting, and formal situations or settings, such as a government office or a military post, and to accompany the actions of the *sheng* and *ching* male roles. The small gong is used to relieve the action, to accompany humorous situations and the actions of young maidens and clowns, and to create a quiet atmosphere for settings such as a household, a temple, or a convent. Generally, the large gong accompanies the actions of important persons and the small gong, ordinary persons (*Travel in Taiwan* 1995).
13. Similar types of passages abound in West African divination. I thank Stoller for this note.
14. Bascom (1969) and others have noted that Ifá divination is a complex communication system between gods and humans that provides hundreds of proverbs and aphorisms that need to be interpreted in very elaborate

dialogic ways by the diviner and the client in order to ultimately make them speak to the client's particular situation.

15. Stoller reminded me that also in West African spirit possession there are usually women called *femmes tranquils* who protect mediums from inflicting harm on themselves or others nearby during episodes of possession.
16. Tártago is a highly toxic plant used in the Middle East to cleanse homes after a birth; its general magic use is meant for protection both inside and outside the home (Murcia and Hoyos 1998–2004).
17. The sacred/profane distinction elaborated first by Emile Durkheim (1964 [1915]) and reworked by Roger Callois (2001 [1939]) and Mircea Eliade (1959 [1957]) has pervaded much of the analysis of religious experiences.
18. Tuesdays and Fridays at noon and midnight are considered the most effective days and times for trabajos, apparently because at midpoints of the week and of the day spirit communication is most favorable. Similarly, certain days of the week were favored in sixteenth- and seventeenth-century England (Thomas 1971). In Songhay, for example, the "days" of the spirits are Sundays and Thursdays, the first and last days of what was the precolonial five-day week. (I thank Stoller for this comment.)
19. Indeed, for this reason sorcerers in Africa, Stoller mentioned to me, are hesitant to utter names, for if one speaks a person's name the vibrations of those sounds render that person vulnerable to sorcerous attacks.
20. I found the expression *¡cará!* in one of Armin Schwegler's transcriptions of Palo ritual speech (2006: 87, 88, 92), where he notes that it is not entirely clear whether the exclamatory *¡cará!* (translated as "gee!" or "shit!") is just a phonetic distortion derived from the Spanish *caray* (a euphemistic variant of *carajo*). When asked, non-initiates were not able to identify the meaning of *¡cará!*, but due to its high frequency of use in the ritual speech of one of Schwegler's informants, he concluded that "its primary function is that of a filler" (92). For my purposes, this cross-cultural coincidence suggests that bozal Spanish occurs in various Afro-Latin religions, not just brujería.
21. de Certeau makes a more sweeping argument (1984:131) by questioning the possibility of "the living word" or an "orality" that has not been already inscribed in the scriptural economy of the "modern age."

Chapter Five

1. Brujos invoke in the making of some trabajos "all five senses" of those involved: "I invoke the five senses of so-and-so [a man] in order to unite him to the five senses of so-and-so [a woman]."
2. Essentially based on a pragmatic motivation for believing in God, "Pascal's Wager" states, in lay terms, that if we believe in God and God does not exist,

we do not lose or gain anything; but if we do not believe in God and God does exist, we gain nothing and lose much (cf. Hájek 2004). The pragmatic essence of Pascal's Wager can be identified in other religions such as the forms of Buddhism in which practitioners are instructed to act as if the doctrines of rebirth and *kamma* (karma, action) are valid in order to generate during the course of their present lives the rewards that these two precepts promise for future lives. The Spiritist laws of Cause and Effect, Love, and Reincarnation are based on these very premises.

3. Slavoj Zizek adds to Pascal's dictum a self-referential and a political twist in "With or Without Reason: What's Wrong with Fundamentalism?" part 1 (n.d.). He adds first a self-referential causality: "Kneel down and you will believe that you knelt down because you believed!" And second, "Kneel down and you will thereby MAKE SOMEONE ELSE BELIEVE!" (www.lacan.com/zizpassion.htm). See Zizek 2001 for more on belief.
4. Exciting, cutting-edge research is being conducted on the connections of brain, mind, and body from interdisciplinary perspectives at, among other centers, the University of Texas Medical Branch by the Mind, Brain, Body and Health Initiative, a research network established in 2001, and at Harvard University by the Mind, Brain, Behavior Interfaculty Initiative, established in 1993. These questions are also addressed in popular publications based on scientific theories. *Waking the Tiger* (Levine 1997) suggests exercises for self-healing based on the premise that traumatic experiences in humans are—as in other animals—first and foremost a physiological reaction. (I thank Janet Theophano for drawing my attention to this book.)
5. The various personality traits of the painted-face characters are indicated by different colors: red designates an honest, loyal, righteous, straightforward, and trustworthy character; white stands for cunning, craftiness, and scheming; black for bravery and justice; and green for cruelty, pride, violence, and toughness. The colors of the costumes, which might not follow the color code for facial painting, are significant as well: yellow is for royalty, red for high-ranking officials, green for virtuous persons, black for the tough, and brown for the aged (*Travel in Taiwan* 1995).
6. The *sheng* is subdivided into the elderly sheng, the young sheng, and the martial sheng. The *tan* (female) roles include the elderly tan, the tan dressed in green, the flower tan, the sword-horse tan, and the martial tan. "Although the *ching* and *chou* are supporting actors, they are still very important. The ching role is a strong-willed male character, either straightforward or scheming. His facial makeup is greatly exaggerated so his role can be identified at a glance. The chou, or clown character, is a very special one. The chou is a jocular, satirizing character who integrates his impromptu comic relief into

the performance. He also steps out to make objective editorial comments on what is happening in the story" (*China, an Inner Realm* 1998).

7. The tan roles are characterized by "the high-pitched 'squeaky' voice cultivated to attract the attention of the audience and appeal to the auditory preference of traditional Chinese gentlemen" (*Travel in Taiwan* 1995).

8. David Scott launches a critique (1991) of Bruce Kapferer's theatrical and experience approach to Sinhalese exorcism possession rituals (*Yaktovil*), arguing that these involve, in fact, "the production of social discourses, social practices, and processes of negotiation," which Scott associates with the power relations that create the "experience" of ritual (117).

9. "To pass a cuadro" means to let one's protecciones possess the body and manifest themselves. It is a means of empowerment by letting the protecciones reveal themselves and thereby effect their healing power in one's life (see Romberg 2003b:142–149).

10. I have heard espiritistas científicos use these terms during my fieldwork but not popular espiritistas and brujos such as Haydée. I have discussed elsewhere (Romberg 2003a,b) the differences in these variants of espiritismo.

11. About Saint Elias and his connection to trabajos malos see Romberg (2003b:153, 168, 253).

12. The theatricality of this exorcism and others performed by brujos is startlingly similar to those reported in de Certeau (1990 [1970]), suggesting the continuous if modified force of Christian discourses of possession and exorcism.

13. Sometime in the seventeenth century, folk tradition says, a statue of the Virgin was found floating on the sea off the eastern shores of Cuba by three fishermen, all named Juan: Juan the black slave, Juan the Indian, and Juan the Spaniard. Her statue was later enshrined in a village called Cobre (copper) and became the object of popular devotion over the centuries. Because of the miraculous recovery of the statue of the Virgin by three ethnically different men and the subsequent intense devotion to this saint (especially during the wars of independence in the last quarter of the nineteenth century) and following the many miracles attributed to her intervention, she was eventually canonized, in 1915, as the patron saint of Cuba. She came to symbolize, mainly among the popular classes, the "creole" character of the Cuban nation. (For a study of the contested nature of the meaning of La Virgen de La Caridad among Cuban exiles in Miami see Tweed 1999.) The history of La Caridad in Puerto Rico and her resonance among Puerto Rican women is yet to be researched; but the actual migration of Cubans and the global circulation of religious icons—in addition to the folk narrative associated with her creole trajectory—might explain in part her fame on the island.

Chapter Six

1. Corojo (gru gru palm, *Acrocomia Crispa*) is owned by Changó, Cabrera writes in the glossary of *El Monte* (1974:411). Cabrera supplies the recipe for an offering made with corojo butter (from the nuts of the corojo, or Cuba belly palm) and dedicated to the orishas. Especially for Changó, when he is angry, its *otanes*, or stones (which embody the orisha's essence or aché), should be rubbed with corojo butter.
2. A number of students of Afro-Latin religions have focused on altars, their historical origins in Africa, and their transformation in the African diaspora, as well as their aesthetic and religious significance. See D. Brown 1999, 2003; K. Brown 1995a,b; Consentino 1995; Flores-Peña and Evanchuk 1994; and Thompson 1983, 1993.
3. Although Haydée refers to the sea as the abode of La Caridad, she and others place her in the river when they refer to Ochún, the African side of La Caridad. Yemanyá, on the other hand, is the African orisha of the sea.

References

Abrahams, Roger D. 1968. "Introductory Remarks to a Rhetorical Theory of Folklore." *Journal of American Folklore* 81 (319): 143–158.

———. 1977. "Toward an Enactment-Centered Theory of Folklore." In *Frontiers of Folklore*, ed. William R. Bascom, 79–120. American Anthropological Association Selected Symposium. Washington, DC: Westview Press.

———. 1981. "Ordinary and Extraordinary Experience." In *The Anthropology of Experience*, ed. Victor W. Turner and Edward M. Bruner, 45–72. Urbana: University of Illinois Press.

———. 2005. *Everyday Life: A Poetics of Vernacular Practices*. Philadelphia: University of Pennsylvania Press.

Agosto Cintrón, Nélida. 1996. *Religión y cambio social en Puerto Rico (1898–1940)*. Río Piedras, Puerto Rico: Ediciones Huracán.

Appadurai, Arjun, ed. 1986. *The Social Life of Things: Commodities in Cultural Perspective*. Cambridge, England: Cambridge University Press.

———. 1996. *Modernity at Large: Cultural Dimensions of Globalization*. Minneapolis: University of Minnesota Press.

Aretxaga, Begoña. 2005. *States of Terror: Begoña Aretxaga's Essays*. Reno, NV: Center for Basque Studies.

Augé, Marc. 1999. *The War of Dreams: Studies in Ethno Fiction*. London: Pluto Press.

Austin, John L. 1975. *How to Do Things with Words*. 2d edition. Cambridge: Harvard University Press.

Bakhtin, Mikhail M. 1981. *The Dialogic Imagination: Four Essays by M. M. Bakhtin*. Ed. Michael Holquist; trans. Caryl Emerson and Michael Holquist. Austin: University of Texas Press.

———. 1986. *Speech Genres and Other Late Essays*. Ed. Caryl Emerson and Michael Holquist; trans. Vern W. McGee. Austin: University of Texas Press.

Barth, Fredrik. 1975. *Ritual and Knowledge Among the Baktaman of New Guinea*. New Haven, CT: Yale University Press.

Bascom, William. 1969. *Ifa Divination: Communication Between Gods and Men in West Africa*. Bloomington: Indiana University Press.

Bateson, Gregory. 1972a. "Metalogue: Why Do Frenchmen?" *Steps to an Ecology of Mind*. San Francisco: Chandler.

———. 1972b. "Style, Grace, and Information in Primitive Art." *Steps to an Ecology of Mind*. San Francisco: Chandler.

———. 1972c. "A Theory of Play and Fantasy." *Steps to an Ecology of Mind*. San Francisco: Chandler.

Bauman, Richard, and Charles L. Briggs. 1990. "Poetics and Performance as Critical Perspectives on Language and Social Life." *Annual Review of Anthropology* 19:59–88.

Bauman, Richard, and Joel Sherzer, eds. 1989. *Explorations in the Ethnography of Speaking*. 2d edition. New York: Cambridge University Press.

Beckett, Samuel. 1965 [1959]. *Krapp's Last Tape and Embers*. London: Faber and Faber.

Behar, Ruth. 1996. *The Vulnerable Observer: Anthropology That Breaks Your Heart*. Boston: Beacon Press.

Bell, Catherine. 1998. "Performance." In *Critical Terms for Religious Studies*, ed. Mark C. Taylor, 205–224. Chicago: University of Chicago Press.

Bhabha, Homi K. 1994. *The Location of Culture*. London: Routledge.

Black, Max. 1962. *Models and Metaphors: Studies in Language and Philosophy*. Ithaca, NY: Cornell University Press.

Boas, Franz. 1888. "On Certain Songs and Dances of the Kwakiutl of British Columbia." *Journal of American Folklore* 1:49–64.

———. 1927. *Primitive Art*. Cambridge: Harvard University Press.

———. 1944. "Dance and Music in the Life of the Northwest Coast Indians of North America (Kwakiutl)." In *The Function of Dance in Human Society*, ed. Franz Boas, 5–19. New York: Dance Horizons.

Bourdieu, Pierre. 1990 [1980]. *The Logic of Practice*. Trans. Richard Nice. Stanford, CA: Stanford University Press.

Briggs, Charles L. 1986. *Learning How to Ask: A Sociolinguistic Appraisal of the Role of the Interview in Social Science Research*. Cambridge, England: Cambridge University Press.

———. 1996. "The Meaning of Nonsense, the Poetics of Embodiment, and the Production of Power in Warao Healing." In *The Performance of Healing*, ed. Carol Laderman and Marina Roseman, 185–232. New York: Routledge.

Brown, David H. 1999. "Altared Spaces: Afro-Cuban Religions and the Urban Landscape in Cuba and the U.S." In *Gods of the City: Religion and the American Urban Landscape*, ed. Robert A. Orsi, 155–230. Bloomington: Indiana University Press.

———. 2003. *Santeria Enthroned: Art, Ritual, and Innovation in an Afro-Cuban Religion*. Chicago: University of Chicago Press.

Brown, Karen McCarthy. 1995a. "The Altar Room, A Dialogue." In *Sacred Arts of Haitian Vodou*, ed. Donald J. Consentino, 226–239. Exhibition catalog. Los Angeles: University of California, Los Angeles (UCLA), Fowler Museum of Cultural History.

———. 1995b. "Serving the Spirits: The Ritual Economy of Haitian Vodou." In *Sacred Arts*, ed. Consentino, 205–225.

———. 1999. "Staying Grounded in a High-Rise Building: Ecological Dissonance and Ritual Accommodation in Haitian Vodou." In *Gods of the City: Religion and the American Urban Landscape*, ed. Robert A. Orsi, 79–102. Bloomington: Indiana University Press.

Bruner, Edward M. 1989. "Dreaming: Anthropological and Psychological Interpretations." *American Ethnologist* 16 (3): 602–603.

Burke, Kenneth. 1969. *A Rhetoric of Motives*. Berkeley: University of California Press.

Cabrera, Lydia. 1975 [1954]. *El monte*. Miami: Ediciones Universal.

———. 1979. *Reglas de Congo, Palo Monte, Mayombe*. Miami: Colección del Chichereku en el Exilio.

Callois, Roger. 2001 [1939]. *Man and the Sacred*. Trans. Meyer Barash. Urbana: University of Illinois Press.

Cantwell, Robert. 1993. *Ethnomimesis: Folklore and the Representation of Culture*. Chapel Hill: University of North Carolina Press.

Chapin, Macpherson. 1976. "Muu Ikala: Cuna Birth Ceremony." In *Ritual and Symbol in Native Central America*, ed. Philip Young and James Howe, 57–65. University of Oregon Anthropological Papers No. 9. Eugene, OR: Department of Anthropology, University of Oregon.

———. 1983. "Curing Among the San Blas Kuna of Panama." Ph.D. diss., University of Arizona.

China, an Inner Realm. 1998. "Opera." ThinkQuest. http://library.thinkquest.org/20443/opera.html.

Cicourel, Aaron V. 1974. *Cognitive Sociology: Language and Meaning in Social Interaction*. New York: Free Press.

Classen, Constance, David Howes, and Anthony Synnott. 1994. *Aroma: The Cultural History of Smell*. London: Routledge.

Clifford, James, and George R. Marcus, eds. 1986. *Writing Culture: The Poetics and Politics of Ethnography*. Berkeley: University of California Press.

Cole, Herbert M. 1989. *Icons: Ideals and Power in the Art of Africa*. Washington, DC: National Museum of African Art, Smithsonian Institution Press.

Comaroff, Jean, and John L. Comaroff, eds. 2001. *Millennial Capitalism and the Culture of Neoliberalism*. Durham, NC: Duke University Press.

Connerton, Paul. 1989. *How Societies Remember*. Cambridge, England: Cambridge University Press.

Consentino, Donald J., ed. 1995. *Sacred Arts of Haitian Vodou*. Exhibition catalog. Los Angeles: Fowler Museum of Cultural History, University of California at Los Angeles.

Cottet, Philippe. 2000. "René Girard and the Mimetic Desire." *Alphabestiaire*. http://www.cottet.org/girard/index.en.htm.

Crapanzano, Vincent. 1980. *Tuhami: Portrait of a Moroccan*. Chicago: University of Chicago Press.

———. 1992. *Hermes' Dilemma and Hamlet's Desire: On the Epistemology of Interpretation*. Cambridge: Harvard University Press.

———. 2004. *Imaginative Horizons: An Essay in Literary- Philosophical Anthropology*. Chicago: University of Chicago Press.

Crossley, Nick. 2001. *The Social Body: Habit, Identity and Desire*. London: Sage Publications.

Csordas, Thomas J. 1990. "Embodiment as a Paradigm for Anthropology." *Ethos* 18 (1): 5–47.

———. 1993. "Somatic Modes of Attention." *Cultural Anthropology* 8 (2): 135–156.

———. 1996. "Imaginal Performance and Memory in Ritual Healing." In *Performance of Healing*, ed. Laderman and Roseman, 91–113.

——-. 1997. "Prophecy and the Performance of Metaphor." *American Anthropologist* 99 (2): 321–332.

Culler, Jonathan. 1981. "Convention and Meaning: Derrida and Austin." *New Literary History* 13 (1): 15–30.

Curti, Merle. 1996. "The American Exploration of Dreams and Dreamers." *Journal of the History of Ideas* 27 (3): 391–416.

de Certeau, Michel. 1984. *The Practice of Everyday Life*. Trans. Steven Rendall. Berkeley: University of California Press.

———. 1990 [1970]. *The Possession at Loudun*. Trans. Michael B. Smith; foreword by Stephen Greenblatt. Chicago: University of Chicago Press.

Deren, Maya. 2005 [1985]. *Divine Horsemen: The Living Gods of Haiti*. Filmed 1947–1951; ed. Cherel Ito. Montauk, NY: Mystic Fire Video.

Desjarlais, Robert R. 1992. *Body and Emotion: The Aesthetics of Illness and Healing in the Nepal Himalayas*. Philadelphia: University of Pennsylvania Press.

———. 1996. "Presence." In *Performance of Healing*, ed. Laderman and Roseman, 143–164.

——-. 1997. *Shelter Blues: Sanity and Selfhood Among the Homeless*. Philadelphia: University of Pennsylvania Press.

Devereux, George. 1969 [1951]. *Reality and Dream: Psychotherapy of a Plains Indian*. New York: Anchor Books.

Diamond, Stanley. 1974. *In Search of the Primitive: A Critique of Civilization*. Foreword by Eric R. Wolf. New Brunswick, NJ: Transaction Books.

Dodds, Eric R. 1973. *The Greeks and the Irrational*. Berkeley: University of California Press.

Douglas, Mary. 1996 [1970]. *Natural Symbols: Explorations in Cosmology*. London: Routledge.

Duany, Jorge. 2002. *The Puerto Rican Nation on the Move: Identities on the Island and in the United States*. Chapel Hill: University of North Carolina Press.

———. 2003. "La religiosidad popular en Puerto Rico: Reseña de la literatura desde la perspectiva antropológica." In *Vírgenes, magos y escapularios: Imaginería, etnicidad y religiosidad popular en Puerto Rico*, ed. Ángel Quintero Rivera, 175–192. 2d edition. San Juan: Centro de Investigaciones Sociales, Universidad de Puerto Rico; and Centro de Investigaciones Académicas, Universidad del Sagrado Corazón.

Du Bois, John W. 1993. "Meaning Without Intention: Lessons from Divination." In *Responsibility and Evidence in Oral Discourse*, ed. Jane H. Hill and Judith T. Irvine, 48–71. Cambridge, England: Cambridge University Press.

Dunham, Katherine. 1969. *Island Possessed*. Garden City, NY: Doubleday.

Durkheim, Emile. 1964 [1915]. *The Elementary Forms of the Religious Life*. London: Allen and Unwin.

Eco, Umberto. 1983. *The Name of the Rose*. Trans. William Weaver. San Diego: Harcourt Brace Jovanovich.

———. 1989. *Foucault's Pendulum*. Trans. William Weaver. San Diego: Harcourt Brace Jovanovich.

Edgar, Iain R. 1995. *Dreamwork: Anthropology and the Caring Professions: A Cultural Approach to Dreamwork*. Brookfield, VT: Avebury.

———. 2004. *Guide to Imagework: Imagination-Based Research Methods*. London: Routledge.

Eggan, Dorothy. 1949. "The Significance of Dreams for Anthropological Research." *American Anthropologist* 51 (2): 177–198.

Ekirch, Roger A. 2001. "Sleep We Have Lost: Pre-industrial Slumber in the British Isles." *American Historical Review* 106, no. 2 (April). http://www.historycooperative.org/journals/ahr/106.2/ah000343.html.

Eliade, Mircea. 1959 [1957]. *The Sacred and the Profane: The Nature of Religion*. Trans. Williard R. Trask. San Diego, CA: Harcourt.

Evans-Pritchard, Edward E. 1976 [1937]. *Witchcraft, Oracles and Magic Among the Azande*. Oxford, England: Clarendon Press.

Ewing, Katherine P. 1990. "The Dream of Spiritual Initiation and the Organization of Self Representations Among Pakistani Sufis." *American Ethnologist* 17 (1): 56–74.

Face of the Gods: Art and Altars of Africa and the African Americas. 1994. Exhibition catalog. Berkeley: University of California, Berkeley.

Favret-Saada, Jeanne. 1989. "Unbewitching as Therapy." *American Ethnologist* 16 (1): 40–56.

———. 1990. "About Participation." *Culture, Medicine, and Psychiatry* 14:189–199.

Feld, Steven. 1990. *Sound and Sentiment: Birds, Weeping, Poetics, and Song in Kaluli Expression*. 2d edition. Philadelphia: University of Pennsylvania Press.

Fernandez, James W. 1974. "The Mission of Metaphor in Expressive Culture." *Current Anthropology* 15 (2): 119–145.

Firth, Raymond. 1934. "The Meaning of Dreams in Tikopia." In *Essays Presented to C. G. Seligman*, ed. E. Evans-Pritchard, R. Firth, B. Malinowski, and I. Shapera. London: Kegan Paul.

———. 1967. *Tikopia Ritual and Belief.* London: Allen and Unwin.

Flores-Peña, Ysamur, and Roberta J. Evanchuk. 1994. *Speaking Without a Voice: Santería Garments and Altars.* Jackson: University of Mississippi Press.

Foster, Michael K. 1989. "When Words Become Deeds: An Analysis of Three Iroquois Longhouse Speech Events." In *Explorations in the Ethnography of Speaking*, ed. Bauman and Sherzer, 354–367.

Foucault, Michel. 1980. *Power/Knowledge: Selected Interviews and other Writings, 1972–1977.* Trans. Colin Gordon. New York: Pantheon Books.

Frazer, Sir James George. 1960 [1922]. *The Golden Bough: A Study in Magic and Religion.* Vol. 1. New York: Macmillan.

Freud, Sigmund. 1994 [1911]. *The Interpretation of Dreams.* Authorized translation of 3d edition; introduction by A. A. Brill. New York: Barnes and Noble.

Garfinkel, Harold. 1967. *Studies in Ethnomethodology.* Englewood Cliffs, NJ: Prentice-Hall.

Garrison, Vivian. 1977. "The Puerto Rican Syndrome in Psychiatry and Espiritismo." In *Case Studies in Spirit Possession*, ed. Vincent Crapanzano and Vivian Garrison, 383–449. New York: John Wiley.

Geertz, Clifford. 1973. "Thick Description: Toward an Interpretive Theory of Culture." In his *The Interpretation of Cultures: Selected Essays*, 3–30. New York: Basic Books.

———. 1986. "Making Experiences, Authoring Selves." Epilogue to *Anthropology of Experience*, ed. Turner and Bruner, 373–380.

Geschiere, Peter. 1997. *The Modernity of Witchcraft: Politics and the Occult in Postcolonial Africa.* Trans. Peter Geschiere and Janet Reitman. Charlottesville: University Press of Virginia.

Gibbal, Jean-Marie. 1994 [1988]. *Genii of the River Niger.* Trans. Beth G. Raps; foreword by Paul Stoller. Chicago: University of Chicago Press.

Giddens, Anthony. 1991. *Modernity and Self-Identity: Self and Society in the Late Modern Age.* Stanford, CA: Stanford University Press.

Ginzburg, Carlo. 1983 [1966]. *The Night Battles: Witchcraft and Agrarian Cults in the Sixteenth and Seventeenth Centuries.* Trans. John and Anne Tedeschi. Baltimore: Johns Hopkins University Press.

Girard, René. 1965 [1961]. *Deceit, Desire, and the Novel: Self and Other in Literary Structure.* Trans. Yvonne Frecero. Baltimore: Johns Hopkins University Press.

Goffman, Ervin. 1981. *Forms of Talk.* Philadelphia: University of Pennsylvania Press.

Good, Byron. 1994. *Medicine, Rationality, and Experience: An Anthropological Perspective.* Cambridge, England: Cambridge University Press.

Gossen, Garry H. 1989. "To Speak with a Heated Heart: Chamula Canons of Style and Good Performance." In *Explorations in the Ethnography of Speaking*, ed. Bauman and Sherzer, 389–413.

Goulet, Jean-Guy. 1994. "Dreams and Visions in Other Lifewords." In *Being Changed by Cross-Cultural Experiences*, ed. Jean-Guy Goulet and David E. Young, 6–38. Peterborough, Ontario, Canada: Broadview Press.

Goulet, Jean-Guy, and David E. Young. 1994. "Theoretical and Methodological Issues." In *Being Changed*, ed. Goulet and Young, 298–335.

Grosfoguel, Ramón. 1997. "The Divorce of Nationalist Discourses from the Puerto Rican People: A Sociohistorical Perspective." In *Puerto Rican Jam: Essays on Culture and Politics*, ed. Frances Negrón-Muntaner and Ramón Grosfoguel, 57–76. Minneapolis: University of Minnesota Press.

Gruzinski, Serge. 1990. *La Guerre des images*. Paris: Fayard.

Gundaker, Grey. 1993. "Tradition and Innovation in African American Yards." *African Arts* 26 (2): 58–71, 94–96.

Hagedorn, Katherine J. 2001. *Divine Utterances: The Performance of Afro-Cuban Santería*. Washington, DC: Smithsonian Institution Press.

Hájek, Alan. 2004. "Pascal's Wager." *Stanford Encyclopedia of Philosophy*. Spring 2004 edition, ed. Edward N. Zalta. http://plato.stanford.edu/archives/spr2004/entries/pascal-wager.

Halbwachs, Maurice. 1980. *The Collective Memory*. Trans. Francis J. Ditter and Vida Yazdi Ditter. New York: Harper and Row.

Harney, Stefano. 1996. *Nationalism and Identity: Culture and the Imagination in a Caribbean Diaspora*. Kingston, Jamaica: University of the West Indies.

Harwood, Allan. 1987 [1977]. *RX: Spiritist as Needed, a Study of a Puerto Rican Community Mental Health Resource*. Ithaca, NY: Cornell University Press.

Hazan, Haim. 1986. "Body Image and Temporality Among the Aged: A Case Study of an Ambivalent Symbol." *Studies in Symbolic Interaction* 7 (Part A): 305–329.

———. 1995. "The Ethnographer's Textual Presence: On Three Forms of Anthropological Authorship." *Cultural Anthropology* 10 (3): 395–406.

Herdt, Gilbert. 1987. "Selfhood and Discourse in Sambia Dream Sharing." In *Dreaming: Anthropological and Psychological Interpretations*, ed. Barbara Tedlock, 55–85. Cambridge, England: Cambridge University Press.

Hernández Hiraldo, Samiri. 2006. *Black Puerto Rican Identity and Religious Experience*. Gainesville: University Press of Florida.

Herzfeld, Michael. 2001. *Anthropology: Theoretical Practice in Culture and Society*. Malden, MA: Blackwell.

Howes, David, ed. 1991. *The Varieties of Sensory Experience: A Sourcebook in the Anthropology of the Senses*. Toronto: University of Toronto Press.

Hymes, Dell. 1975. "Breakthrough into Performance." In *Folklore: Performance and Communication*, ed. Dan Ben Amos and Kenneth Goldstein, 11–74. The Hague: Mouton.

Jackson, Michael. 1998. *Minima Ethnographica: Intersubjectivity and the Anthropological Project*. Chicago: University of Chicago Press.

———. 2002. *The Politics of Storytelling: Violence, Transgression, and Intersubjectivity*. Copenhagen: University of Copenhagen, Museum Tusculanum Press.

Jakobson, Roman. 1964. "Closing Statement: Linguistics and Poetics." In *Style in Language*, ed. Thomas A. Sebeok, 350–377. Cambridge: MIT Press.

Kapchan, Deborah A. 1995. "Performance." In *Common Ground: Keywords for the Study of Expressive Culture* issue of *Journal of American Folklore* 108 (430): 479–508.

Kapferer, Bruce. 1986. "Performance and the Structuring of Meaning and Experience." In *Anthropology of Experience*, ed. Turner and Bruner, 188–203.

Kelly, John D., and Martha Kaplan. 1990. "History, Structure, and Ritual." *Annual Review of Anthropology* 19:119–150.

Kendall, Laurel. 1996a. "Initiating Performance: The Story of Chini, a Korean Shaman." In *Performance of Healing*, ed. Laderman and Roseman, 17–58.

——-. 1996b. "Korean Shamans and the Spirits of Capitalism." *American Anthropologist* 98 (3): 512–527.

Kilborne, Benjamin. 1981. "Pattern, Structure and Style in Anthropological Studies of Dreams." *Ethos* 9:165–185.

———. 1995. "Dreams." In *The Encyclopedia of Religions*, ed. Mircea Eliade, 4:482–492. New York: Simon and Schuster.

Kluckholn, Clyde, and William Morgan. 1951. "Some Notes on Navaho Dreams." In *Psychoanalysis and Culture: Essays in Honor of Géza Róheim*, ed. George B. Wilbur and Warner Muensterberger, 120–131. New York: International Universities Press.

Koss, Joan D. 1964. "Puerto Rican Spiritualism in Philadelphia: A Lady or the Tiger Dilemma." Paper presented at American Anthropological Association annual meeting, November, Detroit.

———. 1970. "Terapéutica del sistema de una secta en Puerto Rico." *Revista de Ciencias Sociales* 14 (2): 259–278.

———. 1988. "The Experience of Spirits: Ritual Healing as Transactions of Emotion." Unpublished manuscript.

———. 1992. *Women as Healers, Women as Patients: Mental Health Care and Traditional Healing in Puerto Rico*. Boulder, CO: Westview Press.

Kracke, Waud. 1987. "Myths in Dreams, Thought in Images: An Amazonian Contribution to the Psychoanalytic Theory of Primary Process." In *Dreaming*, ed. Tedlock, 31–54.

Kramer, Karen, director. 1985. *Legacy of the Spirits.* Video. Watertown, MA: Documental Educational Resources.

Kuper, Adam. 1979. "A Structural Approach to Dreams." *Man* 14 (4): 645–662.

Labov, William, and Joshua Waletzky. 1967. "Narrative Analysis: Oral Versions of Personal Experience." In *Essays on the Verbal and Visual Arts: Proceedings of the 1966 Annual Spring Meeting,* American Ethnological Society, ed. June Helm, 12–44. Seattle: University of Washington Press.

Laderman, Carol, and Marina Roseman, eds. 1996. *The Performance of Healing.* New York: Routledge.

Le Goff, Jacques. 1985. *L'Imaginaire médiéval.* Paris: Gallimard.

Levine, Peter A., with Ann Frederick. 1997. *Waking the Tiger: Healing Trauma.* Berkeley, CA: North Atlantic Books.

Lévi-Strauss, Claude. 1963a. "The Effectiveness of Symbols." In his *Structural Anthropology,* 186–205. New York: Basic Books.

———. 1963b. "The Sorcerer and His Magic." In his *Structural Anthropology,* 167–185.

Lincoln, Eric C., and Lawrence H. Mamiya. 1990. *The Black Church in African American Experience.* Durham, NC: Duke University Press.

Lincoln, Jackson Stewart. 1970 [1935]. *The Dream in Primitive Culture.* Baltimore: Johnson Reprint.

Livingston, Paisley. 1992. *Models of Desire, René Girard and the Psychology of Mimesis.* Baltimore: Johns Hopkins University Press.

Lock, Margaret. 1993. "Cultivating the Body: Anthropology and Epistemologies of Bodily Practice and Knowledge." *Annual Review of Anthropology* 22:133–155.

López Valdés, Rafael L. 1985. *Componentes africanos en el etnos cubano.* Havana: Editorial de Ciencias Sociales.

Malinowski, Bronislaw. 1927. *Sex and Repression in Savage Society.* New York: Humanities Press.

———. 1935. *Coral Gardens and Their Magic.* New York: American Book Company.

———. 1989 [1967]. *A Diary in the Strict Sense of the Term.* New introduction by Raymond Firth. Stanford, CA: Stanford University Press.

Marcus, George E. 2001. "From Rapport Under Erasure to Theatrics of Complicit Reflexivity." *Qualitative Inquiry* 7, no. 4: 519–528.

Marcus, George E., and Dick Cushman. 1983. "Ethnographies as Texts." *Annual Review of Anthropology* 11, no. 2:25–69.

Marx, Karl. 1983. *The Portable Karl Marx.* Selected, translated in part, and introduced by Eugene Kamenka. New York: Penguin Books.

Mauss, Marcel. 1979 [1950]. *Sociology and Psychology: Essays.* Trans. Ben Brewster. London: Kegan Paul.

Mieder, Wolfgang, and Alan Dundes, eds. 1994 [1981]. *The Wisdom of Many: Essays on the Proverb.* Madison: University of Wisconsin Press.

Moore, Sally F., and Barbara G. Myerhoff, eds. 1977. *Secular Ritual.* Assen, Netherlands: Van Gorcum.

Mukařovský, Jan. 1964. "Standard Language and Poetic Language." In *A Prague School Reader on Esthetics, Literary Structure, and Style*, translated and selected by Paul L. Garvin, 17–30. Washington, DC: Georgetown University Press.

Murcia, José, and Isabel Hoyos. 1998–2008. *Zona Verde. Características y aplicaciones de plantas.* http://www.zonaverde.net.

Murphy, Joseph M. 1994. *Working the Spirit: Ceremonies of the African Diaspora.* Boston: Beacon Press.

Murphy, Keith. 2005. "Imagination as Joint Activity." *Mind, Culture, and Activity* 11 (4): 267–278.

Myerhoff, Barbara G. 1977. "We Don't Wrap Herring in a Printed Page: Fusion, Fictions, and Continuity in Secular Ritual." In *Secular Ritual*, ed. Sally F. Moore and Barbara G. Myerhoff, 199–224. Assen, Netherlands: Van Gorcum.

Nadel, Siegfried F. 1954. *Nupe Religion.* London: Routledge and Kegan Paul.

Navaro-Yashin, Yael. 2007. "Make-Believe Papers, Legal Forms, and the Counterfeit: Affective Interactions Between Documents and People in Britain and Cyprus." *Anthropological Theory* 7 (1): 79–98.

Nietzsche, Friedrich. 1967 [1887]. *The Will to Power.* Trans. Walter Kaufman and R. J. Hollingdale. New York: Vintage.

O'Nell, Carl W. 1976. *Dreams, Culture, and the Individual.* San Francisco: Chandler and Sharp.

Oring, Elliott. 1993. "Victor Turner, Sigmund Freud, and the Return of the Repressed." *Ethos* 21 (3): 273–294.

Palmié, Stephan. 2002. *Wizards and Scientists: Explorations in Afro-Cuban Modernity and Tradition.* Durham, NC: Duke University Press.

Pascal, Blaise. 1901 [1670]. *The Thoughts of Blaise Pascal.* Garden City, NY: Dolphin Books.

———. 1966 [1670]. *Pensées.* Translated and introduced by A. J. Krailsheimer. Harmondsworth, England: Penguin Books.

Peek, Philip M., ed. 1991. *African Divination Systems: Ways of Knowing.* Bloomington: Indiana University Press.

Propp, Vladimir. 1968 [1928]. *Morphology of the Folktale.* Trans. Laurence Scott (1st edition); revised and edited with preface by Louis A. Wagner, new introduction by Alan Dundes (2d edition). Austin: University of Texas Press.

Quiquemelle, Marie-Claire, writer-director. 2003. *The Education of a Singer at the Beijing Opera.* Video. Prod. Léone Jaffin. Paris: Top Films and National Research Center.

Raboteau, Albert J. 1995. *A Fire in the Bones: Reflections on African American Religious History*. Boston: Beacon Press.

Radin, Paul. 1936. "Ojibwa and Ottawa Puberty Dreams." In *Essays in Anthropology Presented to A. L. Kroeber*, ed. Robert H. Lowie, 233–264. Berkeley: University of California Press.

Rappaport, Roy A. 1979. *Ecology, Meaning, and Religion*. New Haven, CT: Yale University Press.

Ricoeur, Paul. 1977. *The Rule of Metaphor: Multi-Disciplinary Studies of the Creation of Meaning in Language*. Trans. Robert Cserny, Kathleen MacLaughlin, and John Costello. Toronto: University of Toronto Press.

———. 1991. *From Text to Action: Essays in Hermeneutics, II*. Trans. Kathleen Blamey and John B. Thompson. Evanston, IL: Northwestern University Press.

Rivers, W. H. R. 1923. *Conflict and Dream*. London: Kegan Paul.

Romberg, Raquel. 2003a. "From Charlatans to Saviors: Espiritistas, Curanderos, and Brujos Inscribed in Discourses of Progress and Heritage." *Centro Journal* 15 (2): 146–173.

———. 2003b. *Witchcraft and Welfare: Spiritual Capital and the Business of Magic in Modern Puerto Rico*. Austin: University of Texas Press.

———. 2005a. "Glocal Spirituality: Consumerism and Heritage in an Afro-Caribbean Folk Religion." In *Caribbean Societies and Globalization*, ed. Franklin W. Knight and Teresita Martínez-Vergne, 131–156. Chapel Hill: University of North Carolina Press.

———. 2005b. "Symbolic Piracy: Creolization with an Attitude?" *New West Indian Guide* 79 (3–4): 175–218.

———. 2007. "Today, Changó is Changó, or How Africannes Becomes a Ritual Commodity in Puerto Rico." *Western Folklore* 66 (1–2): 75–106.

Rouch, Jean. 1960. *La Religion et la magie Songhay*. Paris: Presses Universitaires de France.

———. 1971. *Tourou et Bitti, les tambours d'avant*. Documentary film. Paris: Centre National de la Recherche Scientifique (CNRS).

———. 1978. «On the Vicissitudes of the Self: The Possessed Dancer, the Magician, the Sorcerer, the Filmmaker, and the Ethnographer.» *Studies in the Anthropology of Visual Communication* 5 (1): 2–8.

Ruby, Jay. 1980. "Franz Boas and Early Camera Study of Behavior." *Kinesics Report* 3 (1): 6–11.

———. 2000. *Picturing Culture: Explorations of Film and Anthropology*. Chicago: University of Chicago Press.

Sapir, J. David. 1977. "The Anatomy of Metaphor." In *The Social Use of Metaphor*, ed. J. David Sapir and J. Christopher Croker, 3–32. Philadelphia: University of Pennsylvania Press.

Scheper-Hughes, Nancy, and Margaret Lock. 1987. "The Mindful Body: A Prolegomenon to Future Work in Medical Anthropology." *Medical Anthropology Quarterly* 1:6–41.

Schieffelin, Edward. 1996. "On Failure and Performance: Throwing the Medium out of the Séance." In *Performance of Healing*, ed. Laderman and Roseman, 59–89.

Schmitt, Jean-Claude. 1994. *Les Revenants*. Paris: Gallimard.

Schutz, Alfred. 1962. *Collected Papers I*. Edited and introduced by Maurice Natanson; preface by H. L. van Breda. The Hague: M. Nijhoff.

Schwegler, Armin. 2000. "On the (Sensational) Survival of Kikongo in 20th-Century Cuba." *Journal of Pidgin and Creole Languages* 15:159–174.

———. 2006. "Bozal Spanish: Captivating New Evidence from a Contemporary Source (Afro-Cuban 'Palo Monte')." In *Studies in Contact Linguistics: Essays in Honor of Glenn G. Gilbert*, ed. Linda L. Thornburg and Janet M. Fuller, 71–101. New York: Peter Lang.

Scott, David. 1994. *Formations of Ritual: Colonial and Anthropological Discourses on the Sinhala Yaktovil*. Minneapolis: University of Minnesota Press.

Seligman, C. G. 1923. "Notes on Dreams." *Man* 23:186–188.

Seremetakis, C. Nadia. 1991. *The Last Word: Women, Death, and Divination in Inner Mani*. Chicago: University of Chicago Press.

Shaw, Rosalind. 2002. *Memories of the Slave Trade: Ritual and the Historical Imagination in Sierra Leone*. Chicago: University of Chicago Press.

Sherzer, Joel. 1983. *Kuna Ways of Speaking: An Ethnographic Perspective*. Austin: University of Texas Press.

———. 1989. "Namakke, Sunmakke, Kormakke: Three Types of Cuna Speech Event." In *Explorations in the Ethnography of Speaking*, ed. Bauman and Sherzer, 263–282.

Silva Gotay, Samuel. 1985. "Social History of the Churches in Puerto Rico, Preliminary Notes." In *Towards a History of the Church in the Third World*, ed. Lucas Vischer. Papers and reports about periodization presented at the Ecumenical Association of Third World Theologians, Geneva, July 17–21, 1983.

———. 1997. *Protestantismo y política en Puerto Rico, 1898–1930*. Río Piedras: Editorial de la Universidad de Puerto Rico.

Silverstein, Michael. 1976. "Shifters, Linguistic Categories, and Cultural Description." In *Meaning in Anthropology*, ed. Keith Basso and Henry Selby, 11–56. Albuquerque: University of New Mexico Press.

Smullyan, Raymond. 1983. *5000 B.C. and Other Philosophical Fantasies*. New York: St. Martin's Press.

Sperber, Dan. 1985. *On Anthropological Knowledge: Three Essays*. Cambridge, England: Cambridge University Press.

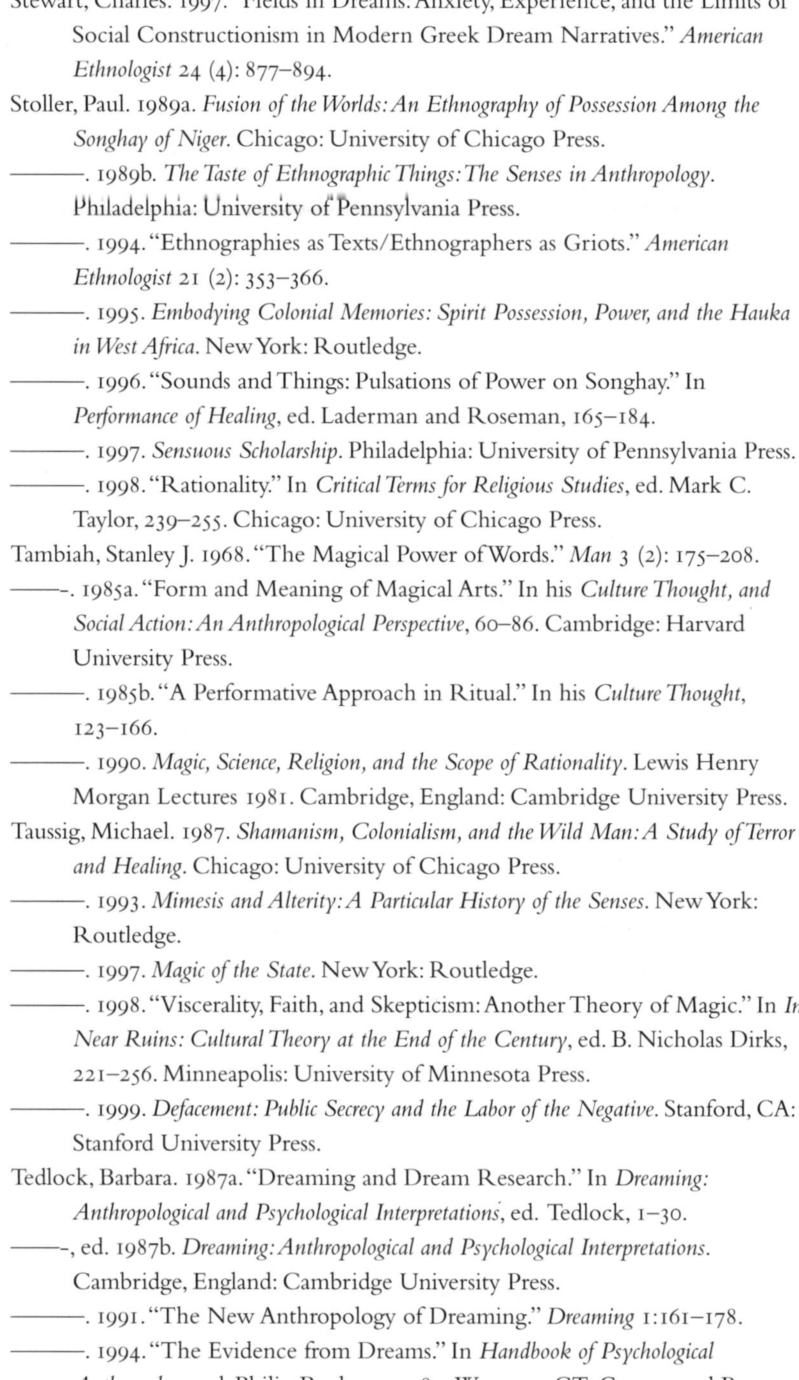

Stewart, Charles. 1997. "Fields in Dreams: Anxiety, Experience, and the Limits of Social Constructionism in Modern Greek Dream Narratives." *American Ethnologist* 24 (4): 877–894.

Stoller, Paul. 1989a. *Fusion of the Worlds: An Ethnography of Possession Among the Songhay of Niger.* Chicago: University of Chicago Press.

———. 1989b. *The Taste of Ethnographic Things: The Senses in Anthropology.* Philadelphia: University of Pennsylvania Press.

———. 1994. "Ethnographies as Texts/Ethnographers as Griots." *American Ethnologist* 21 (2): 353–366.

———. 1995. *Embodying Colonial Memories: Spirit Possession, Power, and the Hauka in West Africa.* New York: Routledge.

———. 1996. "Sounds and Things: Pulsations of Power on Songhay." In *Performance of Healing*, ed. Laderman and Roseman, 165–184.

———. 1997. *Sensuous Scholarship.* Philadelphia: University of Pennsylvania Press.

———. 1998. "Rationality." In *Critical Terms for Religious Studies*, ed. Mark C. Taylor, 239–255. Chicago: University of Chicago Press.

Tambiah, Stanley J. 1968. "The Magical Power of Words." *Man* 3 (2): 175–208.

——-. 1985a. "Form and Meaning of Magical Arts." In his *Culture Thought, and Social Action: An Anthropological Perspective*, 60–86. Cambridge: Harvard University Press.

———. 1985b. "A Performative Approach in Ritual." In his *Culture Thought*, 123–166.

———. 1990. *Magic, Science, Religion, and the Scope of Rationality.* Lewis Henry Morgan Lectures 1981. Cambridge, England: Cambridge University Press.

Taussig, Michael. 1987. *Shamanism, Colonialism, and the Wild Man: A Study of Terror and Healing.* Chicago: University of Chicago Press.

———. 1993. *Mimesis and Alterity: A Particular History of the Senses.* New York: Routledge.

———. 1997. *Magic of the State.* New York: Routledge.

———. 1998. "Viscerality, Faith, and Skepticism: Another Theory of Magic." In *In Near Ruins: Cultural Theory at the End of the Century*, ed. B. Nicholas Dirks, 221–256. Minneapolis: University of Minnesota Press.

———. 1999. *Defacement: Public Secrecy and the Labor of the Negative.* Stanford, CA: Stanford University Press.

Tedlock, Barbara. 1987a. "Dreaming and Dream Research." In *Dreaming: Anthropological and Psychological Interpretations*, ed. Tedlock, 1–30.

——-, ed. 1987b. *Dreaming: Anthropological and Psychological Interpretations.* Cambridge, England: Cambridge University Press.

———. 1991. "The New Anthropology of Dreaming." *Dreaming* 1:161–178.

———. 1994. "The Evidence from Dreams." In *Handbook of Psychological Anthropology*, ed. Philip Bock, 279–285. Westport, CT: Greenwood Press.

Thomas, Keith. 1971. *Religion and the Decline of Magic: Studies of Popular Beliefs in Sixteenth- and Seventeenth-Century England.* London: Wedeifeld and Nicholson.

Thompson, Robert Farris. 1983. *Flash of the Spirit: African and Afro-American Art and Philosophy.* New York: Random House.

———. 1993. *Face of the Gods: Art and Altars of Africa and the African Americas.* Exhibition catalog, Museum for African Art, New York. Munich: Prestel.

———. 2005. *Tango: Art History of Love.* New York: Pantheon.

Travel in Taiwan Monthly. 1995. "Culture: Chinese Opera Experience." *Taipei:* Vision International. http://www.sinica.edu.tw/tit/culture/0895_cu2.html.

Turner, Bryan S. 1984. *The Body and Society: Explorations in Social Theory.* Oxford, England: Basil Blackwell.

Turner, Edith. 1992. *Experiencing Ritual: A New Interpretation of African Healing.* With Singleton Kahona, William Blodgett, and Fideli Benwa. Philadelphia: University of Pennsylvania Press.

Turner, Victor W. 1967. *The Forest of Symbols: Aspects of Ndembu Ritual.* Ithaca, NY: Cornell University Press.

———. 1974. *Dramas, Fields, and Metaphors: Symbolic Action in Human Society.* Symbol, Myth, and Ritual Series. Ithaca, NY: Cornell University Press.

———. 1986. "Dewey, Dilthey, and Drama: An Essay in the Anthropology of Experience." In *Anthropology of Experience*, ed. Turner and Bruner, 33–44.

Turner, Victor W., and Edward M. Bruner, eds. 1981. *The Anthropology of Experience.* Urbana: University of Illinois Press.

Tuzin, Donald. 1975. "The Breath of a Ghost: Dreams and the Fear of the Dead." *Ethos* 3:555–578.

Tweed, Thomas A. 1999. "Diasporic Nationalism and Urban Landscape: Cuban Immigrants at a Catholic Shrine in Miami." In *Gods of the City: Religion and the American Urban Landscape*, ed. Robert A. Orsi, 131–154. Bloomington: Indiana University Press.

Urban, Greg. 1989. "The 'I' of Discourse." In *Semiotics, Self, and Society*, ed. Benjamin Lee and Greg Urban, 27–51. Berlin: Mouton de Gruyter.

———. 1991. *A Discourse-Centered Approach to Culture.* Austin: University of Texas Press.

Van Gennep, Arnold. 1960 [1908]. *The Rites of Passage.* Trans. Monika B. Vizedom and Gabrielle L. Caffee; introduction by Solon T. Kimball. Chicago: University of Chicago Press.

Vico, Giambattista. 1984 [1744]. *The New Science of Giambattista Vico.* Unabridged translation of 3d edition (1744) by Thomas Goddard Bergin and Max Harold Fisch; "Practice of the New Science" added. Ithaca, NY: Cornell University Press.

Vidal, Jaime R. 1994. "Citizens Yet Strangers: The Puerto Rican Experience." In *Puerto Rican and Cuban Catholics in the U.S., 1900–1965*, ed. Jay P. Dolan and Jaime R. Vidal, 11–143. Notre Dame, IN: University of Notre Dame Press.

Vidal, Teodoro. 1989. *Tradiciones en la brujería puertorriqueña*. San Juan, Puerto Rico: Ediciones Alba.

Wagenheim, Karl, and Olga Jiménez de Wagenheim, eds. 1996. *The Puerto Ricans: A Documentary History*. Updated edition. Princeton, NJ: Markus Wiener.

Wallace, Anthony F. C. 1958. "Dreams and the Wishes of the Soul: A Type of Psychoanalytic Theory Among the Seventeenth Century Iroquois." *American Anthropologist* 60 (2): 234–248.

Weiss, Wendy A. 1993. "Gringo . . . Gringita." *Anthropological Quarterly* 66 (4): 187–196.

Winkelman, Michael, and Philip M. Peek, eds. 2004. *Divination and Healing: Potent Vision*. Tucson: University of Arizona Press.

Williams, Raymond. 1980. *Problems in Materialism: Selected Readings*. London: Verso.

Young, Katharine. 2002. "The Memory of the Flesh: The Family Body in Somatic Psychology." *Body and Society* 8 (3): 25–48.

Zizek, Slavoj. 2001. *On Belief.* New York: Routledge.

———. N.d. "With or Without Reason: What's Wrong with Fundamentalism?" Part 1. *http://www.lacan.com/zizpassion*.

Index

Note: Page numbers in *italics* refer to illustrations.